INTEGRITY

INTEGRITY

VOLUME 3
The Second Year
July–December 1947

CAROL ROBINSON & ED WILLOCK, *EDITORS*

AROUCA
PRESS

First Published by
Integrity Publishing Co., New York, 1947
Edited by Edward F. Willock and Carol Jackson Robinson
Illustrations by Ed Willock
2022 © by Arouca Press

ISBN: 978-1-990685-24-8 (pbk)
ISBN: 978-1-990685-25-5 (hardcover)

Arouca Press
PO Box 55003
Bridgeport PO
Waterloo, ON N2J 3G0
Canada
www.aroucapress.com
Send inquiries to info@aroucapress.com

CONTENTS

INTEGRITY

"FOR SPACIOUS SKIES, FOR AMBER WAVES OF GRAIN."

JULY, 1947   Vol. 1, No. 10

SUBJECT—AMERICA

AMERICA TODAY STANDS UPON the threshold of maturity. Her virtues are the virtues of youth. Her potentialities are great for either good or evil. No other country has been blessed as she is blessed in the good things of the earth. A child of Europe, nurtured by its culture and its people to a position of enviable self-sufficiency, she stands now in a position to assume the headship of nations.

Unlike Europe, who fed long at the paps of the Church, America is a bottle baby. She has been weaned on a formula of synthetic spirituality. Despite her physical strength, there is good reason to fear that the necessary spiritual stamina is lacking to carry the load that history has placed upon her. When there is a job to be done, she will do it. We saw that in the last war. It is in vision that she is lacking, and in leadership. America is a lush wilderness looking for a voice.

There are two ways of looking at America. The flattering view is the relative one. Compared to a devastated, bankrupt, despairing Europe, our country really is the land of opportunity that Jerem O'Sullivan-Barra describes in DEAR SIR AND BROTHER.

If the rest of the articles in this issue seem jaundiced or cynical or negative by comparison with the first one, it is because their writers see America in relation to her own unrealized potentialities, her own sins and shortcomings, and the price she may soon have to pay for them.

We begin this month a series of spiritual portraits of American cities, which we shall continue in future issues. After all, America is our native land, and the home of our apostolate, so we must study it in detail.

May the Immaculate Conception, to Whom our fair land is dedicated, help us Americans to become without spot before God.

THE EDITORS

Dear Sir and Brother

FOR THOSE WHO ARE NOT MEMBERS OF unions, it may be necessary to explain the above title is the salutation used by one American workman to another as members of a labor union. The salutation is symbolic of a very real brotherhood and even of a Christian unity of many races who work together in a single nation. "Sir and Brother" gives some inkling of the very basic *Credo* of America regarding the dignity and the work of each individual boilermaker and of the equality of each boilermaker before his God. The very fact that a man is a boilermaker or a fireman or an oiler or a bus driver is the basis of his dignity and gives him the right to be called Sir as well as Brother. This salutation of Sir and Brother seems to be a part and an expression of the American Dream.

THE AMERICAN DREAM

Americans have behind them and in front of them, a great expanse of vision known as the American Dream. For someone who has not lived in America, or who, having lived here, has not entered into the stream of life of our nation, the American Dream may be just a phrase to represent a fiction. To Americans who have lived in other countries where traditions and standards are different, and whose economies are limited and closed, the American Dream is a breathing reality that takes on an actuality in one's daily thinking.

To describe this dream is a task beyond my capacity. Perhaps I can light up a few facets of it. It means that a boy can work his way through college by washing dishes. It means that idleness is not equated with gentility or with position, and that steady work is accepted as an admirable way of life. It means that an American man is not ashamed, but rather, proud, of his sweaty brow and grease-stained overalls. It means that a Child's Restaurant[1]

1 Founded in Manhattan in 1889 and was one of the first national dining chains.

waitress sits down to eat at the table next to the customer and has the same choice of food. It means that an American youth can face his future with an aplomb and careless courage born of at least a tradition of limitless opportunities. It means many more things tangible and intangible, but no one who is seeking an explanation of the achievements and present position of our nation, and of the general attitudes and aptitudes of our fellow citizens, can rule out of the discussion the actuality of the American Dream.

So many local, national, and international spokesmen have taken it upon themselves to deal critically with American life and character, that it seems opportune to underline some of the positive and benevolent aspects of the American people, and of the way of life they have set up in this nation of nations.

OUR IMMUNITY TO OUR OWN DISEASES

Perhaps the most salient characteristic of the ordinary American is his toughness and power of resistance. Americans who have not lived abroad may possibly wonder why this point is discussed first, or discussed at all. Foreign countries feel they know American culture and mores. After all, they have seen American movies. Long-legged girls dance in unison to vapid love songs played by an eighty-eight-piece band. Puppy-love is glorified for all the world to see. The meatier aspects of life are all ground down to a tasteless hamburger before they pass to the American screen. The spiritual aspects of life are quite consistently ignored or are prettied up until they approach an unbearable saccharinity. Foreigners also hear our radio programs, or reasonable facsimiles of them, imitated on local radio stations. They hear recordings of American jazz and ask for translations of the words of our popular songs. Then, of course, they saw our business men on dedicated quests for profit, and immediately classified all Americans as being hypnotized by the almighty dollar.

Not even the transcendence of our technology during the war years, nor the bravery and efficiency of Americans drafted into battle, has radically changed the ideas of the rest of the world about us. Non-Americans, and particularly Europeans of the educated groups, think of us as slaves to the dollar, to ridiculous movies, to fantastic radio commercials, to enticing advertisements, to compelling boogie-woogie music. The happy fact is that while it is certainly true that some Americans, particularly city-dwellers, and the young, have fallen under the influence of such cultural forces as the movies, the ordinary American has developed over the years a really magnificent power of resistance. Merely because a pain remedy is advertised as, "Just like a doctor's prescription because it contains many ingredients," does not prevent him from consulting a doctor when he is ill. What the American accepts most heartily from his radio are jokes, and he is happy indeed when the jokes satirize the radio itself. It would probably surprise program-makers very much to learn how many Americans share the feelings of Lee de Forest, whose inventions made radio possible: "What have you gentlemen done with my child?", he asked the National Association of Broadcasters. "He was conceived as a potent instrumentality for culture, fine music, the uplifting of America's mass intelligence. You have debased this child, you have sent him out on the streets in rags of ragtime, tatters of jive and boogie-woogie, to collect money from all and sundry for hubba-hubba and audio jitterbug. You have made of him a laughing stock to intelligence, surely a stench in the nostrils of the gods of ionosphere; you have cut out time into tiny cubelets, called spots (more rightly stains), wherewith the occasional fine program is periodically smeared with impudent insistence to buy or try."

Though they cannot eliminate the commercial and the senseless chatter of innumerable programs, Americans can and have become immunized against them. Nature often offers its own protection against the hazards of a particular environment. It is reported by medical men that among certain native tribes in North Africa where syphilis is *endemic*, and where all members may be affected by it, the disease loses its virulence. The tribes-men seem to be immune from its effects. Something of this has happened in our culture. It is sad to relate, that where Amer-ican movies, or even American music, are introduced into a new culture, the effect is the opposite. Imitation of movie man-ners, movie makeup, and move dress has often had disastrous effects — particularly in certain regions in South America.

It is interesting to note that English movies, which are pre-pared with at least a little more respect for normal intelligence, are gaining very heavy support from American audiences. It is becoming apparent that our American moviegoers are getting a little tired of picture after picture which offer nothing but a "carefully studied insult to the intelligence," as one of our news magazines puts it. The writer was an interested spectator when a New York audience spontaneously clapped at the end of an English movie. It was not an excellent movie, but was acted and written with discretion, intelligence and a certain verve. On the same program was one of Hollywood's most lavish and studied insults to intelligence, a piece called *The Shocking Miss Pilgrim*. Restiveness and finally laughter met this meaningless technicolor extravaganza, and when a trailer presented scenes from the next feature, *Humoresque,* and the audience was treated to pictures of an agonized Joan Crawford, and a very familiar John Garfield trying to look intense over a violin which everyone knew he was not playing, hooting was heard all over the theatre. This is a small incident, but it is indicative of a wider reaction. It may be argued that the movies and radio are mass media, and are thus an expression of the real soul of America. Nothing could be further from the truth. Both are big businesses, controlled like other big businesses by a few for the benefit of the few. The fact that both draw large audiences is partly, if not largely, due to the fact that they are monopolies, and that American audiences have no other choice but to take what is presented to them. The toughness of the ordinary American is his strength, since he can at least defend his integrity by refusing to take seriously the effusions of men who work quite patently to make money for themselves and for those whose creatures they are.

ARE WE SUCKLED ON LION'S MILK?

That every American is hypnotized by the sacrosanct sign of $ is believed by everyone who thinks that the United States has lived and is living in a period of predatory capitalism of the most primitive sort. A trained and veteran observer of our America has this to say on our business-ordered culture: "Here is a culture suckled on the lion's milk of getting ahead by personal exploitative prowess; a culture which believes that things order themselves best under this scrambling private struggle for pecuniary gain, and that the society as a unit should plan and do as little as possible so as not to interfere with this beneficent private scramble; a culture hypnotized by the gorged stream of new things to buy — automobiles, electrical equipment for the home, radios, automatic refrigeration, and all but automatic ways to live; a culture in which private business tempts the population in its every waking minute with adroitly phrased invitations to apply the solvent remedy of more and newer possessions and socially disintegrating good and comforts to all the ills the flesh is heir to — loneliness, insecurity, deferred hope, and frustration." Robert Lynd, who thus describes the motivating factor in the life and economy of Muncie, Indiana, is of course right in so far as he describes the upper brackets of our business families. Big business, in the persons of its protagonists, is indeed a jungle, where the weak do not survive, and where lion's milk is the most fitting sustenance.

It is ridiculous to say, however, that the United States ever succumbed to capitalism in the same way as England did. The American Dream entered in rather early to prevent the excessive dehumanization of men in mines and factories that was a common thing in Great Britain. Despite the movement of men to cities, there still remains in the United States a strong backbone of hardy farmers whose cultural level is higher than that of farmers anywhere. The preoccupation of federal and local authorities with the farming population has resulted in the foundation of well-equipped Applied Schools of Agriculture for those only wishing the practical training for the land. County agents are stationed in agricultural areas to give advice and help, and universities offer extension courses both to the farmer and to his wife. This network of education and aid is in existence, is functioning efficiently, and is fulfilling its purpose, that of keeping free men free.

The jungle ethos of big business is peculiarly its own and has very little relation to small or family owned business. The element of personal responsibility has not been lost from the hundreds of thousands of family restaurants, of shoe repair shops, of tiny laundry services that dot the country. Here is still the independent worker, even owning his own tools and often his center of operations.

On the farms, in the one-man businesses, the essential spirit of America is not lost. The sense of independence, of freedom, of individual worth and dignity, all are very much alive. Among those who work for wages, there is no less sureness of individual dignity. That factory workers, transportation workers, carpenters and others must sell their work in exchange for money has not yet made them as much slaves to the dollar sign as critics of the U.S. would try to maintain. It is only necessary to go among the American working people to collect for a cause, any worthy cause, to learn the real spirit of Americans. It is true that they have worked hard for their dollars, but they part with them easily and carelessly for almost any cause — for a starving Polish child, for a German child, for the Red Cross, for a new church, etc., etc. There is among them an inexhaustible well of sympathy and generosity that not even the oft-reiterated tents of capitalistic thrift, or capitalistic spendthriftiness have been able to dam up or vitiate.

To some who have studied the long-term effects of capitalism on workers where the capitalistic system is entrenched, the aspect of the American workman is heartening in its independence and courage. As is well-known, the miners of England and Wales are the basic factors in the support of the capitalistic economy of the island kingdom. The writer studied them during the depression years, after many of them had been on the dole for long periods. There was little struggle left in them. They were in the main content to be on the dole, and eked out their pittance by catching rabbits and growing vegetables for the family stewpot. The moral degradation of the half-employed Welsh villages was often unspeakable, and the men, who after all, had known nothing but the daily discipline of the pit from their early teens, rarely branched out into other work, or invented little services, or ploughed up fallow land, or cooperatively entered into any land schemes with their fellow victims. It is true that their resources were pitifully slim, but they had been so successively dehumanized by a long history of exploitation in mines that the full play of their human faculties seem to be stunted.

No such capitalistic discipline cramps the initiative of Americans in similar situations. They always have a faith in tomorrow, in their future, and in themselves — their power to master circumstances. Even the Okies, dispossessed of homes, of land, and of tools, felt that tomorrow would bring them a new life — so they moved on to find tomorrow. It is true that this faith is often more than a little naïve, but it is a faith founded on some reality; the unbroken spirits of American workmen, (in or out of depression) and the great untapped resources of our blessed land.

THE MOST BEAUTIFUL BUILDING IS THE SCHOOL

The emphasis that is placed on the formation of an individual in the American scene is a prime phenomenon of our culture. In motoring though a typical American town, one can note that, in general, the most beautiful building is the school. It is often more beautiful than the local Post Office, and more sturdily constructed than the movie house. Lest country children plead illiteracy on account of distances from the school or on account of weather, regular bus service picks up the children and deposits them safely at home at the end of the school day. High schools are free, and state colleges demand only a small sacrifice of work and extra effort of even the poorest students who wishes to earn a degree. There has rarely been in history a more education-centered culture. Of course, our education system could be improved, but the emphasis on education shows that a secular society is acting according to its own highest principles, and the plant for doing a good job of schooling has already been erected. Certain dedicated souls are already at work proving the inadequacies of our teaching system and of our educational goals. New solutions, integrating the lessons of the past with the needs of the present, are emerging from such studies. As the complexity of our culture and economic system bring more observable tensions, it is to be hoped that educational leaders steeped in truth and idealism will help bring to a real flowering the greatest experiment in mass education that the world has ever seen.

CHILDISHNESS AND GOOD WILL

If there is one quality that distinguishes adult Americans from nationals of other countries, it is a certain childishness that is apparent in their attitudes and behavior. This childishness could only arise in a country where living is not too hard, where manners are elastic, where rigidity of social codes is replaced by an easygoing acceptance of many patterns of behavior. Naturally, there are prescribed limits, because America too has a definable pattern of accepted social behavior (I am referring to surface manners and mannerisms rather than morals), but the latitude is ample enough to permit of wide variation. In older cultures, the classes and professions harden, and those who belong must conform to certain age-hallowed formulas. In the new police states, the necessity of being constantly watchful if one wishes to remain sound of wind and limb, makes for the opposite of the careless, childish attitude exhibited by the majority of Americans.

The childishness shows itself in many ways: in the playfulness generally associated with youngsters; in easy laughter; in an openness in telling about one's life history and aims; in a tendency to oversimplify even the most complex matters, both national and international; and most important, in an undifferentiated good will — the good will that a well-washed, well-fed, plump, child has for people and things that surround it. In passing, it might be well to note that our good will may be turned to all kinds of things, just as a child may, with the best will in the world, drop the baby on the floor in playing doll with it. It was indeed with good will, and without malice or hatred, that we dropped the atom bombs. Our childishness is a help in our thinking and planning — we never think small, or plan small, but think and plan big, just as children do. But we are children gifted with a fantastically wonderful technology, and we can make our big plans come through to reality. Cautious adults are apt to be abashed by schemes of formidable magnitude; not so most young Americans. Very little in this world can serve to abash them; they are willing to try anything once. This open-soul childishness makes Americans anything but a petty people. It is well, however, to keep in mind the distinction between childishness and childlikeness. If Americans were more truly childlike in humility, in simple wisdom, in joy, they could become a people of great vison. We are not *as little children* . . . but childish. We are immature and irresponsible. Either we shall grow up to the splendid manhood our idealism presages, or we shall become irresponsibly brutal in the manner of undisciplined children turned into little brats.

Perhaps the most heartening thing about our life in the United States is that despite all influences to the contrary, right principles and good examples are still honored. Self-sacrifice and service to others are still held up as ideals, at least on commencement day. They have not even lost their context in Christianity. Fidelity in marriage, stability in home life are still honored — if only in the *breach*. The freedom of the individual and the protection of his rights as a child of God are part of our deepest patterns of thinking. This, of course, inevitably brings up our weakest point: the racism that relegates many of our Negro fellow-citizens to a second-class citizenship, and acts to prevent the integration into our culture of our Jewish, Mexican or Puerto-Rican brothers. Though we have far to travel, we are on the road to real equality. The principles under which we will attain this equality have been preserved for us, and are active in our culture. We can still protest, we can work for our brothers-in-Christ without let or hindrance, so the fault is ours if progress in the combatting of racism is not more rapid.

To the Catholic whose heart goes out in love for his country, much of what goes into the American Dream would seem to be firmly embedded in the Judeo-Christian and Catholic tradition of the sacredness of the personality of each and every human being. If the Catholic opposes certain aspects of our development, he would only oppose them as overgrowths on a strong, sound and healthy plant. If he has any apostolic zeal in him, the thought of the harvest to be gained in the United States is a continuous goad of his spirit. Here is a people, surrounded by the worst examples of monopoly capitalism, of incitements to concupiscence, self-indulgence, and sin; where press, radio and movies have already become mere voices for materialism; where factory work with its division of labor tries to rob man of his humanity. Here is a people whose power of resistance and toughness of spiritual fiber have allowed a large immunization as against ever-present disease. Here is a people marked by generosity in the midst of a culture ordered to profit, a people characterized by openhearted childishness, by love and respect for education, by the continued regard for true principles of conduct though powerful forces assail them — a people who have refused to fall victims to the evils that have entered our system of life.

THE APOSTOLATE

If we as Catholics have some things that we know to be good, it is our duty to offer them to our fellow-citizens. They may of course, refuse them, but if we love them as brothers, we must do all in our power to share with them those treasures that we prize most in the world. If we go to them in smugness, we shall arouse only suspicion. If we do not really strip ourselves of money and any desire for power, we may frighten them into thinking that our ultimate aim is not the kingdom of God on earth, but merely some new and glorified Tammany [Hall] whereby Catholicism might wield a more sure political influence.

If we know our own message well enough to be fools for Christ, to go unarmed with anything but the mantle of love and pity, we shall win many who are wandering about, stunned by the confusions of the day, and waiting for the Word. The freedoms of our land are with us. If we want to start a paper, a magazine, a farming commune, a cooperative, a hostel, or if we only want to visit the sick, the fatherless, the widow, and him who is in bonds, we can start as soon as our energies and possibilities permit. There are no restrictive laws to prevent us. The Apostolate is ours to accept or refuse. Dear Sirs and Brothers, have you ever heard of the Catholic Dream?

JEREM O'SULLIVAN-BARRA[2]

---

2 Pseudonym for Eileen Egan.

Why Aren't Americans
Contemplative?

WHEN MOTHER MARY MAGDALEN BENTIVO-
glio, foundress of the Poor Clares in the United States, applied
for permission to make a foundation in Philadelphia in 1876, the
diocesan council refused on the grounds that such a convent was
"not in conformity with the spirit of the people."

That was over a century ago, and an isolated instance, but
it expresses an antipathy to the contemplative life which persists, affecting both the Catholic and non-Catholic population,
although differently. We like our saints to be "normal people."
We prefer Thomas More sans hairshirt and St. Francis minus the
stigmata. Contraception does not seem unnatural, even to many
Catholics who refrain from it, but contemplative nuns do seem
unnatural. We are more at ease with an aspirant millionaire than
with one who hopes to become a saint.

"Why aren't Americans contemplative?" is not an idle question, like "Why do Americans prefer coffee to tea?" It isn't a
matter of idiosyncrasy, or national temperament or genius; it is
much the same as saying, "Why aren't Americans godly people?"
A distaste for contemplation is at the root of the so-called "American Heresy," of modernism and of naturalism.

We hope to show in this paper that there is a real antagonism
between the American Way of Life as commonly understood
and practiced, and sanctity.

The likely saints in America's past (with some notable exceptions such as Mother Seton) have not been conspicuous in the
mainstream of our country's development. Most were early mis-
sionaries; nearly all were foreign born. Mother Cabrini certainly
led a hidden life in New York and Chicago where everyone had
heard of her contemporary, J. P. Morgan. Americans until now

16

have been supremely anti-mystical. It looks as though the tide is changing, both among the Catholics and the non-Catholics (who, when they do not find the Church, go in for a false mysticism, jumbling up Theosophy with St. John of the Cross, or deep breathing with Dr. Emmet Fox). It is good to see an ex-Communist poet leave the New Yorker staff for a Trappist monastery. It is good to learn of the ordination of another Trappist who has a background of Judaism, Psychiatry and the University of Chicago. Among those in the lay apostolate, there is the conviction that all things will not be restored in Christ unless they themselves advance toward contemplation. With these signs, it is not unreasonable to hope that we shall one day as a nation realize that to be anti-contemplative is to be truly un-American.

WHAT IS CONTEMPLATION?

The reason that it is so important that contemplation not be considered "un-American" is that contemplation is the normal process of salvation, so that he who will have none of it, in reality refuses to approach God. Contemplation is the beginning here on earth of the Beatific Vision. It is a simple, intuitional grasp of the religious order of things, and it admits of many degrees between its beginning, early in the life of prayer, and its end in the Beatific Vision.

Salvation is not a matter of doing good deeds or of avoiding mortal sin; it is a matter of sharing God's Life. Thomistic theologians, like Garrigou-Lagrange, teach that the development of the interior life as described by St. John of the Cross is in essence (though not in degree) the same and equally necessary for everyone, so that if we neglect to begin it here and yet manage to save our souls, we are going to have a long period of purification in purgatory. Furthermore, if the body of Christians on earth fails to cultivate the interior life and to advance seriously on the road toward God, the strength of that body will be negligible, and the spiritual health of the nation will be adversely affected. Indeed, our spiritual state is reflected in our national conduct. We are the nation which dropped the atomic bomb (and has not yet repented it). We are the nation which characteristically operates on principles of expediency rather than morality. We are the nation which is famous not for the Cross, but for the dollar sign.

THE ACTIVE LIFE AND THE CONTEMPLATIVE LIFE

The reason why we Americans are not contemplative is usually put this way: that Americans are active people (we get things done) and that activists are the opposite of contemplative.

Certain temperaments, such as the melancholic, incline more by nature than others to the life of the spirit and therefore to contemplation. Conversely, the "shallow" temperaments are more given to things of the body than to things of the mind; to things of the world than to things of the spirit. Superficially, it seems as though Americans incline by national temperament to the earthy, but the influence is more than likely not temperament but the prevailing materialism. We are not racially or temperamentally homogeneous.

On the road to salvation, grace, not temperament, is the all-important factor. Physically energetic people are as touched by grace as those who like to sit around and think. God must become progressively and equally insistently the center of everyone's life.

However, the active and contemplative types will manifest differently the divine life within them. The difference will be marked not by the degree of charity each attains, nor by the fact that one will pray and the other not (both will pray, although the contemplative will spend more time at it). The real difference will be marked by the difference in the gifts of the Holy Ghost which will predominate in each. In the contemplative, the gifts of wisdom and understanding will be especially prominent; in the active person it will be the gifts of fortitude, counsel and knowledge which will be uppermost. This predominance of different gifts is what marks the difference between the sanctity of a Don Bosco and the sanctity of a St. Teresa. It is what should mark the difference between a saintly statesman, nurse or teacher, and a Trappist. The comparison is more clearly seen in those advanced in prayer and holiness because their lives are more noticeably under the guidance of the Holy Ghost.

ARE AMERICANS REALLY ACTIVE?

There is another relationship between activity and contemplation which applies especially to beginners. A truly active life on the natural level prepares for contemplation, which in turn will give rise to better activity.

What is this truly active life? It is activity according to moral virtue, as opposed to what St. Thomas calls the active life of pleasure, or life according to the senses. One cannot escape the realization that much of our American activity is the active life according to sensibility and pleasure. For instance, all the frantic haste and energy which goes into moneymaking as a last end is activity of this type; all the way from running for the 8:17 train to the business conference in the afternoon. The much-vaunted American efficiency fits into the same category, and that is really why we tend to despise it. So much punctuality, so much exactitude, so much precision — for what? Then consider the energy Americans give to sports when they really go in for sports. The tennis match and the golf game are the active life of pleasure, although they may be meritorious if accessory to a life of moral virtue, though apparently they seldom are. Take, finally, the energy we devote to expediency, that contemporary substitute for moral virtue. What a lot of energy has gone into Planned Parenthood! What a lot of racing back and forth in airplanes there is among statesmen who cannot be said to proceed with international affairs along the path of moral virtue.

On the other hand, in some ways Americans are not even active, but shockingly passive.

We never walk if we can ride. We have gadgets to keep from developing skills, elevators to eliminate the necessity of climbing stairs, spectator sports, radios instead of musicians. Our passivity is most conspicuous and deplorable in the intellectual sphere. We work at jobs without ever thinking, and indeed there is usually nothing to think about. We passively accept all our opinions predigested.

WHERE INTEGRATION COMES IN

This is where integration comes in. When we say that Catholics should have an integrated life, we are really saying that they should exchange a passive life, or an active life of pleasure or sensibility, for an active life according to the moral virtues, and that this life according to the moral virtues will put them in line for contemplation, which is the route that they should be traveling toward God.

The basis of an active life, according to moral virtue, is an intellectual comprehension of the relationship between religion and work, family, recreation, reading and all the other phases of daily life. If there is no synthesis between religion and life, a man will be blundering around in the dark, and will save his soul only through ignorance of the undone duty (if he can still manage an invincible ignorance). Meanwhile, our country will not be appreciably bettered by such negative candidates for heaven.

IS PIETY CONTEMPLATION?

There is no doubt but that American Catholics are pious. They stream in and out of churches, are very devotional. The number of Communions is impressive.

Piety, in the popular sense, is largely a matter of external activity — vocal prayer and pious exercises. It is good, of course. But of itself, it stands in the relation of peripheral activity to the real interior life. Contemplation does not usually begin until after a period of meditation, and most devout Catholics have not yet even learned to meditate. The fact that many Americans seem to prefer a novena to Mass is indicative that their piety really is on the external and sensible level. You get out of devotions what you put into them, whereas the sacraments give grace of themselves and are therefore much to be preferred. As for the Americans who frequent Communion and yet do not develop an interior life, their difficulty lies chiefly in that lack of integration which prevents the full exercise of the moral virtues.

WHY AREN'T AMERICANS CONTEMPLATIVE?
1. Materialism

Looked at from the underside, the advance toward God is a progressive detachment from creatures. The "dark nights" of which the mystics speak are purifications in this regard which God arranges. They are for people who are already on the contemplative road. Those who have not yet reached the beginnings of contemplation have to do the first and obvious detaching themselves. They have to mortify themselves in order to lift themselves up from a life bound to the senses so that their spiritual life can get started. This is really the first step: we have to stop loving the things of this world.

Now it is right here that religion and the American Way of Life are at odds. "We're spoiled, thank God," say the advertisements. Don't thank God, thank the devil. God it is Who gave us abundance, but it is the devil who has encouraged us to waste it, to wallow in it, or talk endlessly about it, to forget Who gave it to us, to cherish it and to lay up treasures of it on earth which may prevent our getting to heaven.

Every man has his own struggle against concupiscence. What is vicious in America as presently constituted is that our way of life heaps temptations in a man's path, whereas a godly society, recognizing man's weakness and looking to his salvation, would forbid the exploitation of concupiscence in the interests of avarice. Advertising is the ordinary and most flagrant instrument of our temptations, but advertising is not an isolated phenomenon, it is only the instrument of an industrial-capitalist system which has had to turn to the home market. It cajoles us into buying what we don't need and what is harmful to the salvation of our souls. It cajoles, and that works, but every once in a while one senses the iron hand of force behind the velvet glove of invitation. It is almost as though we were being made to consume in order to keep feeding a monstrously destructive system. As long as our economic system (the tentacles of which are twisted around everything from politics to publishing) is ordered to money as its last end, so long will the spirit of contemplation and the American Way of Life be at odds. There are not enough people yet who have declined to be exploited, so as to disturb the profiteers. But if there were a widespread wave of penance then we would see people showing their colors.

II. Spiritual Blindness

Spiritual blindness is a disease of intellectuals, those people who are the most likely to have escaped the lure of materialism. It is about the worst thing that could happen to those whose lives center in the mind.

First, what is it? It is a punishment inflicted by God for intellectual sins. The sins are intellectual curiosity and pride. The punishment consists in this: that God takes away His light from the minds of those who do not wish to receive it, abandoning them to the darkness which original sin and their own sins pull down upon them. Spiritual blindness is characterized not by ignorance of facts (which is a relatively clear and easily remediable state), nor by native stupidity, but by confusion of thought and defect of judgment. Those who suffer from it are the blind guides of Scripture, who strain out a gnat and swallow a camel, who have every comma in place in an article rife with internal inconsistencies, who concentrate on the artistic elements in pornographic statuary, who feature the delivery of morally bad poetry, and worry about only the medical aspects of venereal disease. Garrigou-Lagrange says of spiritual blindness: "It takes all penetration away from us and leaves us in a state of spiritual dullness, which is like the loss of all higher intelligence."

There are several ways of recognizing spiritual blindness. It is chiefly marked by mental confusion and the inability to recognize implications and contradictions. It also consists in a preference for discussing the trivial over the important, the material rather than the spiritual. It is common among teachers in secular colleges, among liberal Protestant clergymen, among Catholic intellectuals who have higher degrees in social studies, and among Catholics generally who try to serve God and Mammon. It is the obvious punishment of those who lightly disregard the Church's prohibition in the matter of books and movies.

Let us take a gross example of spiritual blindness. Several years ago, an interfaith organization had a brotherhood campaign. They proposed to raise several million dollars to establish a research project to determine the bases of brotherhood (money and research discovered the atomic bomb, why not brotherhood?), after which they were going to arrange to have the same taught in colleges. Now there may exist some simple child of a scientific age so ignorant of religion as to suppose that brotherhood is a fit subject for a research project, or to suppose that the basis of brotherhood has not long since been known and ignored, but such cannot be said of the clergy. "Woe to you, blind guides!"

Evidence of spiritual blindness is at every hand. The double-talk of the radio. The nonsense written in most magazines. The learned palaver of the schools. The fine speeches of statesmen.

Spiritual blindness is the inverse, the opposite of contemplation. As contemplation is characterized by a simple intellectual grasp of truth, so this blindness is marked by multiplicity. It accounts, for instance, for the rash of facts and statistics gathered in contemporary America. Vast amounts of money and energy have been channeled in this direction without adding to anyone's wisdom. People given to this collect thousands of uncorrelated, mechanically arranged facts. They have a lust for stuffing more and more information into already overcrowded memories, without ever going to the heart of any matter. Instead of the passivity of the contemplative gaze, the spiritually blind are always restless in their pursuit of knowledge, reading magazines, attending lectures, weighing the latest theory propounded by the latest paper read at the latest assemblage of experts, joining the book-of-the-month club, keeping up with this and that.

Let us examine the sins which precipitate the punishment of spiritual blindness. They are two: curiosity and pride.

CURIOSITY

Curiosity is a defect of our mind, which inclines us with eagerness and precipitation toward the consideration and study of less useful subjects, making us neglect the things of God and our salvation ... whereas people who have little learning but are nourished with the Gospel possess great rectitude of judgment. There are others who, far from nourishing themselves profoundly with the great Christian truths, spend a great part of their time carefully storing up useless, or at least only slightly useful, knowledge which does not at all form the judgment. They are afflicted with almost a mania for collecting. Theirs is an accumulation of knowledge mechanically arranged and unorganized, somewhat as if it were in a dictionary. This type of work, instead of training the mind, smothers it, as too much wood smothers a fire. Under this jumble of accumulated knowledge, they can no longer see the light of first principles, which alone could bring order out of all this material and lift up their souls even to God, the Beginning and End of all things.

That's what St. Thomas had to say about curiosity.[3] It will come as a shock to many to learn that it is a sin, since intellectual

3 This quote was mistakenly attributed to St. Thomas but is from Volume 1 of *The Three Ages of The Interior Life by Fr. Reginald Garrigou-Lagrange.* — Ed.

curiosity is exalted by the liberalism which prevails in our "best" colleges. It is not a greed for knowledge, but a thirst for truth, which is virtuous. The man who has a thirst for truth is forever seeking to know first principles, to find God. He may be way off the beam at a given moment, taken in by Freud or Yogi, but if he maintains his search and his good will, he will find the ultimate truth. (Here we cannot help but remark on the difference between a pagan searching for truth and seeing, for instance, the glimmer of truth in Freud, and the Catholic who admires Freud in disregard of the fullness of truth which he has and which he has neglected to explore. The former comes through almost untarnished, the latter is a candidate for spiritual blindness.) The curious man, on the other hand, sticks to second, third, tenth and trivial things. He would do well on Information Please, or as a Professor of Sociology at Hunter College, or compiling another volume of "strange facts."

Most Americans don't know (or seem to care) if God exists; which, if any, is the Church Christ founded; what the purpose of life is; and what will happen to them after they die. What they must know is whether the Brooklyn Dodgers won, if U. S. Steel is off ½, the weather report, a five-letter word meaning "to steal," and so on. "Ought we to have a Third Party in the United States?" Town Hall asks. But Town Hall has not committed itself for or against the existence of the Deity, or even ventured to investigate the morality of contraception. And the truth of the matter is that if Town Hall concerned itself with anything really important the radio would frown upon it. Because we Americans originally disagreed about fundamentals, we have come to assume that there is no truth about them.

This mental busyness, this superficial accumulation of facts, this "don't miss anything" attitude which causes Americans to break out in a rash of newspapers and digests, deserves to be punished by spiritual blindness. God is trying to show us, through circumstances, how dangerous our condition is. We are like men who won't look up from the latest work on "How to Make Hatchets"

25

long enough to see the axe descending on our own heads. What wonder then that God takes light away, so that if we should chance to look up, we would only see the unusual contour of the axe handle, or want to measure the wind's resistance to its descent.

PRIDE

The chief condition of learning truth is humility, a certain docility to light from above, a certain mistrust of one's own powers of discernment. But we Americans have even lost the correct meaning of the word humility, and we have striven to set ourselves up as gods. We have self-confidence, self-assurance. We are self-made. All these are reflections of the fact that we no longer look to God but to ourselves. Now the hero of American academic circles is the agnostic, the skeptic, the liberal philosopher. He is the man of tolerance, who regards only one thing with horror, and that is dogmatism. The American liberal exactly fits Ernest Hello's description of The Mediocre Man "… who considers every affirmation insolent, because every affirmation excludes the contradictory proposition." These people are usually gentle by nature, and therefore escape the censure which they richly deserve. We have glorified them, whereas in truth they have done incalculable harm to souls.

Academic pride has given rise to the factory system of teacher-training, to the Ph.D. assembly lines, to the accreditation system and the mania for experts and footnotes in America. Everybody is talking at once, and nobody has truth. You can ask anybody from the ten-cent store clerk to the president of the university this simple question: "What is the purpose of life?" and not get an answer, unless someone has chanced to read it in a catechism. The situation is at once ludicrous and tragic.

Intellectual pride does not seem to have affected the ordinary man directly, but only to characterize his blind university guides. He is more likely to have curiosity. Anyhow, between the two vices, there is widespread spiritual blindness, and almost universal materialism. Why aren't there more miracles around? Where are the saints? You might find them in the byways, but don't look for them in the highways. The American Way of Life does not conduce to their production.

CAN AMERICANS BECOME CONTEMPLATIVE?

"We need a St. Francis of Assisi in America," one frequently hears. Indeed we do. What a delight it would be to have a great barefoot saint helping us to extricate ourselves from the chains of materialism which bind us to the consideration of earthly things.

But we also need a St. Dominic. We need someone who dares shout what we scarcely dare whisper, that everywhere youths are going to college and being graduated as bewildered fools who do not even know the purpose of life. We need someone to give us courage to disregard the latest expert in deference to The First Expert. Then we shall take to our knees and light will be given to us.

CAROL ROBINSON

"But David, aren't you being a little naive?"

THERE WILL BE NO JEW AND NO
GENTILE, NO COLORED AND NO WHITE-

BUT ALL ONE IN
HART, SCHAFFNER & MARX.

A Catholic Culture
for America

THE U.S.A. IS A CIVILIZED COUNTRY RATHER than a cultured one. Culture is organic, personal; civilization is impersonal, inanimate, brittle. If the Church is to be something more in the U.S.A. than simply another denomination, then it must create a Catholic culture. It must be a culture with roots in the soil, and with a vital stake in every public movement.

The most startling observation to a foreigner is the lack of any organized, secular, Catholic life. The Church here is well-organized ecclesiastically, huge numbers attend Mass faithfully, her educational and charitable institutions are richly endowed there is a fruitful spirituality and an intelligent and ardent clergy. The proportion of Catholics in the U. S. A. is one in six, yet their influence on American life is slight. Except in New Mexico and some rural sections of the mid-West there is no evidence of a Catholic culture. The American Catholic is indistinguishable from his fellow Americans — except by refusing to eat meat on Friday.

Catholics are a minority, it is true. Yet the Protestant majority is sub-divided into over a hundred sects, and one-half the population claims no church affiliation whatever. No longer is the timidity of an embattled minority defensible. Catholics can only meet the challenge of the neo-pagan world by a united front battling in the world, not from behind church walls. It is imperative that Catholics come out of the ghetto.

To accomplish the formation of a Catholic culture in the U.S.A. three tasks must be accomplished: the creation of a Catholic aristocracy, the recognition of the traditional Catholic culture in the rural areas, and the conquest of the key intellectual positions. If the first task disturbs those Americans who have succumbed to the modern idea that a democracy must necessarily be a government where all are equal and whose people live in a land of no distinctions; all alike slaves to the mass mind, cogs in the wheel of industry, then we will remind them that the Founding Fathers of the republic intended that there should be representative government by a competent, responsible class of men. The Founding Fathers created a republic on these shores and not a democracy. In the Federalist, Madison defines these two forms of government as follows: " . . . in a democracy, the people exercised the government in person; in a republic they administer it by their representatives." It was the latter that the writers of the Constitution had in mind.

It is an American paradox that in a land where there is continual talk of democracy there is also a desperate attempt to rid itself of the results of democracy. The society pages of the daily newspapers contain more information about the goings-on of the socially acceptable than do the newspapers of monarchies. All the evidence is of a people trying not to be "democratic." Witness the color distinctions, the emphasis laid on the importance of a college degree, the snobbery of fraternities and sororities, the hints at Norman descent and Mayflower ancestors, the whispering campaign against Jews, the restricted neighborhoods. Social ambition is the most important factor in American life and the greatest incentive to the American ego.

So, the notion of a native aristocracy is not too far-fetched. The old families in the country are not as powerful as formerly, but are still vital and a factor to be reckoned with. They are holding their own against the onslaught of the technicians, advertising men and corporation executives who seem destined to be the architects of the future civilization.[4] There are men today who are the worthy descendants of Washington and Jefferson, who prefer to live on their land in modest comfort, who are conscious of their responsibilities and who respect the great

4 For a description of this civilization, read Burnham's *The Managerial Revolution* (1941).

American spiritual and intellectual inheritance. This element in the population possesses all the original strength and élan. They might disappear from the public view for a generation or two, only to reappear on the scene again with all the vitality and purpose of their forefathers. Their influence is considerable even now in some sections; in New England, the border states of the South and on the Pacific Coast.

None the less tenacious is the Catholic aristocracy of the Maryland river valleys, of the Kentucky blue-grass region, the descendants of distinguished Spanish families in New Mexico and the prolific and wonderful progeny of the Spanish-Irish landowners in California. It is to these people that Catholics should look for a way of life that makes no compromise with materialism.

THE PEOPLE

To help the elite get into Heaven, there must be a Catholic populace. Millions of Catholic immigrants brought to this country as their most cherished possession — their Faith. In their mental baggage they brought legends and customs, festivals and Saints' days, ancient ballads and dances. They brought their arts and skills and transplanted intact their family and community life in the traditional Catholic pattern. The Church has been a bridge between Europe and America. The newest Catholic refugee just off the boat has his Faith in common with the descendant of a Chavez in New Mexico or a Carroll in Maryland.

The Faith also binds together the diverse elements of this most unhomogeneous land. It is the connecting link between the French-Canadian mill worker of New Hampshire and the Ukrainian wheat farmer of North Dakota; the Irish saloonkeeper in Boston and the Basque sheep-herder in Idaho; the Portuguese fisherman in Gloucester, the Czech baker in Cedar Rapids, the German brewer in Milwaukee, the Negro janitor in Harlem, the Italian florist in San Francisco, the Polish assembly man in

Detroit, the Magyar coal miner in Pennsylvania, the Slovak steel worker in Cleveland, the Lithuanian refinery worker in Chicago, the Syrian rug weaver in Brooklyn, the Pueblo Indian craftsman in Arizona. The culture of America is largely a transplanted one, and the most cultured people in the U.S.A. are those of the minority groups who have not abandoned their traditions.

To observe these transplanted cultures at their best, we must go to the rural districts. Only when he has settled on the land has the immigrant retained his traditional manner of living. In the cities, he is waging a losing battle. What chance is there in a crowded tenement on a sooty, noisy street in the midst of the least desirable examples of American civilization, for the flourishing of a culture born of an agrarian way of life? The immigrant is frustrated in his attempts to teach his children the homely virtues of the old homeland. He is bewildered by the sight of his children who before his eyes are becoming corrupted by movies, dance halls and the brutal comradeship of the city streets. The children don't know what is happening to them, they only try to conform as one does in a "democracy." The Americanization process is at work, the de-personalization of a human being has begun.

The reaction to such demoralizing processes has set in already. Americans and American institutions do not look favorably upon forced Americanization. They have begun to realize after two decades of bungling and confusion that too rapid Americanization is detrimental to sound development. The younger generations, if cut away suddenly from the traditions of their original stocks do not prove stable elements in the make-up of American society. Juvenile crime primarily finds its victims among those young people whom over-zealous Americanization has deprived of the life-value of nationality backgrounds, without being able to substitute for these sound thinking. Accordingly responsible civic leaders prefer to make haste slowly in this field.

Traditional mores come out second-best in the cities. In the rural areas, however, the old ways have been preserved in more

or less purity. The Czech, German, Polish and Belgian farmers of
the mid-West, the Italian, Portuguese and Dalmatian fishermen
along the coasts are representatives of a traditional Catholic culture. To find Catholic culture in the U.S.A. at its best you must
go among the Mexican settlements in New Mexico and western
Texas; to the isolated hamlets of Cajun trappers deep in the bay-
ous of Louisiana; to the rich farm lands of central Iowa, where
German and Irish families have kept close to the land for three
generations; to the delightful Belgian villages amid the cherry
orchards of Door County, Wisconsin; among the Ukrainian
farmers of North Dakota, whose towns might have been carried over bodily from the steppes; and to Bardstown, Kentucky,
where English Catholics settled in the closing years of the Revolution and to its gracious and dignified Cathedral, one of Catholic
America's historic shrines; and from Bardstown, along the road
north to Louisville, by the venerable Trappist abbey, and through
towns with the holy names of Nazareth, Bethlehem, Gethsemane.

The Catholic rural movement is of great importance to the
U.S.A. The era of great industrial megalopolitan centers is nearing an end. The trend towards decentralization already has set in.
The urban population, predominantly Catholic now, has great
difficulty competing with the high birth rate of the Protestant
rural districts. The rural areas need Catholic families and the
"back to the land" movement needs to be free from the sentimentality that is such a detriment to it. The rural life program
needs the vitality that comes from stimulating activities such as
cooperatives, agricultural colleges, and folk high schools.

THE INTELLECTUALS

The third task, a responsible intellectual class, is more difficult
of accomplishment. We immediately turn to the universities for
the human material. But the prospect is sad. The Catholic colleges have not met the challenge of the times. They seem to turn
out only insurance agents, automobile salesmen and copy writers.

The skeptical attitude of the Church toward mass movements is not discussed in the schools and Catholic students are often not aware of the Church's negative attitude toward the spirit of the times. No attempt is made to destroy the great god Success. Catholic college graduates are no less vulnerable to the effect of the battle to "keep up with the Joneses," than are the graduates of the secular universities. They become civilized at college and ignore or scorn the culture of their fathers.

One might feel some hope in the young intellectuals that foregather in the larger cities, if they didn't become immured in their ivory towers, spending their days (or more often their nights) in endless discussions, stimulating enough to be sure, but influencing no one but their own kind. Catholic intellectual circles are a congerie of groups, each claiming an "apostolate," each one feverish with activity, and each ignoring the other. The Faith that has unified the contrasting minority groups across the land has failed to unite these unregenerate individualists. Working in their own milieu, they have failed to recognize the broader view of an American apostolate. All the "apostolates," whether to the Negro, the poor, the press, the worker, the youth have one goal, the sanctification of society and of one's own soul, yet few of the zealots understand it in its full significance. These eager and intelligent young ones should be the leaders back to culture, but until they work together in the local scene, it will be impossible for them to work on a national scale. The third class should recruit its members from the other two classes. It should be as free of class and racial bias as the clergy. As a peasant's son can be pope, and a prince of the royal blood may be content to be an humble lay brother, so the Catholic intelligentsia should welcome equally the immigrant and his children as well as the old stock Catholic of English-Irish-Spanish-French background. It is only in this way that the tremendous task can be accomplished. It is to the intellectual elite that we should look for the formation of a Catholic theater of the highest standards; based on what is best in Broadway, but not neglecting the provinces; for a Catholic motion picture company, a Catholic lecture forum. It is from this third class that should come a Catholic literature, a crying need. There are Catholic writers in the U.S.A., or would it be more accurate to call them writers who are Catholic? They have been frustrated in their efforts by the lack of a Catholic reading public, by the absence of an enlightened publishing business and an intellectually dynamic press. But must Catholic writers produce only for the negligible Catholic market? Willa Cather has shown what can be done with a fine piece of writing on a Catholic theme. Her *Death Comes For the Archbishop* is the finest American Catholic novel to date.

This, then, is the task for the Catholics of the U.S.A. The country had Christian beginnings and there has always been a ready store of idealism to supply successive generations. This is doomed to dry up under the impact of technological civilization unless great effort is made to bolster the spiritual life of the U.S.A. Catholics must understand their Faith, but equally important they must understand their Faith in relation to the world around them. If Catholic culture is to be taken from the ghetto to be reconstructed in the full glare of public life, then it must be not only Catholic, but American.

Let us come out of the ghetto before we have to take to the catacombs.

LEONARD AUSTIN

Some Fell Among Thorns

*And he spoke to them many things in parables, saying:
Behold the sower went forth to sow.... And others fell
among thorns: and the thorns grew up and choked
them... And he that received the seed among thorns,
is he that heareth the word, and the care of this world
and the deceitfulness of riches choketh up the word, and
he becometh fruitless.*

Matthew xiii, 3–22.

LET US CALL THIS CITY LAKEPORT, BECAUSE
that is not its name, and because it is a port on the Great Lakes.
While this is one city, it represents scores of other cities throughout the country, cities that are in the same spiritual state, where
the seed of the Faith has been sown, and where the thorns are
growing up and choking the seed.

Lakeport is spiritually a dead city, in common with its many
counterparts in these United States, where the love of riches and
the comforts of the American Way of Life choke the spirituality
of the people. There is nothing like luxurious living to destroy
the seed of sacrifice and the spirit of subservience to the Will
of God.

Lakeport differs little from many another city. It has more
gas stations than churches, more motion picture theaters than
hospitals, more bartenders than teachers, and more mechanics
than men of God. It has few wealthy people. The population is
comprised of wage earners, ranging in hierarchy from superin-
tendents (and managers) down to day laborers. Labor unions
are strong and influential, on the American Federation of Labor
pattern, and Catholics play prominent parts in them — more
important parts than they play in Catholic activities. It is largely
a city of small home owners, or those hopeful of owning their

homes. Communism has never been strong, except during the deep depression, and now it is not a problem of importance.

About two-thirds of Lakeport is non-Catholic; about half of these nominally Protestant. There is a progressive weakening of Protestantism. Materialism is the greatest factor in this loss of membership; the trend is toward religious indifferentism, where it matters not whether the church is Methodist or Baptist or Presbyterian. Protestants attend the church nearest their home, and church-going is largely a matter of convenience.

Attempts are made to revive this flagging interest by evangelical crowd-rousers that attract a small core of faithful attendants, but the majority come for a while, and then drift away. The young people are dropping away from the churches. They go to Sunday School when they are small, but since their parents stay away from church few of the children continue when they are older.

Protestantism has little residual vitality. Then what of Catholicism?

A count would show a large proportion of the Catholic population has regular weekly communicants. The churches are filled to overflowing, with long lines of the Faithful awaiting their turn at the Communion rail. Special services during Lent and other times are well attended. The infrequent missions have always had a fine attendance, and generally there could be little complaint regarding church attendance and Communions.

The Catholic parish and city organizations are strong. The Confraternity of Christian Doctrine has a large and apparently satisfactory organization. Programs are scheduled for the various study clubs and groups in the Confraternity, and these schedules are carefully followed by most of the parish groups.

The Knights of Columbus boast a large and successful Council. It attains the Century Club regularly, which means that it adds one hundred or more members each year. Its tastefully furnished club-rooms are often used as a center for Catholic activities and for meetings by other Catholic organizations. Many consider this the best K. of C. Council in the state.

There are Holy Name Societies in almost every parish, with varying degrees of activity. Most of them hold monthly Communion breakfasts after the Holy Name Mass, when the men of the society discuss problems and listen to speakers.

The Catholic Daughters of America are active, with regular meetings, donations to worthy Catholic causes, such as providing Catholic books for the public library, helping the nuns in catechizing during the summer months and holding occasional retreats.

All the parishes have parent-teacher associations, and some Christian Mothers associations, with regular meetings, talks by various priests and prominent laymen.

There are one-day retreats for the men every year and often retreats for the women. Lately some parishes have experimented with days of recollection.

That is the surface. On the surface it seems as though there is a vigorous Catholic life, especially when you add that such Catholic figures as Dorothy Day, Catherine de Hueck Doherty, the Grail Leaders, Vincent McAloon, Therese Mueller, and other have spoken at Lakeport during the past several years. But the surface is deceiving.

Is there any real vitality to all this surface activity — the many Communions, the large memberships in these Catholic organizations? What are the results? Is the real life that exists in the Sacraments taking hold of the Catholic people, turning them into Catholic apostles?

Let's look at conversions. There are few other than those connected with marriages to Catholics. This is not to belittle these, but the scarcity of others indicates that Catholics are not overwhelming their fellow citizens with their Catholicity.

The spiritual outcome of mixed marriages is another measuring rod. There are many such marriages which frequently end as indifferent marriages — even among Catholic school graduates. Some mixed marriages may be expected because there is no Catholic college nearby, and Catholic boys and girls must go to a secular college if they want to attend one convenient to home. But it does question the depth of Catholic beliefs, and even training, when week after week marriages take place in Catholic rectories.

Take a typical instance: The girl is a good Catholic fundamentally, devout, educated in Catholic schools. But she is compromising. All her husband's relatives and friends are non-Catholic and she doesn't want to offend them. She goes to Communion less and less often, although periodically berating herself for her lack of regularity in attending the Sacraments. As a result of this sterile compromise, her Catholicity is lifeless in all but superficial aspects.

Vocations are another test. They have been few, very few for many years, and as a result the city and the diocese are impoverished of priests. The clergy are overworked, often trying to do two men's work, and getting but little help from the laity, who should play such an important role in the Church's growth.

CIVIC CORRUPTION

Another test of the vitality of Lakeport is the state of civic virtue and professional ethics. In both these fields, the trend is basically away from moral virtue.

First, the community as a whole has a spotted past. For years it had a wide open "red light" district, and this was only closed within the last ten years, and not for any religious or moral motives. In the past gambling openly flourished, with slot machines, card games, and elaborate gambling houses. All those were against the laws of city and state, but the laws were not enforced. To my knowledge, there has been no serious protest, serious enough to gain appreciable support, against any of these vicious practices from anyone within the city — whether it be priest, minister, newspaper, public official, or otherwise.

The evidences of civic corruption have been linked with graft and bribery on the one hand and a deplorable indifferentism on the part of the public on the other. This naturally had a destructive effect on the life of the community, lowering its moral tone and exposing its members to temptations of all kinds. Especially vicious has been its effect on the youth, thus subjected to concupiscence of the eyes, ears, and body. Perhaps such things as these account for the venereal disease clinic held each week.

Another indication might be public activities. Generally speaking, they are not religious, they are not "cultural" in any sense of the word, but the ordinary escapist pleasures of the world, and worldly in almost every aspect.

Lakeport has a tavern or bar for about every four hundred men, women and children of the city — a fair indication of the amount of drinking. Some taverns have dance floors, which are the only places youth have to dance, with the exception of occasional school dances. Sometimes a fraternal organization will sponsor a dance for the children of its members.

Generally, then, Lakeport is a community of too much drinking, too little concern for the effects on their children of civic corruption, graft and immorality. Practically all of the corruption, graft and immorality is now past history — though only within the past ten years — but the effects do linger on, for the purge was not a moral one.

SOLUTION BY DISSOLUTION

The divorce rate is high, about three divorces to every five marriages. There are no figures on the percentage of Catholics involved, but they are said to be low. A contributing cause of this high divorce rate is the ease of securing divorces. When divorces are not contested, there is little difficulty beyond the legal waiting time — and most are not contested. Many attorneys have little hesitation in recommending a divorce. Some consider it the practical solution for everything from a petty squabble to more or less serious drinking. To their legalistic minds, marriage is merely another contract, to be dissolved with the proper whereas and be-it-resolved clauses.

There are many Catholic lawyers and judges. Most of them have the political wit of the Irish, a help to survival in a predominantly non-Catholic city. Perhaps this has made them more cautious, but their materialism is strong.

There are some very fine doctors, and some very poor ones. One doctor, for instance, specializes in abortions, but because of "medical ethics" other doctors, including high-minded Catholics, do nothing to attempt to remedy the situation.

The subject of abortion leads to a discussion of birth control, natural or unnatural. Another indication of the spiritual condition of Lakeport is its lack of fruitfulness in marriage.

Parents of large families — and by large most mean four or five children — are considered queer, and such mothers are greeted with comments ranging from "Did you get caught again, honey?" to stories of what others had done through doctors or patent medicines or other means to murder unborn children. The frankness with which birth control is discussed, even among Catholic women, is disgusting.

It is not unusual for families to have only two children — one for the father and one for the mother, as they so calmly express their desires. And there are the usual number of career women, who feel that the world expects more of them than the mere raising of children. Some find to their great sorrow that they cannot trifle with God, and are unable to have children when they feel they can "afford" them.

Others are a bit more fortunate, such as one mother who had one child, apparently with some regret since it interfered with her career. After some six or seven years, she heeded the child's plea for a brother or sister, and brought another into the world. But she is still more devoted to her job than to her family. She hires a girl to take care of the two children, and the mother sees them an hour or two daily, and on week-ends. And this, like other cases, is not one where the mother must work but where she wants a career of her own outside her home to inflate her vanity, or to add luxuries to an already sufficient income.

THE CHURCH FROM THE INSIDE

But let's see if there really is any vitality in the Catholic organizations which superficially seem so successful. And since it is the largest and the most successful, let's take first the Knights of Columbus.

They set the pace for Catholic lay activity. They recognize their prominent place, and meetings frequently resound with the phrase, "the strong right arm of the Church." In Lakeport, the Knights of Columbus are the largest Catholic organization. They are the most active, and they should have the urge to do big things. As Father Gillis remarked at the Catholic Press Association convention this year, "The Knights of Columbus used to say years ago when they were 600,000, that they must do big things or perish, perish of dry rot — or of rot not so dry." The last phrase apparently struck home to his audience, as the ripple of appreciative laughter demonstrated.

The Knights of Columbus in Lakeport draw into their organization the men most likely to work for catholic action. And through these members, the Catholic women of the city are likewise involved in K. of C. activities.

Financially, their position is a most enviable one from a worldly viewpoint. They have probably $25,000 in their treasury. Unfortunately, the possession of this money has hardened the determination of the trustees to resist any attacks against it. At one time, a resolution was introduced to spend $25 of it providing Scout awards. Half a meeting was taken to discuss pro and con this heavy expenditure, and finally after much protest the expenditure of $25 was approved, a prime example of the power of riches to destroy perspective, charity, and even common sense.

Unfortunately, the whole tone of the K. of C. activities is social. Their clubrooms are in the same style as the other fraternal organizations of the city, the Elks, the Eagles, and so forth. The pattern is the same, even to the bar at which beer and hard liquor are sold. The rule of the Knights of Columbus forbidding membership to anyone in the retail liquor business does not keep the Council itself out of that business. Also, the fact that such a bar is definitely an occasion of sin for many of its members is not allowed to interfere with the profits thereof.

The Knights of Columbus followed other fraternal organizations in installing slot machines at a time when they were illegal, complacent authorities suffering it. The theory was that their members would play the machines anyway, and might as well do it in good surroundings. At the time they pointed with justifiable pride to the fact that their machines were set on a minimum percentage — that is, the machines were adjusted so that the house would take only a small proportion of the money played. Thus, it would take you that much longer to lose all your money. The slot machines were later removed — not through the triumph of civic virtue, nor religious scruples, nor an indignant public. A new state law was passed, with sharp teeth, and reluctantly, but with hopes for the future, the slot machines were stored away.

All this has produced a social type of catholic action in the minds of the Council members. Their catholic action consists of a Catholic bowling league in the winter, Catholic dances on Saturday nights, and a Catholic picnic during the summer.

This peculiar Catholic social sense penetrates the minds of all the members. A newly elected Grand Knight once confided that he was determined to effect some reforms, the main one being to close the bar before midnight on Saturday evenings. He realized, of course, that this could not be done immediately, but hoped to accomplish it by the end of his term of office.

Another worthy enterprise was the setting of the fifth Sunday of the month as Communion Sunday for the Council. In justice, it must be admitted that it is expected that the Knights will go to Communion with other men of their Holy Name Societies. But this plethora of social activity vitiates their desire for any other Catholic work. As a result, the Holy Name Societies are anemic, and their activities, small as they are, are subordinate to the social activities of the Council.

The Knights and the Holy Name men do sponsor a one-day retreat, or day of recollection for the men each year. They do get a good representation. Of course, they do not observe silence; there is a convention atmosphere about the intermissions. And they are careful not to schedule the retreat when it would interfere with deer hunting or duck shooting or football games, or any other really important activities. And they choose the retreat master with care. He must not be too demanding, and should be entertaining, and sociable. A painless retreat is wanted. Perhaps it really is needed, because if you drop a man over his head in spiritual waters he may drown. But after six or seven years a one-day retreat can stand intensification.

The women do a bit better with retreats, though they do not have one every year. They have better retreat masters; rather, their retreats are more spiritual, and at one time they had three-day retreats. But that was years ago.

There is no retreat house in the diocese, of which this is the largest city. Some years ago, at the first men's retreat, the Bishop expressed the hope that a retreat house might come out of this new activity. That is as far as it has gone.

There are many other Catholic organizations in the city. The Legion of Mary, which is one of the new excellent apostolic organizations, consists of a few elderly women, whose hearts are filled with charity, but whose activities are extremely limited.

The Catholic Daughters of America include the best Catholic women of the city. Some of their members do excellent work in helping the Sisters in catechizing children in the rural areas, but their influence is not felt beyond that.

The parent-teacher associations are much as they are elsewhere — as are the Foresters and Christian Mothers. Recently a St. Vincent de Paul Society conference was organized, and its influence is spreading. It is too early to tell how important it may become, although the beginnings are good.

The Confraternity of Christian Doctrine is well organized and has many members. Personally, I am disappointed with their accomplishments and feel that it falls far short of its possibilities; others feel otherwise.

Generally, however, Catholic activities lack spiritual fire, while Catholic Action is conspicuous by its absence. Oh, efforts have been made, and speakers have come and gone, and the seed has been planted, perhaps sprouted a bit, but then was smothered by the materialism of the people.

There have been various radio programs, Catholic quiz programs, Catholic news broadcasts, Catholic plays and dramas, and talks and interviews. There have been Catholic newspaper columns and publicity of Catholic events, Field Masses filling a municipal stadium, and city-wide prayers for peace. And the people have reacted to all of these, for a time; and have been interested and enthusiastic, for a time.

There have been various speakers brought by the Sisters in the schools. They brought Dorothy Day to talk ("Why is she so shabby?" they asked) and the Baroness de Hueck ("Why does she use that atrocious slang — and she a Baroness!") and the Grail Leaders ("quaint!") and Vincent McAloon and many others. And they came, and they went and the ripple caused by their coming soon passed away, and it was as though they had not been there.

And he that received the seed among thorns, is he that heareth the word and the care of this world and the deceitfulness of riches choketh up the word, and he becometh fruitless.

And that is the main reason for the fruitlessness of all the seeds planted in Lakeport. It is not hopeless; nothing is, so long as the Gospel is preached. But if the Faith is to take deep root among these people, if the seed is to grow, efforts must be strong enough to overcome the thorns.

And the thorns? This is an ordinary middle-class city, no different except in detail from hundreds of others. It is dedicated to the Good Things in life, as exemplified by the American Way of Lifer and the advertisements in the *Saturday Evening Post.* Here a man wants a new car every year, two children — one for his wife and one for himself; a cottage on the lake, and beer in the refrigerator. The best thing about his job is his pay check and quitting time, when he can drop over to the club for a small one and chat with the boys, and go out for a game of golf, or go fishing.

That is Lakeport — a city of mediocrity, basking in its lukewarmness, unconvinced of the penalty Jesus Christ forecast for the lukewarm.

FLOYD ANDERSON

"But Pope Leo, aren't you being a little naive?"

Advertising and the American Woman

WHEN CONSIDERING THE NATURE OF TRUE womanhood, Catholics have two very wonderful sources in the revealed word of God. The Book of Proverbs sings most beautifully and most realistically of the Valiant Woman—in whose heart her husband trusted, by whose charity and industry, by whose wisdom and prudence, the domestic kingdom flourished prosperously and well in the fear and love of God. St. Luke's joyous account, too, of Mary's visit to Elizabeth is the most exalted yet sweetly simple lesson in the holiness of Christian women whose delight is in their God and in the greatness of their motherhood.

But the modern woman, that Great American Institution, no longer reads the Scriptures — a factor which would not be so detrimental to her spiritual life and to the spiritual life of her family if, then, she read nothing at all. The American woman is, however, a notoriously voracious reader, as a glance at the popular magazine stand or a rush-hour subway ride will indicate. As such she is a much too susceptible victim of another Great American Institution — Advertising — which serves in itself as an inspired text of secularism and a complete education in materialism.

Most advertising is aimed specifically for the American woman and reaches directly at her through the media of her favorite magazines, which have become as indispensable to her as the breviary to the priest.

Since the function of the advertiser is to produce results in the increased sale of goods, his method, generally, is to create a *desire* for goods. Obviously, the stimulated desire must be greater than the natural interest of the woman, who usually controls the family wealth, in providing cautiously and wisely for the needs of her household. That is to say, it must make the purchase of some item appear to the woman as a necessity whether it is or not. Under normal conditions of living, the supply is met only when the demand is a true demand. This simplicity of economics, while intrinsically sane and prudent, is unsatisfactory to the American system of mass production. Industry looks to the advertiser for the remedy.

That the advertiser counts for his success on the use to which he can put the American woman is, as has been mentioned, due to the fact that she does, either as a mother of a family or as an independent wage earner, determine on what the money is to be spent and how much will be spent. Furthermore, it is a relatively easy matter to influence her directly. Unlike men, who read less and more intelligently, she devotes much time, interest and respect to the so-called women's magazines, which constantly formulate her mind and attitudes in keeping with their own worldly standards.

According to the advertisers, there are two types of magazines: those read by the "masses" and those read by the "classes." The distinction made is based on purchasing power. *The Ladies Home Journal, Good Housekeeping, Woman's Home Companion, Cosmopolitan, Redbook,* etc., magazines of enormous circulation belong to the "masses" — the middle-income groups whose needs and whose ambitions are moderate. *Vogue, Mademoiselle, Harper's Bazaar,* etc., are definitely of the "class" satisfying the demands of the professional woman, and the woman of wealth. Nevertheless, recognize the fact that the average American Woman is too well acquainted with all the popular periodicals.

Through observation of the first type magazine and its advertisements certain facts become evident. Whether selling toothpaste, a laxative, rugs, stockings, cold cream, evaporated milk, or mattresses, the technique of the advertiser *is not* at all to supply his readers with reasonably accurate information concerning his product — in fact, the method to his madness is to do everything *but* tell the truth. "Everything" usually is reduced to an appeal made to very human, but not always ennobling, emotions — pride, either personal or social, to the desire for masculine attention, for beautiful things or just for possessions. For example, in the *Ladies' Home Journal* for May there were five advertisements for hand lotion representing five different hand lotion manufacturers. The various copy read: (1) "Now! Keep your *hands* as kissable as your lips. It's new, new, N E W!" (Woodbury's); (2) " 'I'll find you,' he said, 'wherever you go. I'll always know those soft hands.' Chances are such memorably soft hands are Jergens cared for . . . Hollywood stars use Jergens Lotion, New York Models use Jergens Lotion . . . and big preferences for Jergens among other groups of charming women"; (3) He's helpless in your hands with the *New Hinds [sic]!*"; (4) " . . . symbol of noble birth — The Fair and Fragile Hand . . . More Hands use Pacquins than any other hand cream in the world:" (5) "Beauty experts say: Do this . . . for Hands that invite Romance . . . " (Sofskin). With the added enticement of suggestive photographs or drawings and despite the farcical exaggeration of pretended results, a woman, through constant exposure to such nonsense, is approached successfully through her wish for physical attractiveness, her interest in novelty, in her desire to be sought after by men, in her submissiveness to authority (the beauty expert), in her measurement of success-in-life-by the movie star, and the model.

However, a magazine read, chiefly, by the housewife, aims further in the encouragement of an old American custom: "Keeping-up-with the Joneses," where everything from pressure cookers, automobiles, and silverware to furniture must be a matter of pride as well as of beauty and utility. Viewed in its entirety, the exploitation of woman's natural concern for the welfare of her home, through advertising, means the continuation of a false ideal: the sacrosanct American way of life, which is materialistic, ambitious, self-seeking, looking for fulfillment in luxury and leisure and in material and social success.

More ruthless, yet more subtle, is the "class" magazine, particularly *Vogue*, whose pages are dedicated to the task of educating the American woman to its own standards of paganism. It does some curious and rather terrifying things in accomplishing its purpose. At least three-quarters of its content is advertisement. It is a highly specializing magazine; its subjects: women and fashion. Logically, but somehow, strangely, husbands, children and families are simply not considered. *Woman* comes into her own, self-existing in a new world of her own making. Its readers are, of course, career women, whose position in Big Business, demands the sleek sophistication, the poised smartness of a *Vogue* Model and the women of wealth who must keep up the appearance of wealth. In accordance with the sort of culture it affects, *Vogue's* advertisements represent tremendous outputs of genuine artistry and talent, the chief end of which is, again, the exploitation of the beauty and natural desires of women. If advertising is the art of the lie, it is *Vogue* that demonstrates so well that it *is* an art. The *Vogue* woman is the smart woman — successful, beautiful, wanted, admired, adored. But she is this too — selfish, hard, superficial, immodest, and masculine. She is not a mother, she is scarcely a wife — sufficient unto herself, she is not even a woman.

Who shall find a Valiant Woman?
Far and from the uttermost coasts is the price of her.
*　　　* * *

Strength and beauty are her clothing, and she shall laugh in the latter day. She hath opened her mouth to wisdom, and the law of clemency is on her tongue. She hath looked well to the paths of her house, and hath not eaten her bread idle. Her children rose up and called her blessed: her husband, and he praised her. Many daughters have gathered together riches: thou hast surpassed them all. Favour is deceitful and beauty is vain: the woman that feareth the Lord, she shall be praised. Give her of the fruit of her hands: and let her works praise her in the gates.

How remote our *Vogue* woman is from being a Valiant woman! And how far more remote from possessing the purity and womanliness of Mary who could worship God in this manner:

> *My soul doth magnify the Lord*
> *and my spirit rejoices in God my Savior;*
> *Because he has regarded the lowliness of his handmaid;*
> *for behold, henceforth, all generations shall call me*
> *blessed; . . .*

Advertising remains one of the most serious barriers to the conversion of the American woman to the Christian life, for she is subject to its overwhelming presence. Setting up luxury and security as a goal for pursuit, advertising is a publicity agent for materialism and a determining factor in the constant formation of women in a way of life, while it may be American, is not Christian, and is certainly pagan.

Feast of St Paschal Baylon,
DOLORES BRIEN

"But Mother Cabrini, aren't you being a little naive?"

Hints for Converting America

THE CONFIRMED CATHOLIC IN THESE UNITED
States, as he sets about the task of restoring all things in Christ,
must approach each problem fully aware of this specific duty
that is his alone. The expert, whether in theology or economics,
cannot solve *his* problems for *him*. Beyond the factor of a specific
duty lies the greater and more glorious factor of specific grace.
With a humility beyond belief were it not for Divine testimony
to its existence, the Holy Ghost waits upon our instrumentality.
God has chosen to act through us. If we do not manifest Christ,
each of us in his own specific and peculiar fashion, then it follows that our associates, who are pagan, cannot know Him. It is
through us that God is seen, or not seen; it is dependent upon us.

The conversion of America will wait until this lesson is learned.
There is no substitute for personal responsibility. When the
moment comes for John Smith, heir to Heaven to speak, the universe and the angels hold their tongues, and wait. His neighbor over
the back fence may have asked the question, "Do you think that
life has any meaning?" Through John's mind flow many thoughts,
and his emotions are mixed. He may recall a sentimental piece of
goo spoken by a dilettante which had been reprinted in the Sunday
supplement under the picture of a herd of sheep. The temptation
is strong to quote these slick and silly phrases as a substitute for an
embarrassing testimony of faith. He may shift the conversation to
baseball or gladioli. The angels wait. John takes a deep breath. His
words may be slow and uncertain but in the colloquial speech of
his times he tells his neighbor of the promises of Christ, just as he
himself knows them and understands them. In that simple and
homely fashion Christ is made manifest to the world. The entire
power of the Church, the Sacramental system, the hierarchy, and

indeed, the Passion and Death of Christ, are marshalled behind the faltering words of John Smith at the moment when he makes his declaration of faith. In his quiet monosyllables is imbedded the fish-hook of Peter the Apostle. For one awe-full moment John Smith speaks for God. If he had not spoken, there would have been a silence which no sound could ever fill.

AN ORGANIZED ATTACK

A sense of personal responsibility increased by an active Faith will lead the lay apostle to spend many hours with the sages of the Church and learn from them the nature of the Faith and the temper of the times. He will see from experience as well as from the wisdom of the Popes that sporadic personal attacks can hardly serve to turn the tide of materialism which itself is so powerfully organized. Consequently, he will agitate among his fellow-Catholics until he can form a nucleus of like-minded people.

At this stage of the game, the will of the majority instead of the Will of God is liable to become prominent, for that is an old American custom. Counting noses is the weakest of methods for ascertaining truth, especially when the end is a spiritual one. When the majority has its way, the danger increases that the very habits of thought which militate against the Faith will become part of the technique of the apostolate. The tools of the world are always clumsy in the hands of the Christian. If the apostolate chooses to use the weapons of the world, the battle will resemble a duel with marshmallows at fifty paces. It will be another children's crusade, just a boy on a man's errand. An error already strong in the apostolate which flows directly from the spirit of the times, is that of placing too much emphasis on natural means and natural ends. This is a formidable obstacle that deserves our attention.

THE SPIRIT OF THE THING

Suppose that two men who were neighbors went into their adjacent back yards and each began to dig a hole. Now, the

intention of the first man was to erect a statue of Our Blessed
Lady, and his excavation was to hold the base of the pedestal. The
purpose of the other man was to dig a grave for his mother-in-
law whom he was planning to strangle on her next visit. To all
appearances both men were doing the same thing. Actually, what
they were doing was altogether different. It is conceivable that a
charitable Christian might come down the road and, seeing the
men at work, say to both of them, "The sun is warm. Why don't
you rest and let me dig for a while?" His offer being accepted,
the good old soul proceeds unconsciously to give honor to Mary
in one yard, and, in the next yard, to be a minor accessory to
murder. The point I wish to make here is that cooperation in
any work demands, if it is to bear good fruit, that the man be
fully aware of the end and purpose of the endeavor.

If this counsel is not observed, the Catholic apostolate may find
itself used as a mere tool in the hands of those who know what they
are about. For instance, an apostolate for better unionism must
operate within a secular framework, because we do not have Catholic labor unions, nor are they feasible in the United States. Consequently, it will be but rarely that the Catholic unionist can give his
whole-hearted, unqualified support to union policy because in its
immediate ends or the means to attain those ends there will usually
be an un-Christian, and therefore anti-Christian, ingredient.

I do not for a moment imply that this is a unique condition
in unions. Other institutions are much more liable to err on the
side of the fallen angels. Secular colleges, political organizations,
chambers of commerce, cultural societies, and even nominally
Catholic groups with merely social ends, must be regarded with
charitable suspicion by the vigilant apostle. The presence of the
apostle within these institutions is not so much to *conform* as to
reform. A Catholic unionist is not primarily for unionism, but
rather diligently strives to see that the union is an instrument
toward those ends which have his greater loyalty: the furtherance
of the Faith, the salvation of souls, and the common good of

society. Bear this in mind, that the basis of all sin is the making of a secondary good *an end in itself;* and then name if you can one secular institution today that is not doing *just that!*

The primacy of the spiritual cannot for a moment be forgotten. Temporal conditions consonant with the nature of man, property, and the state, can be achieved *only* by those who seek first the eternal salvation of souls. Social Justice can only come as a fruit of Charity. Again, temporal conditions favorable to man's dignity will be occasions for spiritual growth only when they are used as instruments to that end. Good working conditions, frugal comfort, education, race equity, civic liberty, or even, in fact, the ascetic life, do not *automatically* produce better men. In searching for these we had better be careful that we do not lose sight of our goal. It would be better to leave the worker to exploitation than to foster hate for his boss. It would be better to remain bourgeois than to become proudly poor.

Yes, we do want to see God's Will done upon earth. We want all men free, acting freely. If we did not, we would not be integrated Christians. But we know that the Will of God can only be achieved by God with men as His docile instruments. We may rest assured that the Will of God will never depend upon any of the capital sins for its accomplishment.

LET'S SET OUR OWN RULES

The American virtue of initiative is fast becoming a myth. The apostolic Catholic might be doing his God and his country a service to revive this disappearing self-motivation. Is it inevitable that Catholics must go around trying to improve the ethics of purely arbitrary commercial enterprises whose standards are set by pagans? Must every lay Catholic without professional talent be content to be a job seeker instead of a vocation seeker? This is not to advocate social anarchy, but to arouse from apathy those Catholics who imply that we must inevitably be playing in somebody else's game. A married man with ten children might find it difficult to leave the pleasant home-like surroundings of the General Motors' family, and seek greener pastures for a growing brood, but why should we prepare the wrists of our Catholic school students for the fetters they could quite easily avoid? This bowing to the inevitability of wage-slavery is a blasphemous indifference to the efficacy of grace. In a case where it is unavoidable, at least for the present, let's take it patiently and graciously, as a penance imposed by God. For us, God's Will alone, and nothing else, is inevitable and unavoidable. Let's be content but not satisfied, looking for a freedom, if not for ourselves, at least for our children. Many Catholics are kicking against the goad which God has given them because they refuse to abandon the yoke imposed by Mammon. What boon does society enjoy from the contributions of pagan, self-seeking, de-humanizing corporations that could not better be accomplished by men getting together with Christ in their midst working hard in Charity? Of what worth is that shiny gadget or denatured food measured in the price of the human degradation which is its by-product?

There are some enterprises that can be restored to Christ, and we must supply apostles to do it. There are others which serve no good purpose. Aside from profit, they serve no other purpose. Either they are too large, dependent upon a degrading automatism, dependent upon an unnaturally stimulated demand for an unnecessary product, or else they cater to an undiscriminating concupiscence. It is questionable prudence for an apostle to jeopardize his own soul to save the souls of those who choose deliberately to participate in such enterprises. Whatever good he could do, he could do better from the outside unstained by his own reluctant service to their insatiable idol.

AGAINST THE SPIRIT OF THE TIMES

It is fairly obvious to the Maryknoll missionary, when he attempts to win the natives of the upper Yangtse to Christ, that he must avoid conceding too much to the spirit of his potential Catechumens. In everything that is good he will be all things to all men. If they are indolent, he will stop short of that. If they are murderous, he will not encourage target practice. If they are unchaste, he won't distribute copies of *Esquire* to win their friendship.

The apostle at home can learn as much. Unlike the missionary, we are not strangers to this pagan country. We are at home here. Consequently, we have taken certain habits and customs for granted which, if we are to be apostolic, we must disavow.

BIGNESS

Bigness, the virtue of quantity, has become a mysticism in our time. When people forget how to integrate, they learn how to multiply. We cannot integrate the work of numerous craftsmen into a jewel-like cathedral, so we pile one office building on top of another and gaze upon it in holy awe. Periodicals are measured by the quantity printed, rather than the quality of the contents. It has gotten so that we can overlook any mistake if it is big enough (like New York City), or any lie if it is big enough (like the Atlantic Charter), or any injustice if it is big enough (like Industrial-Capitalism). The materialist always goes for size, for he denies the validity of anything that cannot be measured with numbers. The apostolate must begin small, and its progress must be a growth, not a multiplication. It would not be strange to the Church if but a handful of men were to convert America. For the apostolate to puff itself up so as to imitate the proportions of the Metropolitan Life, the American Legion, or the Luce publications would be to place ourselves in as helpless a position as these institutions to bring about social reform. Christ chose Bethlehem, and so should we. Men who think big, don't think; they just add a few more zeros to the end of a number. What we have to bring to the world is Charity, and Charity is found in groups, not in mobs.

The true measure of an apostolate is the increase in spiritual maturity of its members, and the growth of charity between them and in their work. If this growth is apparent, then there is no need to worry about size.

DISPLAY

Americans are given to display. Advertising has made us self-conscious of our appearance and the appearance of the things we do. A sixty-piece symphony orchestra heralds the arrival of a new soap-powder. As magazines become more colorful their literary content becomes more anemic. Five more pieces of chromium, and an extra yard of sheet metal, will raise the price of an automobile from one level to another. For the sake of display a perfectly good coat will be abandoned for a new coat that looks better. The sepulchers require a new coat of mirror-gloss white enamel periodically, just for appearance's sake.

The temptation will be constant within the apostolate to improve the appearances of the apostles, the stationery, the headquarters, and the Faith itself. This will only serve to confirm the opinion of the non-Catholic (as expressed by Eric Gill), "The outside of Peter's Bark frequently looks like the entrance to the Ritz." A Communion breakfast for office workers in the Waldorf-Astoria at five bucks a throw, gives the Church the misleading appearance of a society for social uplift.

If the apostolate is not a penitential movement, then it is not an apostolate. Our Blessed Lady in her three apparitions, at Lourdes, Fatima, and La Salette, insisted upon prayer and penance. Although there might be an excuse for keeping penances private, there certainly is no excuse to hide them behind a public display of luxurious extravagance. The spirit of poverty should be so strong in the hearts of those who seek for Christ's Kingdom on earth, that it would necessarily be reflected in the appurtenances of their surroundings. A pagan world dedicated to the accumulation of shiny new gadgets would be halted in its tracks by a dignified but obvious return to frugal living by Catholics. Every unnecessary possession is an obstacle on the road to Calvary. Both our hands should be so busy with the Cross not to allow for any other impedimenta.

CONFORMITY

Americans have a horror of being different. Catholics *are* different and nothing can be gained by their pretending that they are not. St Paul's practice of "being all things to all men" can and has been ridiculously misinterpreted. I doubt if he changed for dinner while among the rich, or laughed at dirty jokes while among the rabble. It is questionable if he assumed an erudite air among the learned, or confined himself to monosyllables when talking to the illiterate.

The way for a Catholic to be all things to all men is for him to be Catholic, because all men are *potentially* Catholic. He must weed out all pretense and ulterior motives. If he is charitable, he will make himself intelligible to whomever he speaks. His very purpose must set the manner of his approach to all men. Since it is his purpose to win souls to Christ, let him, if the occasion arises, speak lovingly and reverently of God, Our Blessed Lady, or the Saints. Simplicity and clarity in speech and manner, provided with no more ornamentation than is necessary to hold his audience, should be his aim.

The apostle must place the eternal salvation of his neighbor before any temporal amenity. It is not charitable to avoid speaking of adultery to an adulterer. It is not neighborly to let your neighbor's children run riot under your nose for the sake of keeping peace. It is not humility to understate your inmost convictions. It is not kindness to mind your neighbors' baby while they go out and get drunk.

A sincere Catholic life lived out to a full measure is bound to stand out like a sore thumb in these times. The apostle must appreciate that fact and try to steer a middle course between pride and timidity.

American democracy is tending more and more toward anarchy. The cry of "Equality" has come to mean equal privilege, not equal responsibility. For every ten men who desire the privileges of the rich, there is but one willing to assume the moral responsibility that goes with the possession of wealth. This desire for privilege without responsibility is as corrupting an influence on the people as tyranny ever would be. It would be better, in fact, for a people to be enslaved to a man, than to be the slaves of their own unchecked desires. Anarchy inevitably leads to tyranny, because even self-interest is served better by the latter.

The apostolic Catholic will see in society an organic thing with many parts and many functions, complementing each other by their very inequality. In his endeavor to serve God first, he will not deny the hierarchical authorities that God has made normal to society. Democracy, like every good thing, is only achievable within limits. The emphasis should be placed upon responsibilities, not upon rights. Corruption within political circles would never lead him to the erroneous conclusion that political office is any the less worthy of respect. Zeal in the cause of any one group should not rob him of the realization that the common good comes first. As an apostle, he acts under the authority of his Bishop and the authority of those priests who are the delegates of the Bishop. As a citizen he acts under the authority of those men who, through the privilege of their office and the responsibility they exercise, justly demand respect. He is a part working to cure the ills of the whole of which he is part. The only alternative to this is to suppose he is God, a law unto himself, subject to no man. This is the greatest of all sins.

Summarily, the apostle must cut across the spirit of the times. He must place quality before quantity, content before form, reform before conformity, and responsibility before rights. All of which should make him very conspicuous indeed!

ED WILLOCK

JIM CROW SECTION

"They're all right in their place"
Quoth the Southern Belle.
And so "they" went to Heaven,
And she, alas, to Hell.

What's the Matter with Miami?

"Thus saith the Lord: Behold I will raise up as it were a
Pestilential wind against Babylon and against the inhabitants
Thereof who have lifted up their heart against me.
O thou that dwellest upon many waters, rich in treasures,
Thy end is come for thy entire destruction."
  —*Jeremias 51:1, 13.*

W
HAT'S THE MATTER WITH MIAMI?
Nothing—that the Holy Ghost couldn't cure, were
He permitted to treat the patient. But the time is rapidly approaching, we fear, when He will say of this twentieth
century city dwelling upon many waters, as was said of ancient
Babylon, "We would have cured Babylon, but she is not healed;
let us forsake her…"

Miami, America's playground, is a festering point; a spot
where the slow disease of worldliness, which is spreading through
more and more of the body of the nation, has openly broken out,
where it makes itself manifest in a rash of dollar signs, in a fever
of profiteering, in the scabs and pus of profligacy, wantonness
and every other type of immorality.

What throws this sin into even blacker relief is the fact that it
obtrudes upon scenes of the most perfect natural beauty. Miami
is famous for winter sunshine and blue skies; for royal palms, for
hibiscus, jacaranda and poinciana flowers; for exotic mangoes,
papayas and kumquats; for breathtaking beaches; for unique
causeways and inland waterways. All these things are good. God
made them and they are beautiful.

How the tender love of God, in providing such a playground
for His children, should be borne in upon the frigid business

man, fleeing from a Chicago or a New York gripped in zero cold to the smiling shores of Miami! How his heart should sing, in fitting thanksgiving, as his train or plane approaches Miami, "He hath set His tabernacle in the sun and He is as a bridegroom coming out of His chamber"! But it is a rare man whose heart is set upon anything more other-worldly than the lineup for the daily double at Hialeah Park or plans for night clubs to be visited on his first night in Florida.

Miami is primarily a tourist town. Good people there are, but they are overshadowed by the get-rich-quick gang and by the "snow-birds" who drift down from the north to eke out a precarious winter living around the race tracks, night clubs and beach casinos. The home town folks relax almost visibly in late May and June when the last tourist has vanished toward the north. Their work is done for another year. The sheep have been shorn; the suckers milked of their money. How can a city which quite openly lives by making as much as it can out of the great American public for four or five months of the year change its spots, as it were, for the other seven or eight months and become a self-respecting, independent municipality? The answer, of course, is that it can't.

The effects of civic laxity and worse are clearly visible in the periodic shakeups of the police department, in the disgraceful conditions obtaining in the municipal hospital and worst of all, in the squalor of the Miami Negro section, where only the sunshine and clean air of Florida save the inhabitants from the worst effects of tuberculosis, and other diseases of deficiencies, dirt, and poverty.

What is the status of the Church in Miami? The whole state of Florida is still officially accounted a missionary area, with many towns completely without priests, with Catholic schools and Sisters still a rarity, but Miami is in a somewhat different position from the rest of the state. Because of her yearly influx of tourists, she is much more like a northern than a southern city in her

63

attitudes. Therefore, the Church in Miami does not contend with the blind prejudice and hatred so typical of many cities in the South. Rather than hatred there is indifference, which is in many ways harder to combat that outright opposition.

Certainly, Catholics in Miami are not persecuted; but certainly, they do nothing to bring persecution upon themselves. They do not speak out against any of the evils which are brought to a focus right under their noses and which, unless they are deaf, dumb and blind, they cannot help but notice. It is hard to escape the conclusion that Miami Catholics *should* be suffering persecution for justice' sake. They should be loudly vocal in their protests against the corruption which is their city. They should do something, in the name of God, about sky-high rents, about veterans with little children cramped into trailers and tent-houses, about Ku Klux Klan activities, about organized profiteering and rackets. But the kingdom of God and His justice are difficult to find at the parish bingo game or bridge party. What Miami needs is less Catholic inaction and more Catholics in action!

A bright spot upon Miami's Catholic horizon is Barry College, a Dominican institution. Founded in 1940, it is the only Catholic college in Florida and it has already earned its place in the Miami community. Its graduates and former students include teachers, social workers, cloistered and active nuns, scientists, wives and mothers as well as a Florida journalist who has been singled out as likely to become one of the foremost women reporters in the nation. To their varied careers these Barry students have brought the principles of right reason learned at a Catholic college. They can accomplish a great deal, and even more as their numbers increase, towards restoring Miami and all of Florida to Christ.

But this job of restoring cannot wait until Barry College, in the course of time, supplies a plenitude of young apostles. *Now* is the acceptable time, *now* must be the day of salvation in Miami.

Jehovah's Witnesses, who are very active on Miami's Flagler Street (where are Catholic Evidence groups?), are fond of saying, in connection with the end of the world, which they anticipate as a very imminent event, "Many now living will never die." This conviction lends their actions an urgency, a now-or-neverness. It would be all to the good if Miami Catholics could become infected with something of their spirit, of their impatience for the kingdom to come — *now!*

The sin of worldliness comes under a magnifying glass in Miami and appears in its worst aspects. The spirit of the Miami "season" was not badly summed up in a newspaper report of the actions of a young couple who came to the Magic City for a winter vacation a couple of years ago. Unable to find any sort of housing accommodations, they solved their problem by spending their nights in Miami Beach's night clubs and their days sleeping on the sands. (Presumably the Atlantic Ocean supplied a handy plunge to chase hangovers.) Could the pursuit of pleasure go farther?

Miami is in peril, the more because she does not realize it. She is full of the unheeding and foolish who enthusiastically pursue fluorescent and neon will o' the wisps but are willfully blinded to the Light that shines far too brightly and purely for their comfort. She is crowded by thousands who listen eagerly to strident voices shouting of win, place and show, of jai-alai, and of night club revues, but who cannot slow down and quiet down long enough to hear a less audible Voice saying, "Be still and know that I am God."

O Miami, may you see and hear before it is too late. May you even now be spared the pestilential wind, the entire destruction, the fate of a Jerusalem unwept, a Babylon forsaken!

PATRICIA MACGILL

All Men Are Created Equal

WHAT AILS MANKIND?

By Gustave Thibon
Sheed & Ward

This is a small book of essays by one of the greatest contemporary Catholic minds. The author analyses the disintegration and perversion into which modern society has fallen progressively since the French Revolution. Taken as a whole it contradicts all the current platitudes about democracy and the good life, with devastating logic and analysis.

One is tempted to demonstrate the excellence of the book by endless quotation, chosen almost at random. I chose the following on work not because work is his main preoccupation (it isn't), but because it makes a point that we have been trying to make in *Integrity*:

> The proletarian of today hates work. Even when he is well-paid, his dissatisfaction is not appeased. He suffers not so much from being an exploited worker as simply from being a worker, and his endless material demands are but superficial and misleading manifestations of this fundamental malaise. The reason for this malaise is that the proletarian's work is unorganic and inhuman. And the remedy proposed by the socialists is better distribution of profit, higher wages! As if this were all there could be to the labor problem.... Until working conditions in industry — and also in trade — change, it will but injure the proletarian to raise the wage level.... You cannot remedy the ills resulting from work which is inhuman by

increasing the worker's economic well-being. On the contrary, this is a good way of aggravating his boredom and easing his decline.

Most of the book deals with the political structure of society, especially with the weaknesses inherent in democracy and the harm (in the form of envy and insecurity) which results from declaring all people to be equal when they are obviously not equal. The author shows that the breakdown of the traditional classes which were based on organic function and responsibility (even when the corresponding privilege was abused), has led to our present hierarchy of wealth with all its accompanying disorders. He proposes that a class system be reinstated on the basis of privilege and honor carrying in its wake responsibility, insecurity and asceticism, so that only selfless men will desire to gain high position. He does not suggest how this new order of things is to be brought about.

Does this book sound reactionary? It isn't. It is bitter realism. But it isn't a cheerful book, obviously. Every so often the author can't help remarking how like Hell modern civilization is becoming.

CAROL ROBINSON

Authentic Mysticism

ST. JOHN OF THE CROSS
By Father Gabriel of St. Mary Magdalen
Westminster Bookshop

The main thesis of this book is to establish the validity of acquired (or active) contemplation. It is the direct fruit of meditation — that state in which the soul is absorbed in a simple, loving regard of God without resorting to any particular ideas. Since acquired contemplation comes normally between meditation and infused contemplation, its role in the soul's progress in prayer cannot be overestimated. St. Teresa of Avila never discussed it. In speaking of contemplation, she referred solely to that prayer in which the soul is experimentally conscious of God's working in it in a distinctly supernatural manner. St. John of the Cross used the term in the wider sense, however, to include acquired as well as infused contemplation. Steeped in these masters himself, Father Gabriel, one of the ablest Carmelite theologians in Rome, elucidates the intricacies of St. John's doctrine with the greatest authority and unction. As good teachers do, he repeats his essential points a hundred times, and without the least monotony! He knows how vital his discussion is and will be to many souls, and he makes the most of it.

To the soul exacerbated and neurasthenic from 'making point' (i.e., continuing to meditate when the time for contemplation has come) due to misdirection or to a stubbornly and exclusively cerebral notion of the life of prayer, this book will be of incalculable aid. The three signs indicating the aridity preliminary to infused prayer — inability to meditate, lack of consolation in God or creatures yet an anxious desire to serve Him perfectly — are discussed most helpfully. Those who are terrified that they are 'wasting time' or succumbing to an oblique indulgence of the emotions by enjoying God in pure and simple faith need reassurance. Here it is. Every director should have a copy.

FRANCES CLARE O'REILLY

INTEGRITY

AUGUST, 1947   VOL.1, NO. 11

SUBJECT: THE JEWS

HE STORY OF THE JEWISH race can only be told religiously. The problem of Jewish persecution can only be solved religiously. The Promised Land for the Jews can only be regained religiously. The course of Jewish history, like that of the other branch of Israel, the Catholic Church, is an inscription made by the Finger of God on the sands of time. It is in the light of His Revelation alone that the marks are intelligible.

The miracles that saved Israel from extinction while she awaited the coming of her Messias have been recorded in the Old Testament. What, short of miracles, could have saved a few tribes of Semites confined to a narrow strip of land between desert and sea from extinction at the hands of powerful militant neighbors? Could any historian dare to explain her survival apart from the miracle of the Exodus? . . . or the super-humanity of her prophets? The mystery of her monotheism is a vast sea of polytheistic cults, this religion which was her reason for being, cannot be considered as an evolutionary process. This vessel of belief in a Personal Heavenly Father was borne aloft through centuries of different materialism within and ruthless war and enslavement from without. At the time when the Machabees established their dynasty, Israel was reduced to but a handful. Yet she survived. And when her unwelcomed Messias did come, she was occupied by Roman conquerors, and had a usurper for a King.

After the Passion and Death of Christ, Israel was split in two. A few accepted Christ, followed Him, and in the midst of persecution founded a Church to continue His work of Salvation.

The majority, however, refused to honor His Divine credentials, repented not at all for the death sentence they had imposed upon Him, and became in their consequent dispersion and persecution a living testimony to the retributive Justice of God. Today's descendants of the divided Israel are on the hand the Roman Catholics, on the other hand, the Jews.

The histories of these branches, spiritual Semites and fleshly Semites, run as parallel lines through the history of Europe. The survival of the Jews through this period testifies to two important facts:

1. That God has a special and specific concern for His Chosen People.
2. That the specific love was recognized by the Church, for it was through her temporal power alone that the survival of the Jewish race was made possible.

The habits and way of life of the Jews were foreign and often inimical to the otherwise homogeneous Christian society which harbored them. The ghetto was as much a sign of privilege as of imprisonment. It was a place of refuge for the Jew to protect him against secular and personal enmity more obtuse to the will of God than was His Church. Against these secular powers the Papacy was constantly pleading in behalf of the Jews. A society dominantly and ubiquitously Christian, to an extent incomprehensible today, could not help but look upon the Jews as a thorn in its side. Yet they survived. They survive even until today when again the same pattern has been repeated, for no one has labored more selflessly or diligently in behalf of the Jews persecuted by secular Germany, than has Pius XII. History shows that this is not a new or peculiar altruism on his part, but in keeping with a centuries-old tradition.

A concern for the present plight of the Jews as displaced persons and grist for future demagogic mills, if it is to be toward their lasting good and their souls' salvation, must make this distinction: between the Jews as the victims of human judgements, and the Jews the objects of Divine Judgement. If this distinction is not made, then, with the greatest good will we shall seek in vain to protect them from a wound which is self-inflicted. Human good will, brotherhood, tolerance, or charity in this case is inadequate. The severance of the Jew from His Blood Brother Christ cannot be cemented by some modern plastic but will await the Divine surgery by which the transfusion will be made sacramentally. The Hebrew blood of guilt will then become the Sacramental Blood of Redemption. Within the Church of Christ, the Jews will find their Promised Land.

What is our part as Catholics in the redemption of the Jews? The first direction is negative but it represents the minimum. We must not bear false witness against the Jews, adding our rash judgements to those of our pagan neighbors. If we take refuge in human judgements and try to reduce the Jewish problem to a natural equation, we shall be denying to the Jews the supernatural love and Divine pity which alone can bring them to at-one-ment with Christ. As Catholics, we are members of Christ and thus the instrument for Divine Love. As members of Christ, we are the living testament of His Crucifixion, and if we bear witness to this before the Jews, they will see in us both the Cause and the Resolution of their plight.

Christ Our Lord, The Lion of Judah, said, "Salvation is of the Jews." We Catholics who are the newly chosen, the second born, can only merit salvation through the Jew Christ, Son of the Jewess Mary, testified to by the Jews Peter and Paul. The Blood shed upon the Cross was Hebrew Blood. The salvation of the Jews is in the same Blood.

THE EDITORS

COOPERATION

Mrs. Babbitt spends her days,
Helping those who are in need,
Mr. Babbitt works hard too,
So she can find enough to do.

The Fortress

I FOUND MYSELF BORN IN A COMMON ENOUGH Jewish community on the east side of the Bronx. It was not such an orthodox place that the men wore little curls above each ear in the strict Hebraic fashion, but the Jewish way of life was faithfully kept, all the laws and all the customs. My first fear of the Lord came one Saturday when I was about five years of age: I had a cut a piece of paper on the Sabbath. As far as I can remember, that fear was the first act I ever made as a person with religious bearings.

Several years later when I first walked into Harlem, I can remember being shocked into the realization of a Negro community. The man who sold orange juice from a stand was a Negro; the people who sat on camp stools in front of the apartment house were Negroes; even the street cleaners were Negroes. It was a though you had put a mirror to America and everything was reflected back in black. This is what it was like where I was born and grew up except that everything was reflected back in Jewish color. But in all such places there are several openings through which the outside world leaks in. we had such openings too and these were the movies, the schools and the printed word.

In the movies people neither spoke Jewish as we did, nor even English with our kind of accent. All weddings were performed in front of Christian altars and there was a culture represented generally that was clearly not ours. Books made it even more clear to us that in the world of heroes and heroines, Jewish people were far from being the ones with whom might, right and glamor sided.

The schools we went to were neighborhood public schools and therefore nearly all the pupils were Jewish, but few of the teachers were. Most of them were Irish. On the days the schools were closed for the country's religious holidays, Christmas and Easter, we had none of our own to celebrate, though sometimes

Passover, a feast day on a different calendar, did coincide with Easter in an accidental sort of way. And on the days we had our holidays, the schools stayed open though only the teachers and one or two children in each of the large classes went to school. We were out of step.

To a child, the written word, the school and the movies all bring authority. Gentile heroes, strange holidays, love that ends before a Christian altar only — these were inconsistencies I never understood while I was in grade school. Constantly we seemed not to do the right thing.

In school we used to sing "My Country Tis' of Thee," which had little meaning to us. There was even one particular phrase, "Land where our fathers died." That made me mortally embarrassed. I had a feeling that the line belonged to those few who went to school on our holidays and not to us. We never sang a song about our fathers who chose this country to die in in the nineteenth and twentieth centuries.

It wasn't until I was eleven years old and in high school that I found out that I, as an individual, was Jewish. I had known that somewhere outside were all kinds of people who were not like us, and most of these were teachers. But on this day, my friend told me that most people were not Jews and that most people hated Jews. The embarrassment came to the surface and was gone forever because I understood now. Terror, more real and more tenacious, came instead and I imagined an enemy who would kill us and me. The big world erupted into tiny pieces and it took many hesitant moments to build it up again bit by bit. From that day I never doubted that we were hated because we were in small numbers and from that day there has been no security for us or me in a world where people are sorted and counted.

Until that day I had enjoyed many things without question. God gave a beautiful life to each child in our community. I loved the solemnity of Friday nights when the candles made up flickering dances in the kitchen and the house was burdened with cleanliness. Daytime Saturday, which had begun at sunset on Friday, was an anti-climax. I delighted in every one of the thousand times my mother took out my father's praying shawl and prayer books and my father accepted them proudly and went off to the synagogue with a man's pomp. Passover was a dream that came true only once a year and was full of special foods, long days of ceremonies and the smell of spring. I had childish curiosity and frequently demanded to go with my father to the synagogue to see what was going on in this place of awe. Men chanted beseeching melodies there that subdued me with sadness. Men swayed as they chanted.

We never talked about God at home. Perhaps they did in other homes, but in none that I knew. My friends would have told me. I think we talked about "holy." There were holy days, holy things and holy laws that could not be broken. I knew an awful lot about holy because I was conscientious and asked questions so that I would know the proper things to do. I think I knew that God was behind it all, in a remote way, but He was an awe-full God who did not encourage familiarity in our particular community.

I was so conscientious that although I was a girl, I went to the synagogue on Saturday mornings when I was about eight or nine. Boys had to go. The rabbi's two girl grandchildren went and we were the only girls ever present. In the Jewish religion, it is the man who bears the burden of responsibility in keeping the laws. The woman is taught at home and she is not the one who carries on the business of religion except in one potential way; she might one day bear the Messias.

It really was my conscientiousness that sent me off to the synagogue on Saturdays to hear the Bible stories along with the rabbi's grandchildren. I don't know what my parents thought of this strange girl of theirs. I think my father was pleased, though I would have pleased him more could I have become a boy. It was these stories that made glory grow inside me and endowed me with a hunger to know more. I was proud of our Jewish history and I kept hearing God mentioned in the stories and I was proud of Him too. He was not hidden any more. God who opened the Red Sea for the Jews and closed it for the Egyptians was obviously full of authority the way the schools and the books and the movies were. I began to admire Him and then I loved Him for what He had done for my ancient people and then I loved Him, just like that.

I must say that I never felt Jewish in my whole life. I always felt myself. I felt a belonging with my people, and American in nationality and Jewish in religion when the occasion arose to be one or the other. But all the time this thing that was me was me. In school, it is true that the teachers did their duty by us and told us there was a Jewish type and Jewish characteristics. This was confusing because I looked up every geography book I could find that had a description and sometimes even a picture of the Jewish "type," always next to a picture of an Arab, and I had rarely seen this specimen in real life. My own family was blonde and blue-eyed and hooked noses were as common or not among my friends as they are among other peoples. If one has to generalize, I would say that, broadly, there were from five to ten physical categories in our community; I could be more accurate had I measured everyone's skull. We ranged in types from German to Italian; from fat to skinny; from tall to short, almost like everyone else it would seem! It was harder on those children who by some freak of nature resembled this specimen in some degree, because they were credited with proportionately more Jewish "characteristics." But then, this curse has even extended to non-Jews who by the same accident also resemble in some degree this arbitrary specimen, and they too have suffered the consequences of being credited proportionately with Jewish "characteristics." For it is true that in world values, it is not what you are that counts, but what people think you are.

I began to observe changes in our neighborhood as soon as I sometimes could say oddly at ten or eleven years that the old days were gone. It was true however. For one thing, the color of the language was changing. Yiddish was no longer the only official language spoken in the stores and on the streets. It was still spoken in each home to some extent and among those whose first language it was. But a new generation was growing up in a lusty American world and spoke a vigorous Bronx English. So, in this way, the language barrier was gone, and seemingly overnight too. The gates were down and the outside world no longer leaked in, it flooded all over us.

Over the same period of time that I noticed the change in the color of the language, I noticed a change in the color of the religion and customs. For instance, the dietary laws which concern themselves with the keeping of a kosher home were very strictly adhered to when I was a young child. But when I was nine, our house became one of the first on our block to become non-kosher. Today, except for the orthodox Jewish sections on the lower east side of Manhattan, I know of few homes where the laws are kept and these only because of some ancient parent or grandparent who would feel betrayed were there any change.

This breakdown came about in everything. It was a real assimilation of a non-national group along seemingly national lines except that the customs this particular people gave up were their religious laws.

Judaism was a religion of law and order. In so far as the laws were kept, orthodoxy was kept. In so far as the laws were not kept, lack of orthodoxy grew. The laws that had once all been part of a mighty bustle of preparation for the day of the inevitable revolution, the day when the Messias would come to the Jews, were no longer bound together by the priests, the Temple, the sacrifices in the Temple and the presence in the Temple of the Holy of Holies. The laws were like skin that hung on dead bones. It was a religion of law and order.

There has been a great cry heard from gentiles who would like to see the Jews return to their strict orthodoxy. The logic of these people seems to be that if the Jews were only religious, they would not be so bad, but since they are no longer "religious," well then, they must certainly be a rotten lot. But it would be an empty religion that the Jews would return to. Their laws do not make sense today in this world, those laws of cleanliness and Saturday Sabbaths, unless they still strongly believe that the Messias will come some day. Christians know the Messias has come. Why do they tell the Jews to go and practice over 300 detailed laws for daily living and thus prepare patiently for the Messias? Though the Jews do not believe in Christ, the Messianic core of their faith started to fade when the Temple was rent in two on the first Good Friday. Today the Jews who would return to their religion would only go back to laws and not to God, or to a kind of "reformed" faith of a unitarian paleness.

When Jews are persecuted, they go back to their religion. I think this is mostly because it is not unlike a situation where strangers find themselves thrown together and must find a common bond. When Jews are allowed to live in peace they stray from each other, their religion dies naturally and they seek a more permanent truth.

And yet it remained a Jewish community, this place where I lived. I don't know why entirely. The religion was fading, and the Jews are not a national group. They come from every country in the world. When I think of "national" I think of a people sharing history, wars, culture, peace, tradition and language in common. Except for language in many cases, today, twenty centuries after Biblical times, this sharing is only true of the Jews who come from one country, not of all the Jews who come from all countries. I learned this lesson of nationality very sharply when the German refugee Jews started coming into our neighborhood in the 1930's. Our community was Russian and Polish until the German Jews came. They did not get along well with us. The nationalities clashed.

I do not know what keeps a Jew a Jew, after he has given up his religion. I do not believe anyone could really know this though I have read some scholarly treatises on the subject. It is something God will have to explain. I think that in part loneliness drives one Jew to seek another Jew, and a desire to be one's self. I think, in part, gentiles make a lonely and even homeless world for Jews and thus keep them in hordes. And I think God is Third Party to it all.

This is the way the gentiles keep Jews together as a group: they build a fortress of the world and outside it are ghettoes. Except for the Negro, no one has ever been as cruelly discriminated against in job situations as the Jew. We were very hungry in our community during the long depression, and even after the depression went away from many other people. I used to try to get a job frequently from the time I was about fifteen. Jobs were hard come by to everyone, it is true, but except for non-paying jobs in law offices and the like, employers did not pick Jews. Everywhere I went I had to answer questionnaires which asked my religion. Was I Protestant or Catholic or Jewish? I was Jewish. Or if I had to account for my descent, I replied that my parents were Russian. Now everyone knew that most of the Jews in New York were Russian and one's name was a give-away too. When the questionnaire did not ask for my religion, it subtly asked for my nationality which I always answered as being American, oddly enough. But at this, I was sent back to the ink pot to report my "real" nationality. Sometimes I was furious but other times I was cunning and would write down the name of the Russian state my father came from. This device with my features would get me past the first desk to second. I would be well treated until I casually mentioned that I was Jewish for the effect. It was always a rousing effect too. Sometimes a Jew would be hired, but by other Jews. The war has changed a good deal of this by creating something of a shortage on the labor market, for the short time being.

In the course of time, I became a Catholic. As I stepped into the green pastures of the Church, I became a freak, a Jewish convert. By now there should be enough of us not to be museum pieces. But still, everywhere I go with my Catholic friends, I am pointed out as a Jewish convert, isn't it wonderful. Except for a handful people, I have never been treated as anything but a Jewish Catholic. Now, I would like to be treated as neither the one nor the other but as myself. My background and my faith are part of me. If I went to a priest for spiritual direction, I was more often than not told that I had to break my "Jewish pride" or that since every Jew was antagonistic and aggressive, I had to face it within myself and tear out these seeds of Satan. I settled into a group of Catholic friends, someone new would come along and I would be introduced as a Jewish convert, isn't it wonderful. It is not wonderful. If a Jew becomes a Catholic, it is not because he wants to mend his "Semitic" ways. It is because the fear of Hell enters into him that he leaves the familiar life he grew up in and goes into a cold and strange new way of life. It is not wonderful; it is very necessary for some people.

God gave a tiny limited soul to each to keep on earth. It is so limited because it is almost like everyone else's. But God also put in each a little precious bit of individual. Nothing is so priceless in all the world. When we look at each other, this is what we must look at. But people do not really look at you when you are Jewish.

PAULA CEILSON

Christian Anti-Semitism

THE RECENT SLAUGHTER OF SEVERAL MIL-
lion Jews in Europe still has some power to shock the Christian
world. But mostly it is forgotten, assimilated like the bombing
of Hiroshima and grown dim in the short memory of modern
times. It is true that the devastation occurred in spite of Christianity, that anti-Semitism persists in defiance of the Gospels and
in accordance with the spirit of the world. And yet we know
that it is the spiritual shortcomings of an entire civilization
which calls itself "Christian" that is, if not the cause, at least
the occasion for the power that evil has in the world of today.
And are not we Catholics, who bear the fullness of truth, of all
the most guilty for cooperating in this work of destruction by
the tepidity and mediocrity of our lives? For we who, in the
grace contained in the Mass and in the Sacraments, and in the
teachings of Christ interpreted by generations of saints and wise
men, possess the cure of all the "isms" of our time, have been
tried and found wanting. And in the name of the very truth we
have abandoned, we have not hesitated to criticize unqualifiedly
the remedies propounded by the secular world for the allevi-
ation of human ills. The tolerance of the liberal as a solution
to the racial problem, we claim is insufficient, but we have not
yet manifested the charity required for the Christian solution.
Despite the continual warnings, appeals, and condemnations of
the Holy Father and the Hierarchy, there exists among Catholics
a certain antipathy towards the Jew, mild it is true as compared
with the maniacal hatred that finds expression only in physical
extermination or the abrogation of civil and naturals rights, but
equally at variance with the spirit of Christ and His Spouse.
Too frequently the Christian reaction to the Jew is one of fear
of his "subversive activity," resentment of his "grasping nature,"
jealousy of his economic success (even though this is limited to

a small proportion of its members) or envy of his unquenchable zeal in all fields of endeavor.

And even if there is some truth in these accusations, have we not had enough of such Pharisaical weighing of merits and defects? There is no denying the admirable intentions and even the good accomplished by Christian writers who extol the Jewish people for their temporal and spiritual achievements, but such attempts reach only those already disposed to friendliness. There can be no solution to the Jewish problem on this level. For it is not a question of whether the Jew actually possesses the defects attributed to him. In the measure that we make this consideration primary, we unwittingly serve the cause of the anti-Semite, who relies upon the contingent nature of such a search, and the consequent difficulty of precisely determining the facts, to fit the results into his own unsympathetic interpretation. Anti-Semitism is not a simple prejudice based on the dislike of a few personality traits, or even on jealousy, resentment or fear. It is complex, because it has its roots in a mystery, the mystery of God's election. The Jew forgot this mystery and failed to recognize his Messias. The Christian forgets this mystery and re-crucifies his Lord in persecuting His fleshly lineage.

It is the epistle of St. Paul to the Romans, Chapters 9–11, that reveals this mystery to us in describing the past history and future destiny of Israel. The Jews are a chosen people, because God freely elected them and gave them a Law and a mission. The mission was primary, and the purpose of the Law was to enable them to fulfill it. The mission was no less than the salvation of mankind, forfeited by the sin of Adam. Israel was to bring this about by giving to the world a Messias who would establish God's kingdom on earth, a kingdom whose subjects would be Jew and Gentile alike. Essentially, then, to be a Jew meant to be freely elected by God to redeem the world. Emphasis must be laid on the freedom of God's choice, for it was not because of any merit of works (either outside or within the Law) that

Abraham and his posterity received this election. They remained the favored of God not, as they thought at the time of Christ, because they were Jews obedient to the Law; rather, they were Jews by virtue of God's choice and faith. The choice was made manifest by a fleshly mark, that of circumcision, and the Messianic mission promised to the fleshly descendants of Abraham. But as St. Paul points out (Chapter 9, 6–13), not all of Abraham's descendants will be Jews, inheritors of the promise. Ismael, Abraham's son by the bondwoman, Agar, is excluded, as is Esau, who sold his birthright, thereby forfeiting his election. And does not St. John the Baptist warn the Jews that God is able out of the stones in the desert of Judea to raise up sons of Abraham? Although the election of God will be manifest in the flesh, God is not bound by the flesh in this election. To bear God's word to the world is a gift freely given; it was this mark of the spirit that primarily distinguished the Jew from his Gentile neighbor.

Despite many spiritual passages in the prophetical writings, this primary of the spiritual in the destiny of Israel was not understood by the Jews at the time of Our Lord, nor is it understood by those who adhere to the Jewish faith today. The basic reason for their rejection of Christ was, and still is, the claim that He did not fulfill the Scriptures because He did not obey the precepts of the Old Law and because He did not give to Israel the earthly kingdom they believed God had promised them. The Scribes and Pharisees were scandalized at the freedom of Jesus' interpretation of the Law because they had come to believe that their salvation lay in a detailed execution of all its prescriptions which was alone sufficient to render them just in the sight of God. They no longer remembered that the Law was a means to salvation and that it was ordered to the love of God who had freely chosen them as His sons. It limited God's election to a select people, for, after all, it was only the Jews who possessed the Law and who, therefore, could be justified by it. Thus, they no longer realized that their works were meritorious because

God freely chose to find them so and they no longer recognized that theirs was a more universal purpose, the redemption of the Gentiles. That is why the Messianic kingdom was conceived at this time as a temporal kingdom whose purpose was to restore Israel to earthly felicity. The Scriptures were interpreted literally, for their spiritual meaning, the establishment of an Israel of the spirit, was directly opposed to the nationalism of the times which restricted God's free election. Our Lord came specifically to the Jews to recall them to the knowledge of God's freedom and to free them from the narrow confines of a nationalism which denied it.

The Church has condemned the wilful hatred of one's neighbor, which, if not repented, will cut off the offender from the eternal vision of God. The offense takes on an additional seriousness when the object of "Christian" hatred is the Jewish people. The Jews are still the chosen of God, not in the sense in which Catholics are, as constituting the Church through which mankind is redeemed, but because they still play an important, though mysterious, part in the economy of salvation. Although the Jewish rejection of the Messias was not willed by God, it served as the occasion for the election of the Gentiles.

> "But by their offense salvation is come to the Gentiles,
>   that they may be emulous of them."
>   (Romans 11:11)

Israel still serves this purpose. God permits the blindness of His first chosen, in order that the grace of the Holy Ghost may abound more fully among the Gentiles. It is through the charity of Christians that the Jew will return to the Spiritual Israel, a charity which he will jealously imitate. The Catholic is obliged to seek perfection not only for the salvation of his eternal soul, but for the fullness of God's earthly kingdom to be effected at Israel's conversion.

"For if the loss of them be the reconciliation of the world, what shall receiving of them be, but life from the dead?"

(Romans 11:15)

The Christian who hates his Jewish neighbor, apart from social, cultural, and economic considerations which are of secondary importance, does so because the Jew has rejected his Lord and has accordingly been deprived of his original heritage. The Christian anti-Semite sets himself up as the instrument through which justice is visited upon Israel for its faithlessness. Is this not an equally profound misunderstanding of the freedom of God's election? For here again is the subordination of a free election to the primacy of nation in the persecution of a people because they are no longer completely identified with this election. It is not because of works or race but through God's merciful condescension that the Christian has received faith and salvation. When this is not realized, the Pharisaical hatred of the outsider becomes possible.

The fear that Saint Paul describes as proper to those who have replaced the "natural branches" is based on the understanding that faith and justification depend not upon nation but upon the mysterious will of God alone. If Israel now occupies the role of prodigal in the household of God, it is incumbent upon those who are now the first-born to participate in her restoration by works and prayer. If we do less than this and assume that our own favored position depends on other than the mercy of our Father, we run the risk of losing it. It cannot be accidental that in our time Christ occupies Jewish thought in a way that He has never before. The degree to which we cooperate may well be the measure of our sanctification. For salvation is of the Jews, primarily from its King, and then from His people themselves as they occasion our love, and finally from Israel restored, since the fullness of grace is reserved for that time.

JOURNET KAHN

87

The Editions of the Erudite Elders of Erin

THE EDITORS OF *INTEGRITY*, ALWAYS ON THE alert for articles of interest, take pleasure in presenting this remarkable treatise which they feel sure will cause a furore in academic circles, if not a crisis in politics. Its author, not unknown to our readers, is qualified by both race and background to deal with such a subject, and is known for his earthy approach to world problems. Some may question whether it is protocol for an article of this kind to be given space within our pages. At a time when international politics are being discussed with a vision and clarity unprecedented in history, *Integrity* would be lax in its obligations to its readers were it to fail in saying the things that need saying. This it now does . . . come what may.

Since the days of Alexander the Great, both military and political attempts have been made at world hegemony. These attempts have been easily documented except for those attributed to occult forces. For lack of documentary evidence, the objective historian has been very skeptical about alleged attempts at world hegemony by occult groups. This treatise is unique in that it deals with an attempt at world domination, now under way, initiated by a hitherto overlooked occult group, and is at the same time so thoroughly documented that it should satisfy even the most critical historian.

* * *

In the confused period following the first World War, the noted oceanographer Pluvius Mizzenmast discovered in an obscure Irish tavern the documents known today as: *The Editions of the Erudite Elders of Erin*. These were purportedly a plan for Irish world domination. The finder was suspected of being in the pay of the British Secret Service. His violent anti-Celtic sentiments have been definitely attested to.

To give credence to these documents, it must be pointed out that shortly after their publication by the Printing Office of the Peoples Republic of Outer Mongolia, Pluvius disappeared in the heat of the noonday sun!

The authenticity of these documentations does not concern us. What interests us is their pointed relation to events which have transpired since their writing. "*Post hocum ergo propter hocum,*" as the scholastics would say. All who wish to see history directed into its proper channels and not into Dublin Bay (referred to in the *Editions* under the code name of Channel No. 5) will want to read these documents.

Before quoting the *Editions* directly, it would be prudent to give the opinions of authorities concerning them, both pro and con.

PRO

Salvador Dilli, prominent cuberealist painter, one man exhibitionist at La Galerie des Rogues, Dean of the Anamorphosis School of Painting and Design, highly regarded in *Whose Hue* for his representative canvas La Puce et la Matelas: "Wha dees peebles op to? Dey lacking in heestorical Perspecticles!!!"

Sgt. Babbitt R. Microcosmic, imminent isolationist, occupant of the Chair of Electricity at Pratt Institute of Tautology, author of the seven-volume history at the pecan industry Much Ado About Nutting: "With men who know their history best, it's the Editions two to one. That would be a ratio of one hundred to fifty, if you see what I mean."

Westbrook W. Pepys, radio oracle and columnist, star of the Gherkins Notion Program, Diary of a City Bumpkin, listed in the current Almanac de Gotha as "Sultan of Slander": "The Editions show what a pickle the world is in. everyone should read them from the age of eight upward, along with my column. They are even more accurate than my predictions, and I'm never wrong."

CON

Luigi Emersono Martini, hyperbolic lecturer and traveller, author of *Safe Cycling Through Sicily,* authority on the ruins of Provelone: "Scungilli parmigiana al dente cacciatore" which is the Palermo proverb meaning roughly: "They have the door of cheddar to me."

General Welcgmerz Haas-Settin of Stettin, author of "Jet Propelled Propaganda in Wartime — Victory Through Hot Air Power": "Diss ideas iss ridiggleaus. Logistic broblems are inzermoundable. Deese keppitch petchers haff no oil for it, and I would die rather than use a zubsdidute, namely algohol."

John F. X. Aloysius Kilbride, prominent Galway politician: "How could inywan sa such a thing about the race which gave the world Nick Kenny? Thae are the divvils oan divvice, the worrk of perfijus Albion."[1]

With these introductory remarks behind us, it is now possible to quote directly from the Editions themselves. Because of their length, only significant passages will be quoted, passages which reveal clearly the ends and purposes of the authors.

(Edition One, Page One, Paragraph One) "Gintlemin, be sated. In the world arr two races, the Irish and those who wish they were Irish. We must get into high office wheriver possible to use the power for our own noble ends. Once in our desk jobs, this power cannot be taken from us because possession is nine pints of the law. As long as our inimy England rules the waves, we shall waive the rules. As our motto has been so shall it remain, 'Albion's disthress is Erin's opportunity.'"

With the above to guide us we shall now match it with incontrovertible historical facts, facts with which the layman may not be familiar.

---

1 It should be noted that in *The Cause of World Unrest* published in Italy as *Cimex Lectularius,* Signor I. Nostri-Monti pointed out the significant fact that Kilbride was a frequenter of Gardner's tavern where the Editions were allegedly written, and that therefore he may have helped draught them.

As all know, the Irish have been persecuted for both race and religion. To ensure their personal security, they have resorted to the cover name technique which would conceal their true ancestry. Thus, Sullivan has been changed to Allen, Gaffney and Mullins have become Moon, and Gradner has replaced Duffy, to all intents and purpose. These examples could be continued indefinitely. The cover name technique on a world scale we shall now see, in relation to the Editions quotation.

In Country Callcannon, Erin, the names O'Delan and O'Rosevelt are seen on many tombstones and in incunabula in the Office of Registry. Many with these names have used the cover name technique on leaving Erin. Thus, by removing the prefix, and concealing the O in the body of the name, or by using it as a suffix, O'Delan and O'Rosevelt become Delano and Roosevelt. Those used to such a system of concealment spot such names immediately; those who are not used to it think the name is of another nationality. Thus, we see the clue to the true ancestry of the former White House occupant. Further proof is offered in the fact that he wore a green suit on St. Patrick's Day, and that when asked about his desire for a third and fourth term, he replied with characteristic Celtic candor: "Why, yes, of course I could stand another. But be careful, because the Republicans will also want one on the House, and since they're thirsting for power after the New Deal drought of patronage, it will probably go straight to their heads."

While in office, Mr. Roosevelt matched the Editions word for word in his appointees. One of his most unusual appointments was the Secretary of the Treasury, a Celt like himself who made use of the cover name technique, a man whose real name is Morgan-Shaw. According to documents recently destroyed by fire, he is a half-brother of the Dublin born octogenarian wit and playboy, George [Bernard] Shaw who authored such books as: *"A Dietribe Against Meat Esters — Pygmalion"*; *"The Merchant of Venison"*; *"Diaries of Majors Fred and Barbara Allen,"* etc.

After a period of public office, he took his satiric Irish wit to radio, using the cover name Henry Morgan.

As for the present occupant of the white House, we quote Bartlett Pear, son of Drew, Washington correspondent, in his syndicated column, *The Alluvial Deposit: I am informed by Rogers Pitt of the Senate cloak room that Truman is probably a thirty-third degree A.O.H. (Ancient Oddfellow Hibernian), and is quite likely to be under the influence of some cabalistic Celtic clique, possibly McNamara's band. He, Truman, shrewdly advised Robert Hannigan to conceal his ancestry by speaking to a W.C.T.U. group with the alcoholic's analogous address: "A State Within a State — Delerium Trumens In Inebriation." Following the speech, the proprietor of the ball, an ex-serviceman, removed the local slogan of the group: "Rembmber The Alum Oh," and replaced it with the more appropriate: "Killjoy Was Here." As for me, as a columnist I have achromatopsia, but I frequently see green when Truman sends a list of appointees to the Senate of consternation!"*

We shall now consider Russia, and Irish influence there. Evidence of Irish influence, however, is quite difficult to obtain because of the "Iron Curtin," so called in memory of the Celt whose fears of concealment and strength are legendary. However, it is known for certain that a large section of the "Russian" Communist party must be Irish or at least of Irish extraction, because all refer to each other as T. O'varich, which even the most naïve will see is Irish. The foreign minister, M. O'Lotov, who, by his manner of dealing with Russian and foreigner alike has tried to give the impression of belonging to another race, has so far departed from the traditional Irish bonhomie that it is barely possible that he is of another race, but his name would belie it. A further proof of Irish influence in Russian life is the fact to which foreign correspondents and diplomats alike attest, namely, the endless toasts at banquets, in vodka, a cover name for poteen.

In a global manner, the Irish demonstrate their power in many ways.[2] For example, does it surprise anyone to know that the paper currency system of almost all civilized nations has green in almost all denominations from the dollar bill to the baksheesh of the Barbery States — a gratuitous affront to non-Celts. The less power they have in any individual government, the less green is used, so it is possible to judge their power in America from this alone. Another technique the Irish use to demonstrate their power is this. When the swinging doors of any coalition cabinet in any government are open, they elbow their way in. This was even done in the hermetically and legally sealed cabinet of Dr. Caligari, with the result that it became so overcrowded that all progressive legislation was stifled.

Possibly one of the worst assaults of the Irish is the assault on the species *humanum genus*. They frequently have twenty and thirty year engagements, after which they get married, some waiting so long that they have to be wheelchaired down the aisle together. Some go so far as to wait to get the Sacraments of Matrimony and Extreme Unction together. The effect of this on a worldwide scale is staggering to the imagination when one recalls the statement from the Editions: "In the world arr two races, the Irish and those who wish they were Irish." It is obvious that if the people of Irish blood, or with a desire to be of this race, practiced this constantly, the world would be in a short time uninhabited.

Thus, we see the Irish strategically located the world over, ruling in charming or ruthless power, adapting themselves to all situations. Or else we see them, silently gathering and consolidating information under the sinister mask of guilessness and charm, from the deceptively commonplace Gilhooly's *Third Avenue Palace*, to Gilhooly's *Sign of the Bear* in Omsk, to Gilhooly's *Sapphire Room* in Cairo, to Gilhooly's *Dart Room* in London's

---

2 [Original] Editor's Note: In this connection we have heard it said that the Pope's real name is Pat Kelly.

East End, to Gilhooly's *Onyx Room* atop the Sherry Outlands Hotel overlooking Central Park. *Hic et ubique! Hic! Hic!*

This Gilhooly's saga, international in scope and repeated by many another far flung Fenian family, goes on and on, and the information they gather is piped into an as yet unknown source, for use in the struggle for Irish world hegemony, which will come, unless men of good will unite to crush it like a grape.

BIBLIOGRAPHY

Editions of the Erudite Elders of Erin: Printing Office, Peoples Republic of Outer Mongolia.

Inquiry Into Genesis On The Fall Of Man . . . Apple or Grape?: Teetotalitarian Abstinence League, Martha's Vineyard Press, Ann Arbor, Mich.

The Incidence of Morality Among Freudians, by Virginia Dare, Actuary, Metropolitan High Life Insurance Company.

The Irish Element in Atomic Research, Jan. 1946 Science Review.

Brave New Worldling, by Aldous Huckster.

Political Featherbedding in County Down, by Sheamus Zaslavsky.

The Story Of The Irish Race, by Clement McCarthy, a short and accurate account of the background and running of the Irish Sweepstakes.

The Unscientific Treatment of The Common Cold, by Inhabitants of Celtic Communities and *The Failure of Iodine in The Treatment of German Goitre*.

The former was compiled by the Committee on Research Intro Non-Industrial Uses of Alcohol. Both are published by the Medical Press of Johns Sopkins Medical School.

Economy in The Use of Reasons, by Leon Sturart Marxky, San Mentis Sophist Society, Bedlam, England.

SHEAMUS EGAN

THE MARKET PLACE

The market place is filled with ugly people.
The market place is bursting with their talk,
The market place is fierce with something living,
And I feed my eyes with beauty as I walk.

In the passing faces lies the beauty,
Beauty that I cannot understand,
Cannot understand why tortured faces,
thrill me like an artist's groping hand.

All these Jewish faces hide a longing,
All the faces wait for Him to come,
If they knew the God-man came already,
All the brilliant faces would be dumb.

All the flames of genius would be smothered,
With no feverish quest to swell upon;
Did their wise men know that if they took Him,
The beauty of the faces would be gone?

The market place is filled with ugly people,
The market place is bursting with their talk,
The market place is fierce with something living —
And I curse Christless beauty as I walk.

RAE MELTZER

The Venerable Libermann

"Behold an Israelite in whom there is no guile."

THESE ARE SOME OF THE FACTS WHICH, AS we think, make the Venerable Libermann a God-given teacher for our age: He is a Jew, the son of a Rabbi; he is a co-founder of the Holy Ghost Fathers, a society dedicated to the conversion of the Negro; and he teaches a doctrine of peaceful penance. Perhaps these things, taken themselves, do not seem especially remarkable. But let us bring them together with certain other facts to which they appear related.

Freud, too, is a Jew who teaches a doctrine of peace; but his is a peace which removes the conviction of guilt by denying the reality of sin; hence he must deny the rationality of man which is the root of human responsibility. Freud, as the competent students of contemporary thought recognize, is the moral teacher of our time.

Marx, too, is a Jew. He brings good tidings to the Negro and to all the underprivileged. It is a doctrine of hope founded on hatred as Freud's is a doctrine of peace which must deny reason. And so, as Freud is the authority in the realm of personal ethics, so Marx is the contemporary authority in politics and economics. (Our present difficulty with Russia is only a sign that we have not capitulated completely to these doctrines — also God's way of calling us back to the truth and to Himself.)

But the roots go deeper. There is something common to the teaching of Freud and of Marx which, I am convinced, is the secret of their power over us: they exploit our hidden fear of evil, our sins against Faith. Because we know that, without God, the evil in ourselves, and in others, is too much for us. And we do not turn to God in this knowledge; so that we are pretty much convinced that evil is too much for us — without qualification. Freud and Marx would reach a way to attain happiness for men who are convinced that the evil is too much for them. As long as they admit it to be an evil, they will not know peace. And thus, Freud would teach us how to deny it in ourselves Marx shows us how to exploit it in our neighbor.

That is why, in Communist doctrine, it is necessary to bring about happiness through hatred, the hatred of the "class-struggle"; and, so, their method must be revolutionary in just this sense, that it is founded on hatred. On the surface it looks like "the end justifies the means," which is bad enough in itself. But in truth (Though it is not expedient that this be known to many) the end is to glorify Lucifer, the enemy of God. Similarly, Freud teaches that happiness must be attained by an evil means, the denial of sin. (I do not mean that the means are admitted to be evil, but that they are in fact. But these teachers, measuring everything by the end they adduce — which they assume to be good, and the ultimate good — hold that means to it must be good.) Thus, where Communism is ordered to the adoration of Lucifer in political anarchy, so Freudism tends to a kind of personal anarchy, a false peace which removes anxiety by removing the conviction of guilt instead of the guilt. These are the successful doctrines of our time then, because they are devised to bring the simulation of peace and of hope to the guilt-ridden, tortured consciences of our time. They do this, unbeknown to their victims, by a complete and utter capitulation to evil. Hitler was only a figure held up to us by God, our image in a mirror. We sought peace by smashing the image; now we have another image threatening us, and the likeness is harder to deny.

For all that, men are not devils, and they still seek God. They do not embrace Freud because he denies God and the soul; on the contrary, they drink eagerly of his doctrine because they thirst for peace of soul, a peace which will dissolve their guilt. Neither do they embrace Communism because it denies God and private property, but because it appears to make hope and charity really attainable, for all our evil.

The point is that men turn away from despair as by an instinct, and if they embrace these false doctrines, it is because they "have not so much as heard" that there is a Spirit of Mercy, the Holy Spirit, the Spirit of peace and of love. I do not mean that men are innocent of sin. The very opposite: they are so guilty they are unable to face their guilt, because their hearts have grown hard. And yet, even as I write these words, I cannot give my assent to them unless they are qualified. True, forgetting Christ, we may say the hearts of men have become hardened. But to permit this, even, was in Divine Providence, as it was decreed by God that His Church should be founded on a human rock, so hard that he could deny his Lord three times, and publicly. But God was not embarrassed to found His Church, which was to save sinners upon a sinner.

Even more, while it is true that men, considered as a whole, as a race that is, have been turning more and more away from God, it is also true, assuredly, that successive generations have become more and more confused — by the very errors of their parents — so that the culpability of successive generations seems in some way to have diminished proportionately, even as their acts have become more grossly sinful, considered materially, and even as the race was turning more and more from God. I do not mean to excluding culpability; but I do maintain that the degree of culpability is proportioned to clarity of knowledge, and it is evident enough how confused our unhappy generation is.

However that might be, viewing things naturally, as we see men in Christ it becomes evident that ours is the beginning of a time when Our Lord is calling us back to Himself, pitying His poor stray sheep beguiled and led astray by bad shepherds, loving our generation for all its weaknesses because it was denied so much by its fathers. And if this is true, then it is a time for the

Gentiles to see that what the Jews did long ago is denying their Messias, they too have done, this in order that the Jew and the Gentile may, like the lion and the lamb, lie down together before their Lord. The Jews are particularly important at this time, then, because it is becoming clear that St. Paul's warning to the Gentiles has not been heeded, so that now, what happened to the original branches has happened to the engrafted ones. Now both Jew and Gentile may acknowledge together that they have crucified the Christ. For that reason, Jew need no longer fear Gentile as bearing a guilt unshared; and the Gentile need no longer be tempted to judge the Jew in the illusion of his own innocence. For the trouble with the world now seems to be, in principle, not so much that they deny Christ as that they no longer know how to bear the burden of their guilt in relation to Him.

Yet He Himself has taught us from the cross how to bear this burden. He assures all men who will look into themselves to see what they have done, that He pleads for them with His Father: "Forgive them, for they know not what they do." But this consolation is only for those who acknowledge what they do. The burden becomes light because Christ bears it, for those who look upon their sin as their burden.

But in practice the order is reversed. We do not turn to Christ to help us after we have acknowledged our sins by our own strength. Rather, we do not so much as dare to look upon ourselves until we are abundantly reassured that, whatever we shall find (even before we have looked, we fear the worst, and rightly), we are loved without measure, that is, by God Himself. Mary, the Mother of God, is the pledge of that reassurance, of a love that becomes greater, not less, as the need is greater. Thus it was that Mary Magdalen loved much because she was forgiven so much, and her sorrow for her sins was as great as her love.

The Venerable Libermann first founded a Society which was dedicated by name to the Immaculate Heart of Mary. Then it was assimilated to the Congregation of the Holy Ghost — as if to show our generation that the Spirit of Mary is the Holy Spirit, and that God is pleased now, after these many generations, to begin to call back His people, and to manifest Himself, once again, through their instrumentality. The writings of the venerable Father have most wonderful unction to quiet and reassure the anxious children of our age, to convince them that, for all their apprehensions and conviction of sin, they are acceptable to God, yes even more acceptable, if only they will come to Him through His Son. God is indeed a God of justice, demanding penance therefore. But above every other, He looks for the penance of a contrite heart. And even now He stands ready to make hearts contrite by an incredible pouring out of His mercy. Sinners that we are, we find it hard to believe these good tidings. Yet what is sin, finally, if it is not the instrument by which Our Father fashions His humble little children? Like orphans we look up incredulously when we are told how much we are loved. Therefore, our hearts need to be thawed; and now once again God has chosen a Jew to communicate His warmth. The Saints among the Gentiles have won grace for the fallen people, and now we are beginning to see what their conversion will bring, whose falling away was redemption to the Gentiles.

HERBERT THOMAS SCHWARTZ, T.O.P.

LAUDABLE INTENTIONS

When I am rich, I'll give my wealth
   To any man in need,
I'll even help the fellow out,
   Who suffered from my greed.

A Modern Jew
Comes to the Faith

EDITOR'S NOTE: It is said of the University of Chicago that it is "a Baptist school where Jews go to become Catholics." The University has actually been the occasion of the conversion of quite a number of people, including Jewish students of outstanding ability. This is because of the emphasis given, under President Hutchins, to scholastic philosophy. One of the Jewish converts, baptized, baptized in Chicago in the fall of 1936, is now a Trappist monk and has recently been ordained a priest. Before entering the monastery, he was a practicing physician and psychiatrist. The story of Father Raphael's conversion will be published this fall by Macmillan, under the title of The Glory of Thy People. The author has kindly given Integrity permission to print excerpts from the book, and we have chosen three which show the influence of the University of Chicago and the study of philosophy in turning Father Raphael toward the Faith.

SCIENCE AND PHILOSOPHY

The years 1934 to 1936, I spent at the University of Chicago. Professor McKeon had been appointed Dean of the Division of Humanities. My work with him had been subsidized by the Josiah Macy, Junior, Foundation, and I was zealously studying philosophy.

President Hutchins was encouraging the development of a more unified and intelligent educational system. The scientific division had developed a co-ordinated syllabus. In the Division of Humanities, philosophy was receiving a more important place. Dean McKeon taught Aristotle's Ethics and Logic, Plato's Republic, and the intellectual history of the middle ages. Dr. Hutchins and Dr. Adler conducted an "Honors" course in the Classics, in which were read Plato, Aristotle, St. Thomas

Aquinas, Galileo, Newton, the Old and New Testaments, and other great works of science, philosophy and theology. The modern preconceptions of the students were subjected to the scrutiny of reason; the students were obliged to form, express and defend their opinions. Dr. Adler and Dr. Malcolm Sharpe conducted a "pre-law" class in which the students were trained in grammar, rhetoric and logic, and in which philosophy, morality and even theology (to a limited degree and in a "non-sectarian" way) were discussed.

I found this educational program very stimulating. The need of modern education, as envisioned by these men, for order, agreed with the need I had experienced at the University of Michigan. And here, the power inherent in traditional philosophy for providing order for modern sciences, was recognized.

In Dr. Adler, Dr. Hutchins and Dean McKeon, I found men who, like Herbert S., had, in virtue of native talent and traditional philosophical training, the ability to rise from facts to principles and thence to obtain a rational bird's-eye view of great tracts of subject matter.

As my studies in logic proceeded, I saw clearly that truth, eternal changeless truth, existed. I saw that it was attainable, contrary to the opinion of sceptics who assert that no truth is certain. I realized that its foundation is in the really existing order of being, contrary to the idealists and subjectivists who, as I had found, place an impassable gulf between our minds and things existing outside our minds. I now discovered that there is in each natural thing a natural principle, the thing's nature — e.g., human nature in men as their principle. The definition of the thing states it, the name signifies it. From it proceeds all the properties and powers of thing — in men, e.g., their human reason and will, the bodily powers which sustain life, etc. the intellect perceives this natural principle as well as all the properties of things (known first through sense); and it also perceives the order between these properties — thus, I understood, scientific knowledge is formulated. When this knowledge agrees with the reality to which it refers, the mind, which possesses it, possesses truth.

During this period of time, I was forces to re-examine many of the ideas which I had taken for granted in my earlier education, e.g., concerning the origin of the universe and the human race, the nature of the mind, the existence of immaterial beings. I had once firmly believed that the world began, by itself, from clouds of matter which gradually formed themselves into the present universe. I also believed that simple living organisms had arisen from non-living matter under especially favorable conditions, that from these the more complex species had developed through the course of ages, and finally that from apes, man had arisen, through certain intermediate stages. These intermediate stages, according to the theory I accepted, had left certain clues of their existence before they become extinct. The wonderful graduation of living things and the apparent "recapitulation" of the course of evolution in the embryological development of the higher animals and man, had appealed to me as proof of evolution. When, in medical school, an anatomist-surgeon who had done special work in embryology had laughed at this theory, I was taken aback. However, he based his rejection of it upon embryological specimens, and pointed out that Haeckel, who had proposed these views with great violence in the nineteenth century, had gone so far as to introduce falsified evidence.

During my studies in philosophy, however, I reconsidered the validity of the theory of evolution. Embryological recapitulation did not prove but supposed the evolutionary theory. The supposition of evolution has no direct evidence and no direct logical proof to sustain it. In the recorded history of the world no instance of a species has been known to give rise to an offspring of a higher species. On the contrary, when living offspring which differs from the parent stock are produced by breeding experiments — for example, hybrids — they tend to lose their fertility (the mule) or to revert in their characteristics to the parent stock. Analogies between the successive stages of embryonic development and the gradation of living beings exit in the nature of things, without requiring evolution as an explanation. For both must proceed from simple to complex forms, from unicellular to multicellular. Both require in the higher members of their series organs and systems. The theory of rudimentary organs did not have sufficient evidence to support it (i.e., the supposed rudiments of gills in air and mammalian embryos never show a tendency to become respiratory organs, but are probably associated with the development of non-respiratory organs). So with other evidences of evolution. The vermiform appendix, like the thymus in man, proves, not that man has remnants of organs signifying from lower ancestral species, but that structures not used by the fully formed individual, perhaps useful in its embryological development, atrophy. The various clues (for example, fragments of skeletons) to the supposedly missing links in the conjectured origin of man from apes, do not prove the existence of intermediate stages, since they are not outside the range of possible variation of the species (ape or man) to which they belong; i.e., the characters of these bones are not essentially different from the species now existing and, hence, do not signify a distinct species intermediate between apes and men.

As I studied the first principles and natural things, my understanding of their simplicity and uniformity increased and, with clearer ideas, I realized the intrinsic impossibility of a natural evolution of species. Species which are really distinct have an essential difference — color, for example, is only an accidental difference constituting different races of man, who are united nonetheless in all their essential characters and characteristics in one human species. Again, a natural change proceeds in accordance with a natural principle, and is determinate — i.e., proceeds in the same way. Each being has as its natural principle the nature or species by which it is constituted as a certain

kind of thing, and which is the principle of all its natural operations. Reproduction is a natural operation, proceeding from
and in accordance with the nature of a living being, and it also
must therefore be determinate — the offspring must be of the
same nature as the parents. Thus, evolution of new species as a
natural process is impossible. Neither could it occur by chance,
since the more perfect (a man, for example) could not arise by
chance from the less perfect (a lower animal). Again, an effect
cannot exceed the perfection and power of its cause, as all experience and science prove. But the perfect design of a new species
can only be accounted for by supposing the Creator as a cause,
Who has the perfect Intelligence to design each kind of natural being, and the all-powerful Will to execute His design — by
creation — an act befitting Divine Nature. I understood that
the addition in the theory of evolution of an extended period
of time — an age — during the course of which what otherwise
is inconceivable could be supposed to occur, does not alter the
absurdity of the theory. For if the evolution of a new species
is to occur at all, then at some generation a new nature would
arise in some individual, without an adequate cause, and would
be the offspring of parents of a different and lower species.

This left open the question: how then did the human race
originate? It was a question which science had not answered, and
I felt that the creation of two parents of the race best explained
its origin.[3]

3 On the grounds of natural philosophy this proof seems to me to rule out
any other possibility that human beings originated from the lower animals,
and proposes, therefore that they must be the direct work of God's hands.
However, the teaching of the Catholic Church tolerates an alternative explanation (permitting it to be taught as an hypothesis). This is the mitigated theory of evolution which proposes that God immediately created the primitive
species of plant and animal life, and that He endowed them with the power
of producing species distinct from themselves; (which latter He thus created
mediately). This theory acknowledges that without the intervention of God,
animal life could not have evolved from mere vegetative life; nor the human
body from lower forms.

MORALITY AND PHILOSOPHY

My interests now extended to the moral order. At one time I accepted the behavioristic doctrine, then current, which denied the existence of the will, and of freedom of choice.

In my earlier life, I had much difficulty in controlling disorderly inclinations. I had experienced a lack of freedom within myself. In my first study of philosophy in Berlin, I had learned that interior liberty presupposes knowledge, since the man who is ignorant is not free to choose or refuse what he does not know. Now, in Chicago, as my knowledge of divine things and the moral order became more clear, I also found it increasingly easy to conduct myself consistently with my inner convictions and desires, which also were clearer. Hence my experience in that earlier time was in accord with the behavioristic doctrine which I then professed, while now it bore witness to the will and its freedom which true philosophy asserts.

Thanks to my early religious training and especially to my parents, I had always had some moral sense. I was very fortunate in having upright parents with a strong sense of honesty, of fidelity to obligations, love of country, love of race, etc. Thus, I had formed good habits in my early which were of great assistance. However, I had no reasoned convictions to support these good habits or to strengthen me to withstand the allurements and viewpoints with which I came in contact later. Thus, when I had met the attacks of Voltaire against a "personal" God, Who directed all the events of the universe, I thought his arguments very clever and I adopted a mocking attitude towards religion and even denied the existence of God. Thereafter, I settled down to the common belief that if there was a God, I did not know enough to assert His existence. Likewise, when I read of the materialistic theory that sexual relations were as natural as eating and in both cases, it was merely necessary to avoid excess, I accepted this as true. It was only a few years later when a person, whose judgement and character I respected, manifested a different opinion that I changed my mind. This person had shown a violent disgust at the evidence of such laxity. My "innate" moral sense, which I hardly realized existed, heartily approved this reaction. Later, I understood that the mean of a virtue is not necessarily a mean with respect of quantity (a moderation in quantity), but may be a mean through due regard to the pertinent circumstances; it is unnatural and unreasonable, for example, to seek the pleasure attached to a natural function while precluding the achievement of the end of the function. In regard to sex, the end of the biological function is the procreation of children; an essential circumstance whose fulfillment reason requires, is this, that the exercise of this function take place in the marriage state.

Erroneous teaching with regard to the control of thoughts and desires also had misled me up to this time. Thus, I had the false notion that it was dangerous to put away undesirable thoughts and desires — that "repressions" were thus formed. At this time, I did not understand the distinction which psychiatry makes between suppressions and repressions. The calm, deliberate exclusion of unreasonable thoughts and desires is essential to mental health; this is suppression, not "repression." Oscar Wilde's maxim, which had previously appealed to me as very witty and true, that the only way to get rid of temptation is to yield to it, had shown itself in my experience to be very poor counsel. On the contrary — I had discovered that temptations, yielded to, become very severe masters which exact increasing homage, and that to be really free one must despise and cast them out at once.

None the less, although I thus discovered that I had an innate moral sense and that it was extremely valuable, I had not received in my education any reasoned support for it until my philosophical studies in Chicago.

At this time, in addition to discovering that reason alone sufficed to prove the existence of God, the creation of the world, and of the human race, and the existence in each man of an immaterial, immoral soul, root of his reason and will, I discovered that the moral order was a reality, discernible by reason. I learned that the Ten Commandments express the natural moral law. For at the root of human nature is the fundamental desire to seek happiness, to do good and to avoid evil, and in the intelligence are the germinal ideas of those things which are good and those things which are evil. This is the natural moral law, expressed by the Ten Commandments. These latter state the outstanding instances in the classes of things good and evil, as for example the commandment not to kill states the most striking instance of doing bodily injury to oneself or another. I had never previously received such an explanation of the natural moral law and of the Decalogue which expresses it. In my high school and early college years I would perhaps have denied it. Yet my experience had shown me that I did have a moral sense, and this moral sense was evidence of these germinal moral ideas in the intelligence, which false and contrary reasoning had obscured in my mind, but had not radically destroyed.

* * *

PHILOSOPHY AND CONTEMPLATION

That (1936) summer, I was sitting on the balcony of an Italian hotel overlooking Lake Maggiore. The sky was clear with a beautiful pale blue tint. The mountains surrounding the lake were visible in detail conveying the impression that no medium existed between them and the spectator. Uncle Ben had ordered breakfast. He said, "I am trying to show you how a millionaire thought and felt. On the French Line steamship, the Normandie, I had met many men and women who were frequently very tired, seemed to feel very empty and had missed the point of life. Their children, young men and women, were still young enough to hunger for something beyond. They had, however, begun to follow in the tracks of their parents. These people who took elaborate means to seek relief from their cares and trouble were certainly not happy. Jesus had said, "Blessed are the poor in spirit."

For my part, I had enjoyed eating giant snails, which tasted like meaty mushrooms, and found the Normandie a very comfortable boat. At Venice I had enjoyed sightseeing in a gondola with an acquaintance from out hotel, a young woman, who was also in Venice for the first time. At the hotel itself, I had had a great deal of fun with some English friends with whom I always took tea before retiring. Yet the enjoyment was superficial, and was followed by fatigue and boredom. My true happiness and peace, deep, substantial, I found in the retirement of my heart, in the contemplation of Divine truths.

In contrast to my present surroundings were those of the University of Chicago. Bill's room, for example. He had a room in the back of "Grandma's" house, as the boys called their landlady. It was small and square. Around its yellow walls Bill had placed small postcard size reproductions of Fra Angelico's paintings. Here he sat, smoking his pipe and studying St. Thomas' tracts with great contentment. "For my part," he had said one day on returning from the richly furnished room of a fellow-student, "I would be content with this room for the rest of my life." No one who knew Bill could doubt that he meant it. "For my part," I had thought, "I can see my carnality in contrast to Bill's spirituality. On another occasion in Chicago, we were having dinner together, near a table occupied by two ladies and a gentleman. The husband and wife were fashionably dressed; she wore jewels. Their chests were thrown out in that attitude often seen in those who have "found their place" in the world. The other lady was small, modestly and poorly dressed, but with a sweet and lovely countenance. She was listening graciously. Bill had expressed his love for the poor. I realized how foolish was my love for the rich. Certainly, the poor in spirit, like Bill, like this poor little lady, undoubtedly poor from birth, had the better part. Bill's peace and joy were deeply rooted in his heart and were not to be disturbed by changes in circumstance, in position, by humiliations. His peace was not disturbed by restless desires for honor, distinction or riches. If he remained faithful to the part he had chosen, nothing would impede him from constantly advancing towards his sublime destiny — the sublime destiny open to the poor. Just as in Chicago I had experienced the superiority of the humble, holy life of the spirit to the worldly life of the senses, so again in this trip through Europe I found the contemplation of Divine truths alone complete and satisfying.

FATHER M. RAPHAEL SIMON
Monk of the Order of the Cistercians
of the Strict Observance
Abbey of Our Lady of the Valley

The Jews and the Hidden Mary

THE JEWS AND WE CHRISTIANS HAVE THIS IN common, that we both possess the Old Testament. The orthodox Jew may have very definite views about it and the Zionist Jew may feel somewhat ill at ease in its presence, but both have this book with us. It is in the interpretation of the book that the differences come. The task is then to find the common ground of agreement.

In the Old Testament, we have the story of the wanderings of the Jewish people until they reach the promised land. We have the story of the covenant with Abraham; the tales of Esther and Ruth and the mother of the Maccabees; of Rachel and the mysterious bride of the Canticle of Canticles. And even before these stories, we have the wonderful description of the creation of the world, of life in the Garden of Eden, and the terrible fall from grace of our first parents.

The Jewish people treat of these characters of the Old Testament merely as historical personages. They do not consider them as persons symbolic of the greater truths of the New Testament.

A few Jewish writers today have come to accept Christ as the Messias. Only the other day, we heard of a well-known Jewish novelist who, in a conversation with a priest friend, said that he accepted Christ as the Messias. May more Jews have come to accept Christ as one of the prophets of their people.

But it isn't Christ and the sixty or more prophecies concerning him in the Old Testament that we propose to discuss, but rather His mother, Mary, who in a wonderful moment which must seem to have been madness to one not of the Faith said, "Behold all generations shall call me blessed." And all generations have called her that.

In the world of art, we have the outpouring of Madonnas. Musicians have tried their best to do justice to this Jewish woman who became the Mother of Jesus Christ, our Lord and God.

The Old Testament is filled with stories of valiant women. We have mentioned some. As we have said, these personages are only people of history to the Jews, but to us they are symbols of Mary. We shall take some of these Biblical stories and try somewhat to show how the Fathers of the Church and the Catholic tradition have looked on these women.

It will be a revelation of the story of Mary hidden in the Old Testament.

Today, the Jews are going through a time of tremendous suffering. They are being crucified and Mary is most certainly beside them, praying for them as she stood sadly beside the Cross of her Son on Calvary.

It has been the constant tradition of the Catholic Church that at the end of the world, at least a remnant of the Jews will enter the Catholic Church. The tradition is that Enoch and Elias will come to bring them to the truth. But when these men will come, they will certainly work the conversions through grace and not through physical force. Since conversion is a matter of grace, the change ultimately goes back to Mary, the Mother of God, who the Church holds is the dispensatrix of all graces.

It is a rather curious fact that today when the question of Zionism is so much written about, the very name, Zion, is one which has been used by the Fathers of the Church to symbolize Mary. How wonderful it would be if the Zionists were in reality what they are in Mary's intention — her children, Marianists!

The Jews must certainly be mystified when they hear Catholics speak of Mary, the Blessed Mother, in such sublime terms. We call her Gate of Heaven, House of Gold, Ark of the Covenant, Tower of David, Queens of the Angels, Queen of Patriarchs, Queen of the Apostles. We are always trying to outdo ourselves in our praise of her. To crown it all, we speak of her as the Immaculate Conception of God.

It was a little Jewish girl who under the inspiration of the Holy Ghost spoke the wonderful words of the Magnificat, which has a tremendous place in Catholic devotion. When the Jews discover this woman of their race, they will have found the woman of whom God spoke in the Garden of Eden right after the Fall.

When God had questioned Adam and Eve about the Fall, He immediately softened the punishment of exile from the Garden of Eden with a promise of a Redeemer to come, the Messias. He said that He would place enmities between the seed of a woman and the seed of the serpent, the Devil, and she would eventually crush his head.

Even sinned by disobedience, and Mary atoned by obedience, obedience unto death.

THE STORY OF ESTHER

Let us go from the scene in the Garden of Eden to the story of Esther.

In the Book of Esther, it is related how Vashti, the Queen, sins by disobedience to the King, and is driven from the royal court.

The King becomes sad, and his seven counsellors suggest that another woman be chosen to take the place of the fallen Vashti. All the beautiful women of the nation are chosen and brought to the King. Each goes in dressed in her best, but, let it be noted, her best. Esther makes no pretence, accepting only the clothes and accessories that the royal eunuch places at her disposal, but despite her personal abnegation, she appears to the King as the most beautiful and she becomes the Queen in place of the banished Vashti.

Esther is a Jew, and she has been brought up by Mardochai. She doesn't, however, tell the King that she is a Jew until a situation arises which compels her to take her place as the pleader at the royal court for her people.

Aman, the chief noble of the court, had plotted against the Jews of the nation and had told all manner of lies against them.

He had even obtained the death warrant for the Jewish nation.

Mardochai then begs Esther to reveal herself to the King and to plead for her people.

Esther decides to do this, and, although she is fearful, she goes ahead. Dressed now in her best clothes and ornaments, she goes into the King's presence resting on the arms of two servants. It is forbidden to appear in the King's presence without his command and Esther is ready to swoon with fear as she enters the royal chamber. The King, moved by her fear, rushes forward to meet her and lets her hold his scepter — the sign that she is accepted into his presence. She tells her story and the King frees her people and has Aman hung from the highest gibbet.

In honor of the freeing of the Jewish people, Esther decrees a yearly feast to be held, called Purim, and she sings a canticle of the Lord's mercies, reminiscent of the Magnificat.

Even today, the Zionists celebrate this feast day at least with Purim balls. Near Teheran in Iran, Esther's grave is still honored, and the story is told thereabouts, much as we talk about heroes of the early days of this country.

The Jewish people think of the feast of Purim as the story of their deliverance, but the persistency of the tradition over thousands of years can scarcely be accounted for except by the influence of the Holy Spirit.

The great heroes of the Greeks and the Romans are told of in history books, but we have no yearly celebration of the mother of the Gracchi, for instance. Yet the celebration of Purim goes on and on, and we believe it will until the Jews come to the realization of the true meaning of the story, its symbolization of the place Mary must play in their salvation.

THE CANTICLE OF CANTICLES

Let us go from the story of Esther to the story of the woman of the Canticle of Canticles. This work is usually attributed to Solomon, and he is noted for his wisdom so that the phrase "as wise as Solomon" is a tradition. The Canticle of Canticles is a poem which outmatches all human poetry for the profundity of its thought. It is probably the most sublime piece of literature ever penned and we as Catholics know that it was written under the inspiration of the Holy Ghost, and that it has a deep mystical meaning.

Cornelius a Lapide, in his great work on this canticle, collects what the different Fathers of the Church have said of it, and he tells us that the true sense, the sensus verus, of the poem refers to the bride as Mary, the perfect soul, which God, the Lover, loves more than all the other concubines, the elect.

Because of this continued tradition, the Church has continuously applied the texts of this poem to the Blessed Mother. Cornelius a Lapide, quoting the Fathers, speaks of the different adornments of the bride loved as the graces and gifts of Mary.

The whole story of the union of a soul with its God is there told under the aspects of human love and when we ponder on the canticle in this light, we realize the significance of St. Paul's words about the Sacrament of Marriage resembling the union of Christ with His Church.

As the elect are the children whom Mary protects and brings to God through the dispensing of the graces which Christ has left in her care, so we come to understand the meaning of the phrase so often used today by spiritual writers — to Jesus through Mary.

THE BOOK OF WISDOM

Saint [Louis] Grignion de Montfort, whose canonization took place on July 20th of this year, says in his True Devotion to the Blessed Virgin Mary that whenever we see the word "wisdom" in the Old Testament, we can take it out and replace it with the word Mary. If we do this, we find startling new insights coming to us. We realize why the Church takes those long quotations from the Book of Wisdom and applies them to Mary, using them in the Masses in her honor.

Thus, on the feast of Mary's Nativity, September 8th, the Church uses this quotation from the Book of Wisdom in reference to Mary.

> The Lord possessed me (i.e., Wisdom) in the beginning of His ways, before He made anything from the beginning. I was set up from eternity, and of old, before the earth was made. The depths were not as yet, and I was already conceived; neither had the fountains of waters as yet sprung out, the mountains with their huge bulk had not as yet been established; before the hills I was brought forth. . . . I was with Him at all times, playing in the world: and my delight is to be with the children of men.

A very mysterious quotation indeed, but one that has some light for us when we ponder the words of Saint [Louis] Grignion de Montfort, that God looked forward from all eternity to the moment when He would come to dwell in Mary's womb. It would be the best tabernacle on earth for Him for it perfectly reflected His perfections. The Fathers have called Mary the House of God for this reason, and the quotation, "Lord, I have loved the beauty of Thy House and the place where Thy glory dwelleth," refers to Mary, the perfect temple of the Holy Ghost.

We can meditate almost endlessly on this subject — the hidden Mary — and through this meditation we can come to a greater understanding of the profound depths of the Divine Plan. All things have been created according to Wisdom. Before there ever was a mountain or a saint or a fountain of water or sanctifying grace, the thought of Mary was in God's mind, and it gave Him continuous delight, for there He derived His greatest extrinsic joy from creation.

When the Jewish people know what we know — namely, that the Old Testament is but a shadowing of the New

Dispensation — they will have found the hidden Mary. They will reach the true Promised Land, the Catholic Church.

Saint Augustine says of the Book of Genesis that in the most minute detail, it is a prophecy of Christ and of His Church. With this thought we can conclude, except for a quotation from St. John Chrysostom, who is speaking of the Garden of Eden said these words:

> The word Eden signifies virgin land. Now such was the region in which God planted Paradise. For it is written that God planted Paradise in Eden toward the East that thou mayest understand that Paradise was not a work of human hands; since the earth was virgin and had known no ploughshare; but without tillage — at the Divine command alone — it put forth its vegetation. For this cause He called it Eden, which means virgin soil. This virgin earth is a type of the Virgin. For as that land without having received any seed, blossomed forth for us Paradise: so too Mary, without having conceived of men, blossomed forth for us Christ.
>
> When then a Jew says to thee: How did a virgin bring forth? Say unto him: How did the virgin earth put forth trees?
>
> ARTHUR SHEEHAN

A Letter on Lakeport

TO THE EDITOR:

I just read Floyd Anderson's article about "Lakeport" in your July issue. I know enough about some of the cities on the Great Lakes to recognize its authenticity. Sure enough, "Lakeport is spiritually a dead city." Still, I thought you might be interested to hear about something that happened in Lakeport this very morning, July 9, 1947 at 7:12 A.M.

At that moment in St. Mary's Church, Father Murphy came out, late as usual, and proceeded to say what should have been the seven o'clock Mass. He did not say it with much devotion because he was distracted with thoughts about whether the convent needed to be repainted now or could wait another year and who would be a good speaker for the coming Communion Breakfast of the Holy Name Society.

It was not a particularly edifying Mass, but the effect was cataclysmic! There were nine Seraphim in the sanctuary and sixty-three Cherubim. There was a respectable attendance of Thrones, Dominations, Principalities, Powers, and Virtues. The Archangels and Angels just couldn't be counted. When Father Murphy started to mumble Hoc est enim . . . the Seraphim veiled their faces with their wings, a group of Archangels swung invisible censers, and twelve Angels with torches knelt reverently in a semi-circle in the sanctuary. The whole affair created quite a sensation in Heaven; for, unlike ourselves, the Blessed never get used to the Mass and they see no reason why the billion-and-first Mass should not be quite as remarkable as any other. In the meantime, the soul of Mrs. Muldoon, for whom the Mass was offered, was liberated from Purgatory and winged her way up through the empyrean to the presence of God and eternal beatitude.

In the sleepy-eyed congregation was a girl with yellow hair, a red-and-white striped dress and too much nail polish. For six months, she has been going to Communion daily. Last night she was the life of the party. She doesn't look very spiritual; but the Bread of Life accomplishes remarkable results with second-rate material. Her friends will be surprised when she enters Carmel next fall. That man with a soiled sweater in the end pew works in the filling station around the corner. He is tired because he has been working all night. His friends know that he has turned over a new leaf recently, but no one except his confessor knows about his frightful physical penances. That shabby, middle-aged woman straining her eyes over a worn prayer book has grounds for divorce ten times over against her faithless husband, but the thought of divorce never occurred to her. She offers up her troubles cheerfully in expiation for her sins which are tiny enough, God knows, and her soul is so effulgent with sanctifying grace that Angels bow reverently when they pass her on the street.

Yes, I suppose that Lakeport is spiritually a dead city. At least I get that impression when I read the papers and talk to Lakeport Catholics. Yet there must still be some spark of spiritual vitality there if things happen such as happened at St. Mary's this morning.

Very sincerely,
PAUL HANLY FURFEY

121

Living the Liturgy

DURING THE COURSE OF LAST YEAR, I HAP-
pened to hear some discussions on the subject of *living the Liturgy*. They followed two papers, one read by Miss Teresa Gray and one by Dr. H. F. Rance.

Miss Gray is Headmistress of a modern school in northwest England. She makes all of her school work enter toward and derive from the Liturgical Year. The result is an enormous success. The children's religion becomes a really potent one. They see the life of the Church, and their own lives in a true perspective, because under the direction of a woman of genius and a very keen Catholic, the life of the Church flowers and fruits, to a greater or less degree, in all their activities.

Miss Gray says that she has a fine staff which carries out her ideas ably and generously, that the parents of the children become infected with enthusiasm too, that there is hope, as far as she can see, of fewer lapses from the Faith when the children come to the age for leaving school.

Dr. Rance's paper — he is a scientist and a fairly recent convert — was about *Liturgy and the Family*. My impression of this paper was that the family to which Dr. Rance referred was a specially favored one, in that, unconsciously, he was thinking of a family existing in a special section of society — that of the professional class. I do not think that Dr. Rance intended this. His paper was couched in theological and philosophical rather than concrete terms. But while I agreed with his thesis as wholeheartedly as I did with that of Miss Gray, and while I have among my friends an example of a well-nigh perfect family, which is at the same time a well-nigh perfect liturgical family, yet my mind turned sadly to the vast majority of Catholic families who do not possess the physical, mental, social, or religious amenities of Dr. Rance.

I turned the matter constantly in my mind until I became obsessed with the thought of these unhappy people who, while they might live liturgically if they could, are powerless to do so.

"Cannot live liturgically?"

That was perhaps a rather sweeping statement. They can live liturgically in one sense — but not with body and mind, as well as soul, as a true and complete participation in the Liturgy of the Church demands. The only way these people of whom I am thinking can live liturgically is by a life-long supreme identification with that supreme desolation on the Cross, in which body and mind are tortured to the annihilation of almost every semblance of humanity, and life remains in the supreme point of the spirit alone.

I think of a story told to me recently by a school teacher in a Glasgow slum. It refers to a child in her class to whom she gave a holy picture.

"Thank you, Miss," said the child. "But, Miss, I haven't anywhere to put it."

"It's to pin on the wall."

"We haven't got a wall, Miss."

"?"

"We're in the middle."

The point is that there were five families to the room, one to each wall, and one in the middle of the room. It is true that a liturgical movement of a sort would have to develop if so many families were to be able to share a room without getting all mixed up with one another. But is this a liturgical movement according to the full mind of the Church?

I think of the American factory workers whose lives are so vividly described by Dorothy Day in her *House of Hospitality* — how, for instance, in motor factories the building of a car is so subdivided and so speeded up that no worker is able to leave his work for a moment for anything less than dire necessity. Is their's liturgical living?

I think of other factory workers — perhaps more fortunate, some of them certainly more fortunate — of the girl who stands day long, week long, year long, at a hatchway door through which, on a moving belt, comes an endless procession of boxes. The girl's only function is to keep her eyes on the hatchway and see that the boxes are straight; if one of them is crooked, with a little movement of the hand she puts it straight again.

Is that life? Above all, can it be liturgical life?

I think of more factory workers. They are everywhere, all over the world, wherever there is an industrial town. They turn a little screw perhaps. They press a lever. They fill a box or a can. They fix a label. No need for skill or responsibility. No need for aiming at perfection. No room for creative activity. No choice. No adaption of means to end. Let them make no deviation from the task the machine has set them. If they do so it will get them. They must themselves become a perfect piece of mechanism in order to work at the machine. Let them assume a sense of responsibility at their own peril.

"They can contemplate, because they have no distraction from contemplation."

Yes, by a miraculous grace. But let them not have ecstasies. They would be into the wheels at once.

Did God, when He created Adam, intend that he and his descendants should work like this? I know that God permits this evil, but that is by no means the same thing. He permits murder. He lets the enemy sow cockle but, if we are his children, we must not sow it ourselves. We must even refrain, as *far as it is in our power,* from *conniving* at the sowing of the cockle. Above all, we must not allow ourselves to be convinced — much less shout it from the housetops — that the cockle is first-grade wheat.

"They are workers. They must remain workers. We must not try to take them out of the class from which they come. Otherwise, they will no longer be able to influence that class. The industrial world can once again be opened to Christianity." I quote from a Catholic magazine. But how is it possible to Christianize the institution which is annihilating those very faculties in man which essentially make him a potential member of the Mystical Body of Christ—his memory, his understanding, and his will? The sacrifice of man's life to his God must be not only a pure sacrifice but a whole sacrifice. Man should be the possessor of his own body, mind and soul before he can *offer them up*. It is the perfect creature who is the fittest victim of sacrifice. Only God Himself has the right to approve the crucifixion of His creatures.

The factory worker of today is not a whole personality. This must be obvious when one considers how little of him is needed in his work. He leaves outside the factory all of himself except a certain bodily strength, the act of will that takes him there and keeps him going through the day, and those sub-human reflex actions which, unerringly and undeviatingly performed, link him up with the machine. His human power of making varying decisions and adapting means to ends are all unnecessary. To attempt to use them would be a handicap. Thus, he is weary with a boredom of mind from which he is tempted to take refuge in various forms of excitement.

His wife's lot is slightly better than his. She can still bathe the babies if she wishes. But more and more, she tends to relegate the lovely and civilizing functions of mother-care to a state control that is only too anxious to shoulder her responsibilities. More and more as the cheap chain store provides her with food from a can and garment from a peg is her initiative dulled, her task perverted. "*Who shall find a valiant woman?*"

She can still have babies.

Yes, if there is room in the house for babies. But houses near factories are, in the main, built on expensive land sites, and therefore the houses are small. And so, there are not so many babies. Husband and wife must live in a state of heroic continence or they must fly to contraceptives. Yet this is mortal sin. Only priests and doctors know fully the evils which are the frightful results of the overcrowding in our city. Is it in such conditions that family life can be carried on liturgically?

The children grow. The state takes charge of them — not perhaps overtly, but by subtle, creeping measures — by being, for instance, kinder to the children than the parents are able to be, simply because it gently or forcibly removes from the parents the right and the responsibility to be kind. And when this process of the adoption of the children by the state has been carried sufficiently far, the mother, as well as the father, is free to do factory work. Goodbye, Christian home.

The industrial system, as everyone knows — but few people will face that knowledge — is destroying us, body, mind and soul. It is the industrial system with its economic network and its basis of international finance which has made possible the concentration of power in the hands of the few, the dragooning of the masses, the poison gas of lying propaganda, the machine gun at the street corner, the atomic bomb. It is the industrial system which is destroying the very fertility of the earth. It has made possible and led to the widespread destruction of reasonable human activity. It has made modern Russia possible — the greatest enemy the Church has ever known.

Ah! Poor world! Can you live now liturgically except in the paradox of crucifixion! Surely God never intended *that* for the common life of man! Otherwise, why, drawing nigh to Jerusalem, did He weep over it, saying, "*If thou hadst but known, and in this thy day, the things that are to thy peace: but now they are hidden from thy eyes.*"

"But," you may protest to Him, "I can't put the clock back."

Chesterton, whom I would venture to compare in some ways with St. Thomas Aquinas, pointed out that you could. The trouble is that, like Christianity, we haven't tried sufficiently. What is more, we don't intend to try. And yet we have already witnessed, in this our day, the fulfillment of the prophecy made so long ago to Jerusalem— *"For the days shall come upon thee, and thy enemies shall cast a trench about thee and compass thee round, and straighten thee on every side, and beat thee flat to the ground, and thy children who are in thee. And they shall not leave in thee a stone upon a stone; because thou hast not known the time of thy visitation."* And entering into the temple, He began to cast out them that sold therein and them that bought, saying to them, *"It is written, My house is the house of prayer. But you have made it a den of thieves."*

AILEEN MARY CLEGG
Sussex, England

Christ Without Caricature

THE LIFE OF CHRIST

By Guiseppe Ricciotti

Translated by Alba Zizzamia

Bruce

May God shower His Tender compassion and light on those of us who carry upon our hearts and lips our personal caricature of His Divine Son. Though there is a more grievous sin than presumption (despair, for example), we who are the presuming type may one day find we really had no great cause for relaxation into this peculiar brand of mental "well being."

The followers of Christ when He walked the earth were surrounded by far greater reality and intensity of life than we are in our age. They talked about Him, studied Him, asked Him questions, and pondered His words in their hearts. Many, having done this, became His disciples or, on the other hand, thinking the price too great, "walked no more with Him."

Just inasmuch as man is a caricature of himself in this mechanized, urban culture, so is Jesus, our Brother, too frequently made over into our own image and likeness — and only then do we proceed to refer to ourselves as His "disciples."

Two caricatures of our Redeemer immediately come to mind as I write. For some there is the long-robed, long-bearded, phlegmatic caricature walking about with thin, frails hands, His lowered eyes avoiding all conflict and noticing no mischief. This is the devil's specialty in South America and other Latin countries. How far this conception is from the reality of "Jesus our Brother, strong and good" — the Son of God and the Brave Hearted Maid — the Foster Son of a skilled carpenter! But this misconception is one of the reasons why so few men are found in churches in Latin countries and why piety and a certain lack of masculinity are often associated in their minds.

On the other extreme is a misguided "leader" complex. There's the frequently strained masculinity in the rehearsed, clear-headed objectivity of the good-Catholic-college graduate. He wishes so much to serve Christ and His Church that he works very hard to become a millionaire, real-estate dealer or head of the stock exchange. Thus, cloaking his worldly aspirations, his plan is to bedazzle those who formerly ridiculed the Faith into realizing what practical hard-headed people the followers of Christ really are.

There is very obvious need for Catholic laymen to know their Leader — and it will logically follow that they will then know what life wants of them.

In order to avoid, as much as possible, coloring the Life of Christ in his own particular manner, as so many authors have, Father Ricciotti says " . . . it has been my wish to write an historical and documentary work. I have studied the ancient fact and not the modern theory, the solidity of the documents and not the flimsiness of any interpretation presently the fashion. I have even dared to imitate the famous dispassionateness of the canonical Evangelists, who have neither an exclamation of joy when Jesus is born not a word of lament when He dies. It has been my intention, then, to write a critical work."

The Life of Christ is a scholarly book written with utter clarity and simplicity. The author is an Abbot and Procurator of the Canons Regular of St. Augustine. Throughout the book, the countryside of Palestine is shown in numerous photographs. While hovering between life and death on the battlefield in the first World War, Father Ricciotti thought that, if he might live, he would write a life of Christ. The book is the culmination of a lifetime of study and meditation and was completed during the second World War. The author possesses a depth of knowledge in Oriental literature and languages (Hebrew, Aramaic, etc.), as well as Greek, Latin, English, French and German.

The first part of this book deals with the historical, social and geographical background of Christ's life, followed by an examination of the sources of our information about Him, a chapter on His physical appearance, and a discussion of the rationalist's interpretation of the life of Jesus. The second part is a detailed and chronological consideration of Christ's life.

Each chapter is equally full and detailed. One can merely outline the contents of this learned contribution to Catholic thought — brief complimentary sentences are not sufficient to describe a life work of this nature. This book is a real source of food for meditation. It shows us the *real* Christ.

MAUREEN GIL

Genesis of the Contemporary Chaos

A HISTORY OF THE CHURCH, VOL. III
By Philip Hughes
Sheed & Ward

This third volume deals with the revolt against the Church, from Aquinas to Luther, that period which preceded and made possible the Reformation. It does not make pleasant reading, for it is an almost unrelieved tale of men's betrayal of Christ in His Church. But it is fascinating and profitable reading with constant present-day implications. What was then beginning is now finishing completely in our generation, attended by, on one hand, final horrible perversions and barbarism, and on the other by the fruits of the purification of the Church, and new spiritual beginnings.

Father Hughes' treatment of Church history is impressive. Obviously, a scholar, he is acquainted at first hand with all the researches on key questions and, where necessary, he can and does give detailed facts. He is completely objective, never betraying the slightest anxiety to color the facts. His chief concern is to show the origin and development of trends rather than to interpret events from an apologetical point of view, although he occasionally does that, as when he points out how Popes, good and bad during this period, rise to the defense of the autonomy of the Church against the threat of the princes. The author is a man of judgement, knowing what is important and what is not, and a man of charity, notable throughout but especially in regard to Luther.

He treats the history chronologically, by periods, with time out three times to discuss Christian life, thought and sanctity. Here is where most of his interpretation comes in. The only weakness the book has is that these philosophical and spiritual considerations are separated from, rather than integrated with, the general history.

Two themes run through the history at this period, both culminating, in a way, in Luther. One is the struggle between Church and State and, although the author does not stress it unduly, it is quite clear that it is not a case of the Church trying to usurp temporal power, as of the State trying to subordinate the spiritual power, which the revival of pagan ideas abetted. Luther, then, represents the capitulation of religion to the political arm with what ultimate results the daily papers bear witness. The other theme is the progressive departure from truth, first in opposing faith and reason, and so on down to the intellectual anarchy of Luther. Philip Hughes shows this as a movement away from and neglect of St. Thomas. He has an interesting discussion of the "Devotio Moderna," apropos of "The Imitation of Christ." Here the application to our own day is obvious. We have been the recipients of the tradition of devotions separated from theology, with Garrigou-Lagrange among other champions of a new return to St. Thomas.

Good will is what saves men's souls, but the reader of this history will learn the disease to which good will is liable in the absence of good understanding.

CAROL ROBINSON

Salt, Not Soup

AUTOBIOGRAPHY OF THE BLESSED VIRGIN
Compiled by Peter Resch, S. M.
Bruce

Only God in His inspired word can adequately describe Mary, His Masterpiece, the crown of His creation. The appropriation by the Church of Scriptural passages as found in the Breviary and attributed to Our Lady make up this entire work. Otherwise, the title would indeed sound presumptuous. With the self-effacing restraint of the Woman whom the Old Testament unconsciously describes, Father Resch writes his modest preface. A striking footnote follows the excerpt from the Canticle of Canticles "I am black but comely": "The reference here can only be to the darkness of her unconscious beauty. For as the sun which fills the earth with light has power to turn to blackest night the white bodies of men upon whom its rays fall directly, so Mary was rendered invisible to herself by the brightness of the sun which envelopes her. The result is complete oblivion of self. . . . She looked into the translucent depths of her own nothingness and saw only the might of God; all else was blotted out." The austere beauty, the elevation and the vigor of Scripture are a relief after the sentimentality that taints much Marian literature.

FRANCES CLARE O'REILLY

The Fact of Fatima

OUR LADY OF FATIMA
By William Thomas Walsh
Macmillan

This is one of the most important books of the year, perhaps of any year, and deserves a high place on any best-seller list. This is partly because of the excellence of Dr. Walsh's presentation, but much more because of the subject. Dr. Walsh came home from Portugal convinced that nothing is so important as making known what Our Lady asked in these apparitions that have been so neglected, so distorted, so misunderstood. The future of our civilization, our liberties, our very existence may depend upon the acceptance of her commands, he wrote. And he has done his share in making these facts known in an excellent, most readable book.

The story is fairly well known: The appearances of Our Lady in 1917 to three shepherd children in Portugal, in the hill country called the Serra de Aire, near Fatima. There were six appearances in all, and at the last, before 70,000 people, Our Lady performed a startling miracle to prove the truth of what the children said. And what did the children say?

That Our Lady asked the consecration of Russia to her Immaculate Heart. If this were done, Russia would be converted and there will be peace. If not, Russia will scatter her errors throughout the world, provoking wars and persecutions of the Church. And people must pray the Rosary, perform sacrifices, make the five first Saturday Communions, pray for the Holy Father, and after each mystery of the Rosary say, "O my Jesus, pardon us and deliver us from the fire of hell. Draw all souls to heaven, especially those in most need.

This would be a fascinating story, delightful and charming, if it were fiction; but it is fact, and fact that concerns all of us. Dr. Walsh has caught the flavor of the country, the simplicity and sincerity of the children, and gives you the feeling that you too were there. You must read this book.

FLOYD ANDERSON

The Subtleties of Newman

NEWMAN, FAITH AND THE BELIEVER
By Philip Flanagan, D. D.
Newman Bookshop

"The present work is an attempt to show whether or not there are solid grounds for accusing Newman of Modernism or even

Semi-modernism." In his Introduction, the Reverend Henry Tristan of the Oratory points out that "from the first page of his book until the last, Fr. Flanagan, fearing lest his love of and veneration for Newman should in the smallest degree bias his judgment . . . has forced himself to be severely critical. . . . " This severity reaches its culmination in the following two passages (pp.97 and 112):

> Apart from the fallacies in the examples, there appears to be a much more serious error underlying Newman's assertions: his apparent does not seem to have understood what is meant by abstraction, for his universal man is just an aggregate of all men that he knew.
>
> It is clear from passage that Newman did not understand what was meant by a universal idea.

However, we may definitely affirm that the author triumphantly exculpates Newman from the accusation of Modernism or even Semi-modernism.

The body of the work is devoted to a detailed examination of the accounts of Newman given by the French "Newmanists" who treated him as Jansen treated St. Augustine. There are two appendices: the first is an exposition of Modernism, and the second is a most luminous discussion of the "conscience argument" for the existence of God. There is a useful explanation of the true doctrine of abstraction as opposed to conceptualist errors (pp. 110-113), and a rather detailed study of the rational basis of belief in children. This last (pp. 83-90) is rather terrifying, because it seems to conceal skeptical implications utterly destructive of all infallible certainty.

The gist of the whole work is expressed in these words: "What Newman emphasises above all is the importance of background and environment in our study of the evidence for the Church."

ALAN C. BATES

A Guide to the New Testament

THE GOSPEL OF JESUS CHRIST
By Père M.J. Lagrange, O.P.
Newman Bookshop

The revived interest of Catholics in the Scriptures, and particularly in the New Testament, makes this work a very timely one. The reputation of Père Lagrange as a Biblical scholar is too well established for me to attempt to add it. His many years of study in the Holy Land have made him perhaps the prime authority on Biblical history, language, and customs. He is consulted by archeologists and other research students throughout the world.

In this study in two volumes, the four gospels are treated harmoniously as a continuous narrative with interesting historical background material. Père Lagrange is slightly apologetic to his more scholarly readers for what may seem insufficient arguments and refers them to his more complete synopsis of the Gospels with the explanation that this work is intended for popular consumption. It is this fact which I especially liked about these books; they are so very readable. They elaborate and explain the Gospels and should be read along with your New Testament in order to obtain the greatest benefit and delight. As permanent additions to your library, they are well worth the price.

DOROTHY WILLOCK

Leaders in Liaison

WARTIME CORRESPONDENCE BETWEEN PRESIDENT ROOSEVELT AND POPE PIUS XII
Macmillan

These messages have lasting historical value, revealing the parallel endeavors of our late President and His Holiness Pope Pius XII, in their respective spheres to alleviate the sufferings of those innocent peoples engulfed in the greatest of all wars.

How much encouragement His Holiness received from Mr. Roosevelt's letters and from his personal contacts with our envoy, the Honorable Myron C. Taylor, is reflected in the letters an in the achievement of their common purpose.

The introduction and explanatory notes by Mr. Taylor show the framework of events and fill in the correlating information and describe various developments arising in connection with the messages.

The love and trust in God expressed by our late President was very encouraging and consoling to His Holiness, in the face of so much Godlessness in the world; so also his declaration that America looked forward to a world founded upon the four essential freedoms.

JO ANN HARFORD

Fruit of Contemplation

THE SPIRITUAL DOCTRINE OF SISTER ELIZABETH OF THE TRINITY
Rev. M. M. Philipon, O. P.
Newman Bookshop

If sublimity is the echo of a great soul, Sister Elizabeth of the Trinity ranks with Catherine of Siena and Gertrude the Great. The doctrine of the Divine Indwelling was the center of her spiritual life. This holy young nun died in 1906 at the age of 26 after only five brief years in the Dijon Carmel. Everything she wrote has the breath of another shore. Her letters and retreats are replete with infused wisdom and light. (St Paul was a great source of her inspiration. Considering her complete lack of all formal theological training, her commentaries are amazing. Indeed. in her love of solid doctrine, she was "a Dominican at heart" as she herself once said.) She is a model for interior souls for her own was like a crystal reflecting the Trinity. She was absorbed in her "Three" to the exclusion of and complete forgetfulness of self and she radiated that peace which comes only from divine union. Her "Prayer to the Trinity," written in the white heat of inspiration without an erasure, has in it the power to set one on the contemplative road, as many Carmelites have attested. She has marvelous facility for reaching souls to go out from self and live in God.

There isn't a trace of sentimentally in her, there is nothing "Frenchy," nothing saccharine in her piety. She always views things as a soul at one with Christ. She never comes down. With exquisite grace and tact, she writes to her friends — spontaneously and without the least stiffness of the things of God. Never appointed to any office, her main work was an interior one. Like Mary, she is the silent woman absorbed in the Mystery within her.

Father Philipon treats her with the maximum of respect and penetrative understanding. His appreciation is as keen as his doctrinal analysis is solid.

FRANCES CLARE O'REILLY

Christ in Concrete

GOD'S OWN METHOD
By Aloysius McDonough, C. P., S. T. D.
The Sign Press

".... And a small drop of ink,
   Falling like dew, upon a thought, produces
   That which makes thousands, perhaps millions think."

(Byron)

Taken from the introduction to Father McDonough's book in which he brings "up to date," so to speak, the lesson found in the divine "design for living." This book has been written in the modern manner for the reader of today. The trial of Christ is discussed in modern legal terms, His death in modern medical terms, holding one's interest all the way through. The writer does indeed "give his reader the most knowledge, and takes from him the least time, "leaving him grateful for the "drop of ink" and the time spent in thoughtful preparation.

JO ANN HARFORD

God's Magnet

THIS AGE AND MARY
By Michael O'Carroll, C. S. Sp.
Newman Bookshop

In the chaos of present-day instability, man needs, more than any other thing, an object to turn to, something from which he can drive sympathy, consolation, serenity. Too often, not knowing where to go, in his despair he turns to material things, to friends worse off than himself, to skepticism, all of which can only lead him deeper into the pit. Father O'Carroll, in his book *This Age and Mary,* offers a solution to the problem, one to fill the minds and hearts of men with true hope. He gives us Mary; she who, in the words of St. Bernard, is the "Key of Heaven" and at the utterance of whose name the portals of Paradise open.

How does Mary answer the needs of our times, this age so often called the "Age of Mary"? In his book, Father O'Carroll highlights various titles of Our lady and shows how her particular attributes serve not only as inspiration for men in this age so lacking in virtues, but also as a source of the actual help needed so desperately. Mary's life, her humility, her purity, her charity, her position in heaven above the angels and saints, her maternal affection for men — all her perfections are vividly analyzed and portrayed. Her position as powerful Mediatrix, interceding continually for us before the throne of God, should make us go with hope and love to her who can lead us out of this chaos, if we but ask.

This Age and Mary can well serve as a guide to understanding Our Blessed Mother. No one can read it without feeling closer to her and loving her more. The author writes with clarity and warmth, making of the book a source of comfort to the reader, and a garland of praise for Mary. In the words of Father O'Carroll, she must become a "living magnetic force" in the life of every Christian. If this should happen it would indeed bring joy and serenity to each individual, for as St. Bernard tells us: "God wills that all graces should be bestowed upon us through Mary."

GLORIA TANASO

MEDIAEVAL PHILOSOPHY
By D. J. B. Hawkins
Sheed & Ward

For a neat, clear resumé of mediaeval philosophy, this is excellent. One senses an ease of mastery on the part of the author. What is important, what is new and what is relevant, is quite clear to him, and the whole is related, in an especially good final chapter, to modern philosophy and to present-day philosophical needs. There are occasional lapses into humor and colloquialisms that make you wish the writer would bend yet further in the direction of the ordinary mind.

CAROL ROBINSON

"With persevering prayer to the Spirit of Love
and Truth, We wait for them with open
arms to return not to a stranger's house,
but to their own, their Father's house."

—PIUS XII

INTEGRITY

: the twelfth issue :

SEPTEMBER, 1947   Vol. 1., No. 12

SUBJECT: SECURITY AND GOD'S PROVIDENCE

OR THE PULSE OF AN AGE, study its use of words. Only an age which loves money would coin phrases like "there's no *percentage* in it," and "you look like a million dollars." And only an age which has ceased in practice to respect God's Providence would develop institutions called The *Guarantee Trust* Company, The *Providential* Loan, and The *Security* Exchange. All these words, which today suggest the realm of finance to us, really pertain to the forgotten doctrine of God's Providence. It might be useful to review that doctrine.

Providence is God in respect of His ordering of all things. Nothing happens in the universe unless God wills it or allows it. God even moves our free wills (without, mysteriously, interfering with their freedom). It is not correct to say only of a happy event that "it is providential." Everything is providential. God is never foiled. God is never frustrated. All things work together, ultimately, for God's glory. How this works out in the whole is mysterious, but we can see some of the workings, especially when good comes out of evil.

Security is a word which we have come to consider as meaning "safe," or "certain." It originally meant, and it literally means, "without care." How obviously that change is the result of our growing materialism! To be without care is to have confidence in God, to have the virtue of hope, and in this sense the most secure person is a St. Francis of Assisi, or a contemplative nun, a person with no material possessions whatever, and with a correspondingly deep trust in God.

But we have turned away from God and sought our security in

material things. We thought that if we only had a house, money in the bank, stocks, insurance, then we would be safe, without care. But the more we hope in these things, the further we are from being without care. If you want to find a man who is really solicitous for tomorrow, go see the multimillionaire. Care decreases as you go down the scale of wealth, until you find the poor, as poor, relatively unconcerned. But for the really carefree, you must seek those who have made themselves poor for the love of God. Most people have observed this is so, but being orientated to materialism they can't help hoping that if they increase their $100,000 in the bank to $200,000 in the bank, they will sleep easier at night. The more we try to solve the problem of insecurity on the materialistic level, the more obviously it shows itself to be primarily a spiritual problem. Just as security is a way of expressing the virtue of hope (a man is without care because he trusts in God), so insecurity, by contrast, is a sort of way of expressing despair, which is manifested through anxiety. That is why one of our articles on security in this issue is fittingly called THE ANATOMY OF DESPAIR. We have never had such insecurity. We have never had such despair. We think that if we have social security and tenure and all those other things that we will be happy, but it is really the other way around. It is because we are unhappy and despairing that we seek so desperately for those things, and the fact that we are not satisfied with a few of them, but want more and more, is evidence that we are looking for something in a place where it is not to be found.

Virtue is the key to our role in God's Providence. All things conspire to God's glory, but not all things conspire to our salvation or to harmony in the temporal order. Here things work out happily only in proportion as we obey God's commandments, because His laws reflect, in the moral order, the potential harmony of secondary causes. This whole doctrine of God's Providence is contained in the sixth chapter of Matthew, reprinted on the back cover of this issue. Our duty is plainly stated: "Seek ye first the kingdom of God and His Justice," and our reward promised, that "all these things will be added unto you." It is because Providence operates that way. Hardly anyone believes this any more. Those who practice virtue often do so with a martyred air, as though it were against their own best interests, while most of us just flatly don't believe that all these things will be added (that is, we despair) and run our lives according to the law of expediency, which says "make sure you get yours, and then practice what virtue you can squeeze in." We think it is very important to point out that God's law really does operate, even today when it would seem as though all the cards are stacked against the practicing Christian, so we have included testimony on the subject in AND ALL THESE THINGS WILL BE ADDED. But we must also avoid thinking that obedience to the divine law will be rewarded in worldly success. Everything will come out all right in the end, but the end is the Beatific Vision, not the presidency of General Motors. Nevertheless, for what God wants us to do here he will provide the means, and it is the rare person who is tested unto folly, as was Job. We can often see the uses of unemployment, as did the man in the story in this issue (A JOB'S A JOB). When the generality of men practice virtue, things in general work out well. But even if the generality of men practice vice, it still is true that "to them that love God all things work together unto good," as St. Paul has assured us.

If men won't do things God's way, they run into trouble, and then they try to invent ways of staving off disaster. Our economic history for several hundred years past can best be understood as the efforts of men to build defenses against the consequences of society's sins. Capitalism sought refuge in large fortunes and insurance. Socialism is the development, or if you like, the decadence of capitalism. It is solicitous of every detail of a man's life in the name of security. If life under capitalism was unlovely, life under socialism is dreary beyond measure.

We have two articles this month protesting the inhumanity of such an existence. One (BUILDER IN VAIN) is about life in a government housing project; and other (APOSTATES' HARVEST) comes from England where the mechanization of life is all but complete.

We have also included a remarkably clear exposition of the essential errors of both capitalism and socialism (THE FRYING PAN AND THE FIRE). The author sees what is frequently missed, that the planned state which is almost upon us just couldn't have evolved if men had given God His due. When we deny God's Providence, we start ordering things ourselves, as though we were God. The state which sets out to be wholly Providential must necessarily also be Omnipotent.

THE EDITORS

CO-CREATORS

Men of vision search and grope,
To find a name for a washing soap,
While God takes care of little things,
Like turning Winter into Springs.

And All These Things Will Be Added

TO THE MODERN MIND, NO STATE IS QUITE so terrifying in its aspect as that of being utterly dependent upon God. This state is looked upon as synonymous with hopelessness, destitution, and despair. The cheeks of parents blanch at the thought that such a fate may await their children. Worried business men spend sleepless nights counting on their fingers, or re-examining their inventories, assets, debits, and liabilities, in terror that the near future may find them utterly dependent. It is this fear that sets neighbor against neighbor, each one fearing that the other may carry the contagious germ of insecurity. This fear is the root of many people's worldly ambitions. They are not as much greedy as they are afraid. When the vision of wealth and power grows dim, the fear of dependence comes in to take over. Security, the end of the modern man's labor, is the rosy heaven set up by contrast with the dark hell of being dependent upon God.

Those who claim a special familiarity with God, are often no more remarkable for their trust in His Beneficence than those who deny Him. The timidity of the elect, with all their petty fears and need for reassurance, does not make election appear to be a particularly attractive state. The pagan is confirmed in his non-belief. If the heirs to Heaven distrust their Father, who can trust Him?

This morbid fear of dependence upon God, so current among the moderns, is bulwarked by two theological misconceptions:

1. That God's Mercy is only operative in the breach, when things go wrong.
2. That God is *our* Helper, an omnipotent accessory to *our* plans. Informal research into popular opinion among nominal Christians would lead a pagan to conclude

that God is a supplementary agent to a first-aid kit and a bank account. After penicillin has failed, all you can do *then* is pray; if you have overdrawn on your account, then you had better start making a novena. Thus, a weird phantasm of the Deity takes shape in the modern mind: an administering angel, who, like the shyster lawyer, is always found at the scene of an accident; a beaming philanthropist who comes to the door with groceries when the cupboard is bare; a Santa Claus who frequents sick rooms ready to bestow new livers for old, for a prescribed portion of fervent prayer. Along the road of life, the Deity is looked upon with the same misgivings as the glass-paneled box hanging on the side of buses: "In case of emergency, break glass, and pull down hook!" One anxiously hopes that the glass need never be broken! While this distorted idea of God's Mercy exists, it is small wonder that dependence upon Him will be feared. Instead of the father of the household, God is looked upon as the family doctor or dentist, someone whom you would prefer not to call upon . . . if possible.

The second calumny against God which distorts our concepts of His Mercy is the belief cherished by secularized Christians that God is *their* Helper. According to this theory (it is more a dream than a rational theory), God made the world quite a while ago, then He left it up to us to do with it what we will, at the same time promising us that if we find the going tough, He will send us what we need in the way of goods or expert advice. This places all the *initiative* on us. We say, "Here, dear God, give me a lift." This accounts for the too frequent sight of Christians engaged in shady businesses involving exploitation of the poor, or appeals to concupiscence, going to church for a little Divine help.

This accounts for an otherwise inexplicable practice that went on during the war: both German and American Christians praying to God for victory, as though the motives and end of the war had no interest for God at all!

Regardless of what men may think, God's Mercy is not only operative in the time of emergency, but all the time. God not only restores health, He sustains health. He holds the whole universe in being, bringing it to fruition in an orderly sequence of events. Nothing exists apart from God, not even an atheist, or the idea of atheism. To be real means to be sustained by God. All things begin with Him, continue in Him, and end in Him. The men afloat upon a raft in an endless sea, as they cried out to God for help, were not wailing down the passages of a strange and unknown world. Before they started to pray, God was with them. He held up the waters upon which their raft was held. It was He Who rolled the sun through the sky, and laid over them the blanket of the night. It was He Who aroused in them the hope that He would answer if they cried across the desolation. As He led them to their rescuers, He merely continued the Mercy He had begun when He gave them life.

Regardless of what men think, it is we who are God's helpers. All initiative lies with Him. He has a plan which he reveals to us through His Church, through His teachers, and through the grace with which He moves us and the opportunities He presents to us. This plan excludes *nothing*. All creatures less than man cooperate with God's plan of necessity. They have no choice in the matter. In man, God respects the free will which He placed there, and so we are free to cooperate or not. We are free to obey His laws or not. We are free to share His Love or not.

To deny the omnipotence of God, His everywhereness, is to deny reality. A man may stand before a whirling propeller, and say it is not there, but it is there none the less, as he would readily observe were he to extend his arm. Another man may stand before a tree, and say, "Sure, that's a tree. It's made of wood, leaves, and, once a year, apples grow on its branches." IF that is all he sees, then he is called a "realist." The man who truly faces us to reality sees a tree as an instrument of God's Mercy. He has the humility to see that a tree is essentially a mysterious thing with a very practical purpose. It mysteriously produces apples. Only a fool could ask, "What is an apple?" without asking, "*Why* is an apple?" No other explanation fits the phenomenon than that God has made apple trees and He sustains them so that they might give their fruit to men.

Many people have been brought to know God's Mercy by some unusual or miraculous occurrence. The shrine of Lourdes and the miracles which have taken place there have been the occasion for many conversions. Yet the Faith of centuries has not grown upon miracles. The beneficence of a father may be shown in rare acts of extraordinary kindness, but the trust of his family is earned by his generous conduct from day to day and throughout the years. The habit of Faith nurtures upon a day-by-day observation of God's Mercy being unfolded before our eyes. Hope for the future grows as we recall God's Mercy for us in the past, and as we count the blessings we presently enjoy. God's Mercy is always there, if we but look for it.

If you want to see God's Mercy in operation, just look at the lives of people who trust in Him. The lives of these people who have a living Faith in God are testimony to His daily concern for those who seek the Kingdom of Heaven and its Justice. These people do not debate academically about the Faith but in their very lives every one of today's false doctrines is denied.

I know a young mother who recently had a baby. She is poor and was bedded in a ward with ten other women. As is inevitable, the conversation frequently turned toward a discussion of the ways and means of preventing conception. She didn't take part in the conversation until her silence was noticed. She told them then that she had five children, she was tired but happy, knew all about contraception — including the fact that it is against the law of God, was sure that God would find it no more difficult to feed another mouth, that her husband loved her very much and she loved him, that being healthy she probably would have more children, that she was anxious to get home to her family, and if they would kindly keep quiet for a while, she would like to say her rosary. Her remarks were greeted with silence. In thirty seconds, she shattered every excuse that a woman can devise to soothe a bothered conscience, not by what she had said, mind you, but by being there with them and seeing God's Mercy where they saw disaster.

I know a young man who, as he approached marriage, was warned by his friends against it. He suffered from a serious organic trouble which demanded that he take occasional rest periods away from work. He had a semi-skilled job which brought him in $25 a week. His strong trust in God's Providence was counted as a liability because it neutralized any worldly ambitions he might have. Notations in his bank book, covering a period of one year, soared to the considerable figure of $40.18.

He married a Catholic girl who had the same simple trust in God as himself. They have been married almost six years and have five children. He rarely missed a day's work, the greater part of which was manual labor — that for one period of a year and a half amounted to 68 hours a week. The children are exceptionally healthy. On the one occasion when they found themselves penniless, a diligent search unearthed a half dollar which provided them with a pint of ice cream (to celebrate their discovery) and Daddy's carfare to work.

At one time they were tempted to worry. An earnest doctor warned them that their combined blood factors were unfavorable to the birth of healthy babies. Since then, medical science is faced with the problem of either revising their statistics or giving the couple a medal for accomplishing the impossible. When they moved New York City a year ago, they put an ad in a Catholic weekly, made a novena to Mother Cabrini, and received one answer. This was an entire house which perfectly suited their need and purse.

This family has no bank account. The husband is no more desirous of wealth than before, nor has he acquired any particular facility for acquiring it. This, to my mind, is the most convincing evidence of God's Providence. Nothing here is very extraordinary, yet this family has turned up its nose at every one of the modern security axioms. Their happiness and well-being are obviously from God because that is the only place they sought it.

Just find a man who trusts in God and there you will find God. Every religious order has as its history a long testimony to God's Mercy. The greater and more absolute the trust, the more magnificent is His generosity. Mammon is the god of the slot machine economy: "Ask and you shall receive . . . what you can pay for!" Mammon, the god of insecurity to whom our present system of economics is dedicated, will always give you a nickel's worth for a nickel. But our God is a Just God and a Merciful God.

In God's Mercy there is more than enough consolation to cure all of the despair in the world. God abides with us. His love for us is limitless. His power to make that love manifest is limitless. No matter how many may by their perversity disharmonize the economy and polity of nations, God can reknit the strands they have severed so that not a hair of the head of those who trust him may be harmed.

The combined efforts of all men of good will acting apart from God can achieve nothing, but *with* God all things are possible.

ED WILLOCK

AT EVENTIDE

There's money in the bank,
  The future is assured,
The car is running nicely,
  My jewels are insured,
So now it would be nice,
  After I have dined,
To read Rabbi Liebman
  And pacify my mind.

A Job's A Job
A STORY

"YOU RANG, MR. ATWOOD?" SHE STOOD ON the threshold of the conference room. A dozen solemn faces looked up without interest—they were tense, preoccupied. Atwood sat at the near end of the table, his back to her. He smoked nervously. Irritably he tapped a thin pile of dittoed sheets on the corner of the table.

"Eileen—you can give these out now."

She picked up the pile, left the room. Atwood continued: "So much for Model L. Now about Model R. Roger, you and Hinchliffe tie in with . . ."

She shut the door softly. The tension in the room confirmed her suspicions. It was an axe-swinging session. She stood in the aisle outside the door and glanced at the sheets in her hand. "Copies to: Simpson, Flynn, Gensheimer, Hubbard . . ." She scanned the text for errors—a correction showed up as a smudge. Well, here it is, gang. Read it and weep.

Cynically she surveyed the rows of desks, drawn up like battalions. Almost no one was working. Girls gossiped languidly in twos and threes. The people of Purchasing were fingering their paper-work and daydreaming. Others flipped through technical magazines or visited. Typewriters opened fire at intervals, petered out. Even the rumble of the billing machines sounded drowsy and remote, life summer thunder.

She thought: Precision Manufacturing—what a lot of sad sacks. But she knew what they were waiting for. It was pay day. On pay day at Precision, things had been happening lately . . .

She threaded through the aisles, dropping copies of the notice on various desks.

The office stirred nervously from its lethargy. People went back to their places. Groups scattered, bunched around the bulletin, broke out in rumors.

In the middle of the room, a young man in gabardine trousers and a Barrymore shirt pushed aside a magazine, yawned mightily, and glanced at the wall clock. Two thirty. He peered across the room toward the glass partition of Atwood's office.

"Nuts!"

He reached for his pipe. Absently he tapped the ashes into his hand, threw them under the desk. He pulled apart the stem, blew through the bit, examined the bowl. Then he fished a bent wire out of a drawer and began poking at it.

He stopped—the juice was staining his fingers. He glanced around helplessly, eyed his neighbor across the aisle.

"Fritzie-gimme a Kleenex."

The older man looked over, took in the situation, smiled gently. He pulled open a drawer, picked out two tissues from a half empty box and without comment handed them across the aisle. He smiled again, almost shyly—a small man in a dark suit—and returned to what he had been doing; he was checking off a cancellation order.

He frowned at it a moment, then wrote "File" across it, initialed it "F.G." and wearily tossed it in a letter box on the corner of his desk. The organization chart of Precision Manufacturing looked up at him through the glass top. His eye caught the caption: "Model L. Project Manager, Roger Simpson." A line dropped from it, split into two boxes. He followed the one reading "Tooling—Flynn, Gensheimer." He studied the two names.

Eileen stood between them in the aisle. "I've got something that'll interest you two."

The young man looked up, smirked lazily. "Any time, honey, you know me."

"Fresh!" She pretended offense.

Fritz glanced at her. She grinned at him glibly, flirting casually, from habit. She had a "cute figure"—she knew it. She flaunted

it, an invitation and a dare. The crucifix at her throat guarded
the keyhole neckline. He smiled back vaguely.

The young man asked, "What's news from the firing squad?"
He jerked his thumb toward Atwood's office.

"It won't be good." She dropped a sheet on each desk. "Here's
a preview." The young man leaned forward.

Fritz frowned. "Model L. Production Schedule, Third Quarter." Quickly he picked over the figures. "Oct. 6,000. Nov. 2,400.
Dec. 800." He paled.

Eileen was starting away. The young man swirled in his chair.

"Hold the phone, gorgeous."

"Yes?" She stepped back.

"There's a misprint."

"Don't you believe it."

"Eight *hundred?*"

"That's what the man said."

He stared moodily at the sheet. He said slowly, "That's a hell
of a way to tell a guy."

"Yeah, isn't it wonderful how they do things in this place?"

"I suppose," said Fritz quietly, "there will be engraved
announcements in some pay envelopes today?"

She smiled kindly. "Could be, Fritzie."

He thought: she knows. One of us is going. Both? Something
swooned inside him.

Flynn muttered to himself.

She looked at him warmly. "Don't worry about it, Chuck.
It'll work out. You know — the Will of God, and stuff . . . " She
hesitated, left. Her heels clacked away: tap, tap, tap.

"The Will of God . . . " repeated the young man abstractedly.
Jauntiness drained out of him as the figures on the sheet stared
back. Restlessly he stood up, crossed the aisle.

"Fritzie, m'boy," he announced, "it is later than we think." He
drummed his knuckles on the desk.

The older man smiled. "Perhaps on this new Model R . . . "

Flynn snorted. "Yeah, like the L-2. And that plastic deal. It'll be cancelled before it's off the drawing board. Don't kid yourself, Fritz. We're out of a job." He looked with troubled eyes toward Atwood's office. "The worst of it is," he went on, half to himself, "all the shops are layin' off . . . "

"So Mr. Carver tells me," answered Fritz.

"You saw him?"

"Last night. He is still looking."

"You take it pretty calm."

"When one has seen war . . . concentration camps . . . " He made a vague gesture. But the other was not paying attention. He was still looking toward the conference room.

They were silent. After a moment the older man said carefully, "It is possible, you know."

"What's possible?" asked Flynn absently.

"That God has plans . . . "

"Plans?"

"A better job. A worse one. None at all."

The young man stirred. "What? What? He had lost his thread. "I'm sorry, Fritz."

"Eileen is right," Fritz began again patiently, "you shouldn't worry."

"What d'ya expect me to do? Cartwheels?"

Fritz appraised the young man. He said without humor, "Maybe you should pray."

Flynn snickered, stopped. He thought: the man is serious. It maddened him. He stepped back from the desk.

"Look Fritz—with me a job's a job, see? That's all. I don't know anything about . . . " He broke off, tried to smile away his irritation. "It's no use, Fritz," he went on in a different tone. "I can't sit out that bull session any longer. I'll go nuts. I'm going out in the shop. If the paymaster comes while I'm gone, put me on the autocall, willya?" He strode up the aisle rapidly.

The older man watched him go. He headed for the door to the

plating room. A girl crossed his path; she must have dropped a remark — he was stopping. The exchange did not last long. He was backing away, laughing — they were both laughing now — he was moving toward the door again, his head and shoulders bobbing along behind a row of file cabinets.

The older man put his elbows on the desk and supped his chin in his hands. The words came back to him: "It's no use, Fritzie . . . A job's a job, see?" He frowned to himself. Why was he always so futile? Why didn't Flynn listen?

The difficulty of the language? He wondered if he had said something wrong. Do they have such words in English? He had hardly ever heard such things discussed among Americans, except cynically. It struck him again: even the young people go to church here, but they do not believe in God.

And yet . . . to the young there is no death. Each love affair, each job, is an ultimate. One would think they could see the hand of God in everything.

Thinking of his companion, he looked over at his desk, imagined him in his seat. The dismembered pipe lay where the young man had left it. He could see him cleaning it — scowling, squirming in his chair, crossing and uncrossing his legs, rummaging absurdly through drawers, flailing his nerves into ribbons over the simple task, as he was now doing over the fear of being sacked.

His eye caught the Vargas calendar next to the pipe; he ceased his gentle game of caricature. Flynn had shown it to him in glee. The couplet in gilt letters on the frame and shocked him:
"Backward, turn backward, O Time, in thy flight —
Make me a boy again, just for tonight!"
He had translated it with such difficulty . . . He was fourteen, they were living in Meiningen, before they moved to Erfurt; and as the thoughts became German, the classroom had receded from him, and he had conjured up all the magic that America might be; the immense space, the drowsing cows, the solitary boys fishing up lazy, clear rivers, the freedom . . .

"Pretty sharp, eh?" He had handed it back to Flynn without comment, his heart full of pain that the nostalgic little poem should have been thus twisted to the snicker of a roue's regret. Flynn had caught the look, he had pouted, his fun had been spoiled.

Now he could feel only compassion for Flynn. His failure to reach him was not due to lack of words. It was merely too late.

He thought of the plaster statuette one of the office girls had brought in for a laugh. It was of a child of about fourteen. She stood with downcast eyes, her arms locked behind her, one sandal stepping on the other, a swollen figure of shame. On the base of the statue, "Kilroy was here."

Everything, everywhere, a symbol. Impurity settled on them like sand, they breathed it. He felt the tyranny of evil. It seemed improbable that Flynn would ever see the Will of God in as many places as he saw sex or money or good living. "A job's a job, see?"

The paymaster had come in. He worked his way slowly among the desks, dropping envelopes that were quickly torn open . . . Atwood came out of the conference room. His captains fanned out behind him, returning to their companies . . . the billing machines set up a barrage.

As the paymaster advanced toward him, fear quickened his breath. He found it hard to consider this fat, hot, preoccupied little man as the arm of the Lord. He pondered the sincerity of his own words, "Maybe you should pray." He could think of no prayers. He could think only of his wife, his bank balance, the bleak walls of employment offices. His hands were moist. He knotted them in an attitude of prayer. He closed his eyes, bit his thumb . . .

The fat man thought he was asleep.

"Hey, Fritz!"

The German looked up, embarrassed.

"What is the good word?" he asked sheepishly.

"Save yer money," answered the fat man with a grin, dropping an envelope on his desk. The German looked startled. The fat man moved on.

* * *

"Mr. Charles Flynn. Mr. Charles Flynn."

The loudspeaker carried it all over the shop.

" — and not only that, the chrome peeled all off in six months. No sir, I don't want no Chevvie." George, the foreman of Sub-Assembly, stood shaking his head, not wanting no Chevvie.

"Oh God, there's Fritzie!" The young man ran for a phone.

"Flynn?" It was Simpson.

"Yes, sir."

"Where are ya?"

"Trouble-shooting, out in assembly."

"You are like hell. Come in here, I wanna see ya." The receiver went dead.

He stood by the timekeeper's phone, frowning and pulling at his lip. Then he sighed, smirked irritably and doggedly set off for the office.

"Yeah, yeah, I know. I don't care whether they're checked or not, I want all the Model R prints you got . . . I know, but I can't start cuttin' stock and layin' out tools till you boys . . . "

Simpson sat like an animated Buddha, barking into his phone, his jowls slapping on his neck. His pig eyes fixed on Flynn, motioned him to a chair. He continued his abuse into the mouthpiece.

The young man sat down, tugged at his tie, slumped into a relaxed attitude, thought better of it and leaned forward respectfully. Simpson slammed down the receiver, swiveled in his chair. He spoke rapidly.

"Chuck, Model L is kaput as of Christmas."

"So I've heard," the young man muttered.

"We're making a few changes in the organization."

"Oh?" He wondered if this was . . .

"Model R is breakin' loose. It's gonna be a sweetheart. I'm heading up the project. I'm putting you in charge of tooling.

161

We got four months to get into production, so you gotta get the lead out. It's crazy, but it's what the Old Man wants. Here." He shoved a handful of drawings at him. "These are all I can scare out of Engineering. Rough out your dies, get your orders on tool design, start your load chart for the press room. Pete Benson'll be workin' under you. Better get together with him . . . Hello?" He had picked up the phone. "Gimmie material control." He had already dismissed Flynn. He muttered to himself. "Phosphor bronze! Where the hell — Hello, Bill?"

The young man stumbled out into the office. Eileen came over. She had seen him leave Simpson.

"Hiya, honey!" He beamed broadly. "I'm in!" He flicked her nose with his fistful of drawings. "I'm on the Model R!"

"Good for you," she said, without joy.

He feigned disappointment. "Where's my big kiss?"

It's in the works," she answered, without interest.

"What's the matter?"

"Fritzie . . . " she looked off across the office.

With the twinge, he remembered that Simpson had said nothing about Fritz.

"Cheer him up, will ya?" She walked away.

Slowly, he walked back to his place. What can you say to a guy like Fritz, when . . . ? As he drew nearer to the grey head, bent over the desk, he became conscious of the prints in his hand — Model R. He hesitated, tossed them on his desk, ambled over to his companion.

The envelope lay open. The pink slip was beside it.

"Fritzie, I . . . "

"Congratulations." Fritz looked up at him, smiled faintly.

"You heard?"

"The grapevine," he explained. He seemed amused. "Don't look so unhappy, Chuck. This is a good break for you."

Flynn studied the floor. "Eileen just told me . . . " he began.

Fritz said quickly, "I don't mind, you know. I really don't."

162

"Gee, Fritz, I'm sorry."

"Why? A job is a job, that is all. Isn't that what you say? It is good to be reminded of that, sometimes."

"What do you mean?"

"Oh, one forgets so easy... One is fooled into thinking of all this as... well, safe, secure, beyond pain. And all the time, all over the world... there is starvation, despair, much suffering. It is good, sometimes, to be without, to be cut off, to be joined for a while with those others. Perhaps God is reminding me that there is no security anywhere, really..."

"Is that all you got to think about when you're out of a job?" Flynn was exasperated.

Fritz looked thoughtful. He answered, "It is enough."

The young man fidgeted. "Look, Fritz, I know the chief engineer over at Rite-Way. Why don'tcha — " His phone began ringing. "Oh, hell, excuse me, willya? Look, I'll be right back." He darted across the aisle, grappled for the receiver.

"Chuck?"

"Right." It was Simpson again.

"Dawson tells me we need a new press. Says the Erie isn't big enough for the deep draws. I wantcha to check into it right away. Find out if you can cobble up something that'll fit in the Erie. If not..."

The voice barked instructions. Chuck fished for a pencil, scribbled notes on a pad as he listened. In the corner of his eye, he could see Fritz watching him. The old man looked sad, hurt.

Flynn thought: poor devil!

Simpson talked on.

NEIL MACCARTHY

163

The Anatomy of Despair

A PHILOSOPHICAL LION—WHO PRESUMABLY expressed the views of his kind—once observed that few big-game hunts have been considered from the lion's standpoint. In this matter, we are inclined to an understandable bias which seems, significantly enough, to stem from the first records of paleolithic man. Yet, it is conceivable that that viewpoint could make a very great difference. We find much the same difficulty when the "northern races" look down upon the ways of the "Latins." Consider the shiftless Mexican fruit-vendor, who will close shop immediately his morning supply is sold, even if the first customer should buy the lot. This dismays his Yankee neighbor, to whom the course inevitable and instinctive would be to hustle more fruit, his mind already awake to distant possibilities and visions of Farmers Market. Even without reading the advertisements, he knows that "the future belongs to those who prepare for it."

What appears to be a lack of industry and initiative may be something altogether different. It may be another viewpoint, expressing a tradition that seems to have been accepted at one time rather uncritically. Victor Hugo had the idea when he lectured Napoleon: "No, Sire. The future belongs to God." Though the details of the thing might often have been hazy, it was generally agreed that if a man paid close attention to a few present matters over which he had been given control, certain greater matters over which he had no control, would be managed to his well-being, even despite his own clumsy bungling.

If the future really belongs to those who prepare for it, the present owners are in great danger of dispossession. If the future belongs to those who prepare for it, insurance and sureties, the bureaus of planned economy, social security, old age pensions, and unemployment compensation have made it ours thrice over.

And yet the title is not clear as we could wish. Preparation seems to leave us constantly unprepared. Some future archeologist possessed of an inquiring mind may, in the rubble of ancient New York, discover this morning's newspaper, thereby solving a puzzling point of history, for it is there we find the strange assurance that America has enough atom bombs to destroy the world. Signs admit of the possibility that the post-war world's salvation is not the altogether certain thing we had anticipated. The results of the planning are not always in the plans.

If, from all this, with that logic-chopping for which we Christians are notorious, we conclude that perhaps the future doesn't belong to us after all, the alternate tradition might be worth our casual examination. It springs from certain much-praised words in which some have thought to find something more than a fine piece of poetry.

> Do not be anxious for your life, what you shall eat; nor yet for your body, what you shall put on. Is not the life a greater thing than the food, and the body than the clothing? Look at the birds of the air, they do not sow, or reap, or gather into barns; yet your heavenly Father feeds them. Are not you of much more value than they? But which of you by being anxious about it can add to his stature a single cubit? And as for clothing, why are you anxious? See how the lilies of the field grow; they neither toil nor spin, yet I say to you that not even Solomon in all his glory was arrayed like one of these. But if God so clothes the grass of the field, which today is alive and tomorrow is thrown into the oven, how much more you, O you of little faith! Therefore do not be anxious, saying, "What shall we eat?", or, "What shall we drink?", or, "What shall we to put on?" (for after all these things the Gentiles seek); for your Father

knows that you need all these things. But seek first
the kingdom of God and his justice, and all these
things shall be given you besides. Therefore do not
be anxious about tomorrow; for tomorrow will have
anxieties of it own. Sufficient for the day is its own
trouble. (Matt. 6:25–34)

As this remains an untried ideal, the practicality of its literal
application has not been precisely determined. Quite apart from
this consideration, however, we may be certain that such an
application, if there were any danger of it, would be, broadly
speaking, a moral impossibility. The Christian can hardly avoid
the complicated business of living in the world today as we have
made it. We may be excused of mere facetiousness in assert-
ing that modern man is pretty thoroughly fettered in stocks
and bonds.

Christian tradition, however, has never maintained that we
ought not prepare for the future, though it has been known to
be touchy on the question of ownership. We have been given
the virtue of prudence for the regulation of the secondary causes
through which God customarily dispenses His providence in
men's lives. Holy Scripture consequently admonishes the slug-
gard to garner wisdom from the ant, who in summer lays up
food that he may have whereof to eat in the winter. Christ and
the Apostles carried with them a supply of money for whatever
needs might arise, and over this they appointed one as treasurer
(possibly as a salutary lesson to bankers).

Back in the days when such matters were taken seriously, men
set their minds to determine the extent to which they ought
to be concerned over the goods of the earth. St. Thomas is the
"common doctor" who may be considered the voice of Christian tradition, and he thought that a distinction should be
made. "No good work is virtuous," he wrote, "lest clothed in
the proper circumstances, among which is the proper time, for

as it is written (in Ecclesiastes), 'There is a time and an opportunity for every work' — now this is applied not only to exterior works, but also to our internal solicitude." A man sows seed in anticipation of the harvest, he takes every precaution to ensure a bountiful return, careful of everything in turn, for each occupation in season is a present concern. But the harvest itself will become an object of his care in harvest time, not before. All this is to regulate temporal goods in the providence of God. Not only in making worldly matters an end in themselves do we misuse them (a possibility not unheard of today), but also if we uselessly seek them beyond all necessity, and if we make them the object of a constant solicitude. "Temporal goods were made subject to man that he might use them for his necessities, not that he should find an end in them, or that he should vainly worry about them." Screwtape explained to Wormwood how a certain dear old lady, who ate very little food, was by her picayune preoccupation with what she did eat a great glutton. When a man works to provide his family with necessities and a measure of temporal security, he labors well. But just as a system that forces his whole attention to subsistence will be a wrong system, so, a society that has put its trust in the multiplication and double-checking of "secondary causes," denying outright or at least forgetting the owner of the future to which they are supposedly directed, is a society that has gone wrong. It is the confused wake of an initial and general sin of despair. If a man who professes belief in a provident God labors with the view of making himself self-sufficient just in case — as though Peter had donned water-wings before striding forth upon the Sea of Galilee — it is the sin against hope.

The early Reformers stood aghast before the wild freedom of the human will and its consequent implications of individual responsibility toward a hypothetically uncertain destiny. They pronounced dead and quietly laid to rest the courage and adventure that had made for Western civilization, and settled back into the oldest and most terrible of slaveries that had opposed the rise of Christianity. Because certainty was not vouchsafed by the Christian God Who demanded hope in His predestination, they sought it in a fate that enslaved their will. Despair has proved to be the most fecund of the superstitions. The promised race arose that was a cry: "Give us bread. Take our freedom!" Rather than trust in a Father Who provides for His children who are seeking the kingdom of heaven, we have lusted for the security of fixed and inexorable economic laws, for which we have sacrificed the personal liberties which were the heritage of Christianity. With the promise of economic security, we have been lured to the regimen of the anthill, asking only a comfortable serfdom.

Despair is a lady that deceives. If a man thinks by tugging at his own bootstraps to set himself beyond the transience of this life and be at rest, he has been played for a fool. Instead of attaining peace, he has undertaken a ceaseless activity, dissipated because without direction, doomed to frustration through an attempt to create the uncreatable. God retains a firm grip on the future, despite all the sleep we may lose over it. When it arises, Charles Péguy has said, that God does not like men who do not like sleep. It is an activity that breeds activity forever, a despair that breeds despair. It is a superstition that enjoys its last grim triumph when at last the quaint Christian notion that material things were created for man is reversed, and man is bidden to order himself to their inexorable laws. So, Margaret Sanger sternly advises the stoppage of all human reproduction for a decade—not only as a punishment for the criminal nations who after all brought the war and all that sort of thing on themselves, but also as a discipline for the victors who have made the world once again free.

In our society, an aging parent often can have recourse only to a meager state pension; social security affords a substitute for charity and justice. The individual Christian may not be able to swim free of this complicated maelstrom, but he knows that God, and not economics, is the unchanging. We may have to humor the process, but we must not take it seriously. We do not take spoiled children seriously when they reach for the moon, and the preposterous jargon and pomposity of finance is, when all is said and done, very much like the prattle of slightly impossible children.

What has the Christian in common with a world that refuses to believe and to hope, but must make its own certainties? We cannot have infallible certainty of even the state of grace. Death itself, aside from a kindly revelation, is scientifically only a probability. In that crazy paradox so ill-suited to the serious soberness needed by the man who is to get ahead, it is only in the uncertainty of Christian living that we may find certainty. Only in the unknown mind of God is peace and security. Humility continues to exalt a man; poverty goes quietly about delivering into his hands the lasting wealth. The divine sense of humor is a beautiful thing. But it is never funny.

> Why should we falter? Ours shall be the mirth
> And yours the amaze, when you have thinned away
> Your starving serfs to fit their starving pay —
> And seen the meek inheriting the earth!

BRUCE VAWTER, C.M.

Builders In Vain

"Unless the Lord build the house..."

ACCORDING TO ANY GENERAL MOTORS'
vice-president, the Assembly Line is the greatest thing since Prometheus pulled a fast one on the inhabitants of Olympus. If I were one of the gaskets or spark plugs or bearings turned out so efficiently via A.L., I might agree with the honorable vice-president. I am, however, actually conscious of the fact that I am made in the image and likeness of God. My awareness of this noble heritage informs me with resentment for the Assembly Line which has overflowed its industrial banks to encroach upon the spiritual sphere. The moral implications of this phenomenon are epitomized in that grandiloquent catch-phrase, "human engineering," with all its connotations of life according to blueprint and slide rule and the sharpened pencil. As an "inmate" of government housing for several years, I have been "engineered" to the point of eruption—and this protest constitutes a safety valve.

I have discovered that behind the Utopian façade of its several material advantages (termed "the fat of the land" by the uninitiated), life in a government housing project — and I have lived in more than one — has preponderant disadvantages which all the functional apartments and electric refrigerators and landscaped playgrounds from Greenbelt to Candlestick Cove cannot offset. The days of the uncooperative budget and the balky stove have gone — but they have taken with them the kind of living in which one's personal integrity is not forever under siege by a thousand abnormally demoralizing influences.

In the Hopeful Thirties, the Rural Resettlement Administration, under Technocrat Rex Tugwell, initiated the first wide-scale program of government subsidy of housing in the United States. The project was conceived, undoubtedly, in a lovely aura of idealism amid much talk about improving the lot of the "under-privileged." The program was postulated on the theory that the answer to human ills can be found by relieving material wants. It forgot that you cannot transplant people as though they were primroses along the traditional path. It forgot or, more probably, did not know that the stone of philanthropy is indigestible fare and that only the good bread of Christian charity contains all the vitamins essential to true happiness.

Even this half-a-loaf ethos of philanthropy was abandoned when the impact of war upon the nation's industry necessitated the acceleration of home building for war-workers. Housing became, primarily, a military and economic means of implementing the effectiveness of the State. The State wanted the welders and riggers and machinists close to the factories and the ship-yards — not because commuting long distances is inconvenient to these workers but because it impairs their efficiency and this shows up in red ink on the profit-and-loss sheets.

The current stagnation in home building, a national scandal, appears to be attributable to the fact that the law makers have retained this militaristic concept and short-sightedly continue to concentrate only on the issues of proximate expediency in the interests of the State. The simple motivation of the desire to provide homes for the homeless to atone for the homelessness of the Infant Jesus who found no room in the inn at Bethlehem, fails to carry sufficient force to spur our solons to solve the housing problem. The present policy, as during the war, is to consider the benefits accruing to tenants as a by-product, not an end per se. The housing problem remains a political and economic issue. Its moral aspects are ignored.

A government housing project is predicated on a philosophy of Procrustean adaption. You fit rigid rules without having anything more than a nominal part in their formulation. The qualifications for residence are mainly economic which means that within limited variations, all above the floor of indigence, all residents are in the same economic bracket. This automatically creates the tendency to become self-sufficient for there is not immediate challenge to the practice of charity that is evoked by the presence of the poor. This condition, in turn, breeds selfishness and its correlative materialism. Keeping up with the Joneses has never been the vice of the very poor — but in a community where there is no poor, the class distinctions, though marked off by a hair, are sharply drawn in vertical rather than horizontal lines. The materialistic concept which life in a housing project engenders crops out in the limitation of families, for housing architects evidently consider the three-bedroom family abnormally prolific. Further abetting the trend toward a materialistic rather than spiritual interpretation of life, the fluctuations of population make what Mrs. Grundy says of small concern. Morality, of course, is not based on what the neighbors think, but with the decline of respect for social sanctions, there is a corresponding disintegration of the respect for moral sanctions as well. You mind your own business. The cry of Cain becomes the watchword. You disclaim any responsibility for the welfare of your neighbor . . . a line of thinking evolving from the fact that both of you are cogs in an economic regime. And cogs do not fraternize. The preservation of personal integrity against these odds becomes a losing battle. Most tragic aspect of this defeat is the unawareness of the loser that his loss *is* tragic. For, although he would chafe at the pressure of Christ's cross, he bears the "cross of gold" blithely.

The pursuit of spirituality was never easy. It is made even tougher in a housing project — for the usual obstacles are artificially aggravated. Pragmatic and expedient action, at first repugnant, gradually becomes acceptable. Under the essentially dictatorial regime, it's "put-up-or-shut-up"! For where is the man so brave as to bother to go down fighting for his principles against a system that always wins? Who is there to cut the Gordian knot of government bureaus whose administrative intricacies have long since descended to the stock-pile of cartoonists and radio comedians? Inside looking out, by the way, the humor is more grim than in the spirit of good, clean fun.

In one of the housing projects in which I lived, there was a system of concessions which made it illegal for a private group of residents to hire its own instructor in craftwork or dancing or sewing. You had to use the instructors provided by the official community education board. This board even protested the formation of a Catholic Youth Club on the grounds that this constituted unfair competition with the official, secular program for youth recreation. You were also forbidden to keep goldfish without a permit. They think of everything! Only the pressure of business like this has kept them from seeing whether I swept under the beds this morning (I didn't!).

Save on paper, where they look fine, there are no practical instruments of appeal from either grave or captious dicta. The sanctions that result make conformity more prudent. You can be asked to move. Murmuring, "They can't do this to me!", you find they've already done it.

Life in a housing project is a conscious Marking Time against an unpredictable morrow — and by "morrow" I mean the Tuesday that follows a specific Monday! As long as the qualifications for residence are dependent upon economic status and/or usefulness, you do not say, "Here are the acres I shall pass on to my sons!"

When you plant morning glory seeds, you cross your fingers, hoping you'll be around when the blue trumpet-like flowers make music out of color and their intimation of God's love. You cling, for moral support, to the one idea that this present living is a protracted camping trip and, in consequence, the household gods get little meet adoration. To relax and admit this to be home, is to be lost. For Home is somewhere else. The sense of insecurity becomes, paradoxically, the one security against your capitulation to the life of an automaton to which the ideology of the bureaucratic commissars, in effect if not in intention, would have you conform.

The devil's advocate plays fair, they say. And there is one phase of life in government housing which has immense potentialities for the improvement of the social order. This is the area of race relations. As an example, take the Southerner who moves into a government housing project. He brings along with him his lifelong prejudices against his Negro brother in Christ. He finds himself in a community where, for the first time in his life, he has to compete with the Negro on equal terms on the job, at the movies, on buses. He finds, to his surprise, that not all people think as he does, and he has to whitewash his leopard's spots of fancied superiority. His prejudices may be too deep-seated for complete eradication — but he has to submit them to discipline and control. It happens like this.

In one of the California shipyards, a man was killed in a fall into the drydock. The workers on the bus were discussing the tragedy when one Texan drawled, "Why all the fuss? It was only another burrhead!"

Quietly, another man answered the cruel question, "Sure, only another *man.*"

The Texan blushed. Even this is progress along a difficult and slow journey.

I've been living in a community where I've experienced a fore-taste of life in the totalitarian pattern. I, at least, have the freedom to leave it. What then must life be like where there are bars that prevent escape, and where the administration is not in the spirit of misguided benevolence but in that of calculated exploitation?

Congressman John Taber recently made some startling disclosures on the extent of Communist infiltration into government housing agencies. I know that if I were a Communist, I'd say, "What a sweet set-up!" and roll up my sleeves.

I've been R32A for four years. I've taken walks down blocks and blocks of houses exactly like my own. My husband goes to work when everyone else does, at wages everyone else gets. Our jobs, our interests, our recreation, converge with those of every other family around us. Many of us have already come to accept plenty of hot water and dependable garbage collection as the ultimate in the Good Life. But underneath it all, we are a wandering people who have not yet crossed over into the Promised Land. In the ideological desert in which we are encamped, we eat an ersatz manna.

I miss the kind of a community where there's a friendly grocer who gives candy to the children just before dinner. I miss Mrs. Murphy down the street who has an uncanny intuition about sending up a pie when old friends drop in unexpectedly, and adding water to the soup won't fill the breach in the menu. There are no old friends in housing projects.

Life in a government housing project is sterile and devoid of the integrity and significance which only a Christian philosophy can provide. It will remain thus, pending the substitution of charity which now subserves economics and expediency.

Life like this is reminiscent of the one Aldous "Alpha Plus" Huxley envisioned in his blueprint for a "Brave New World." When society gets around to applying his assembly-line technique for the procreation of the race, the resulting human being will be just the type to identify happiness and the collective mediocrity of life by government directives.

CATHERINE CHRISTOPHER

1.

... AND JESUS SAID "COME"

3.

BUT WHEN HE SAW THE STRONG
WIND, HE WAS AFRAID, AND AS HE
BEGAN TO SINK HE CRIED OUT,
SAYING, "LORD SAVE ME!"

FOUR ACTS

2.

THEN PETER GOT OUT OF THE
BOAT AND WALKED ON THE WATER

4.

...AND JESUS AT ONCE STRETCHED
FORTH HIS HAND AND TOOK HOLD OF HIM.

Apostates' Harvest

ANYONE WHO SPENDS MUCH TIME TRAVEL-
ing about London, or any other large industrial town, with his
eyes open, will be struck by the fact that most people live either
in slums or in the next things to them.

By slums I do not necessarily mean premises which would be
condemned by the sanitary authorities, but depressing regions
in which one must live in a makeshift manner, cramped and
sordid. Generally, one has no room for more than the barely
necessary operations of living, and there is neither time nor space
for the graces. The term may be applied to many blocks of new
flats and to miles of streets of eighteenth and nineteenth-century
houses, built for people of substance and now let off in rooms
and tenements. In the latter you have little privacy and in the
former no room.

Our observer will also notice that nine people out of ten are
ugly. All, that is, except children and some fresh, pretty girls
who are unspoilable. These people are ugly in themselves, and
their clothes make them look even worse. If anything, the more
expensive clothes are worse than the makeshift ones worn by the
real slum dwellers, as those have a certain gaudy charm which
has not yet been refined out of them. Your really respectable city
dweller is not ugly with the pungent, racy ugliness which inspired
Hogarth and Cruikshank, Dickens and the artists who carved
gargoyles on medieval cathedrals. They are just drab, shoddy
and characterless. They live in drab streets, travel daily, packed
like sardines in a tube, and earn their living in monotonous and
unfruitful work. In the evening they return home and dope their
sorrows with novels, films, dance music, spirits and spooning
in corners. True, a few will stand for hours to hear a symphony
concert, or see the ballet, or take a day in the country. Some go
cycling and hiking at week ends — in large parties. A few go by

themselves or in twos and threes. True, every now and then we buy up a tract of lovely country and preserve it for the nation, or a lovely house and turn it into a museum, if we can find the money, but beauty, even when it has lip service and does not interfere with efficiency, is an extra and a luxury. To most people life is ugly and lived in ugly surroundings. That is Real Life. And I am not here even thinking of the raw-ended houses, the hollow shells too far damaged to repair, the streets that have not been painted since 1939, the open spaces in the city, choked with weeds.

The ugliness is not a new phenomenon. It has been with us now for years. Even the insides of Catholic churches are ugly enough to make a convert of even average taste gasp. If a priest, greatly daring, procures pictures or statues by a responsible and competent artist, the cry is raised that these are not devotional. I have often wondered in what this quality consists. In practice, it appears to involve poor craftsmanship, similarity to every other statue one has ever seen, and complete absence of verisimilitude or thought. To be devotional it seems that a work must be mass-produced, shoddy, and guaranteed not to provoke ideas of any kind. It is a horrid thought but I believe people really like their ugliness. Before the war at least you could buy pretty things in gay colors as cheaply as drab ones, and yet many people preferred to be drab.

I have often wondered if this was always so. I think probably not. Ugliness there has always been, but I fancy it was incidental, not ubiquitous. The sixteenth-century religious wars were incredibly ugly, but more local than those of the nineteenth century. I have been told that in Hogarth's London there were slums worse than any we have now for sheer filth, but a city dweller could take a piece of bread and cheese in his pocket and go for a walk among green fields and hawthorn hedges, hear the cuckoo, pick primroses and sleep under the stars. Ugliness was an incident in his life. It did not hem him in on every side. Even now it has not trapped everyone. I remember my suburban childhood; picnics on the common, evenings by the fire, children's parties, and Sundays in the garden, and they are good to remember. But if a young couple expects a little house and garden all to themselves now, they are met with a stare of shocked surprise that they should dare to hope for what other people have not. Apparently, if "other people" haven't a thing you must not want it. If no one has it you lose the right to it. One day we shall have a whole generation to whom Communism looks like a rosy dream, as it has long looked to the industrial poor.

How did we come to this? Most people would say the Industrial Revolution, but that is too easy. How did we bring such a horror on ourselves and how can we overcome it? I do not think the invention of machinery alone would have produced this enormous evil nor that a return to simple living alone would cure it. You cannot unscramble an egg, and you cannot uninvent a machine. If we banned them forthwith, it is doubtful whether we should be much better off. In every walk of life, there is a divorce between truth and beauty. Most people speak as though they could not be reconciled. If you hear that an author tells the whole truth about a subject, you know at once that it will be ugly truth. A realistic writer is always a dealer in mud, corpses and sin. Beauty is a luxury and an extra — tolerated as long as it keeps quiet, unworthy of the attention of serious persons. They are too busy with their politics.

This was the attitude of the men who built and developed the industrial civilization. Art and all that was very well for women and effeminates. Let them have their pretty toys. Men must occupy themselves with such serious matters as cheating in business, lying about politics and suppressing revolt. They were largely extreme Protestants, the children of Puritans who defaced the medieval churches, drove all the joy and beauty out of religion and frightened more people away from Christianity than any other body of people that ever lived. The Borgias were nothing to them. Under them we grew to mistrust the beauty of Catholic ceremony (so pagan), the graciousness of Catholic devotion (how decadent), and the delicacy of Catholic morals (how disingenuous). We learned to mistrust beauty and grace and tenderness and to believe it to be first a seduction, then a luxury. Even Catholics are not entirely free from it. In most people's mind there is a connection between piety and gloom, piety and ugliness, piety and the wet blanket. A cruder and saner age than ours (sometimes known as the Dark Ages) looked on sadness and despondency as a fault — even a sin. The Desert Fathers had a great deal of practical advice on combatting accidia — or, in modern language, the blues.

Now the spirit of gloom has disguised itself as love of the truth, that of phlegm as balance, mental laziness as humility and you may reform the social order till you are black in the face, the next one bids fair to be as bad as this in time. For the shadow of the Puritans has settled down on us like a bad smell, and though we have outgrown their clothes the shadow and the smell remain behind. While it is with us, anyone who wants to open the window and let in a new idea is a troublemaker; if he has ideals based on principles, he is difficult, and a woman with brains who is so rash as to use them (oh, abomination of desolation) does not "fit in." Catholics are tolerated now — so long as they are indistinguishable from pagans, but most people would be less shocked at your living with a man than at your explaining your Faith from a soap box at the street corner. One often wonders whether the saints would have "fitted in."

Gradually all vitality, all character is being ironed out of the human race. He (or still more she) who is not cut to the approved pattern or prepared to be molded to it is not wanted, does not get on, slips out and is forgotten. He is queer, difficult, does not fit in. To a certain extent this must always have been so, but there seems once to have been more relish for oddities and more tolerance, and certainly more respect, for character as distinct from mere usefulness. Did that amiable quality, respect for man as such and enjoyment of him as he is and not with reference to his use to one's self, go out with religious dogma? Or has it perhaps not quite gone out? They are still to be found among the poor and the outsiders, these eccentrics who do not fit in. They are of no practical use, and they are swept into a corner where they cannot get in the way.

It is becoming increasingly evident that without dogmatic religion, and the Catholic is the only dogmatic religion that is not covered with mildew by now, beauty and truth do not walk together. To the Puritan and his offspring, beauty is vain and truth unpalatable. Most people have forgotten that there should ever be a connection between the two and raise the cry of "wishful thinking" should truth by chance be sweet. Created beauty should have led us to the truth, and truth to Eternal Beauty, but they feel that medicine, to be of any use, must be nasty and they become heathens instead — and talk as if there were something very noble about this bleak lack of faith.

One wonders how any cure is to be administered. Perhaps is will be started by those who break away from the machine and start afresh, perhaps by those who, unable to leave the machine, stay in it. An idea that has always fascinated me is that of a soul who achieves holiness in the machine and as part of it, in no way cut off from the other cogs, or unlike them as far as anyone can see; of that spirit spreading like wildfire through the whole inhuman structure of a society that means to turn men into dummies; of holiness braking out and laughing at the monster which tries to drain the life out of our souls. I can imagine that its first hold might be among the misfits and the unsuccessful, among those who are branded as unsuitable material for promotion — obscure folks only known to a few friends, but spreading everywhere, till there was not a man or woman who had not known at least one of them. I can imagine the Young Christian Workers operating in this way, but the plan might be extended to include Old Christian Pensioners as well — queer old maids relegated to back bedrooms and carefully forgotten by their friends, and seedy unsuccessful men who have lost their chance now of having families of their own or who have lost them. I think they would not be a very respectable gathering and they might be a very odd one, but these odd people might have the holy lightheartedness of the saints, a lightheartedness spreading like sparks from a conflagration, lighting here and there and breaking out into new fires everywhere till the planned and standardized world, the planners' paradise and the prison of men and women, would seem to burst into flame and be shaken down by the laughter of regenerated men. And then we shall be able to begin.

C.M. LARKINS
London, England

The Frying Pan
and the Fire

Either for God or against God — that is once more
the point at issue, and upon it hangs the fate of
the world. For in every department of life, in
politics and economics, *in the sciences and the*
arts, in the state and domestic life, in the East
and in the West, everywhere the same issue arises.
(Encyclical, *Caritate Christi Compulsi,* 1932)

CONFUSION AND DISORDER IN CONTEMPO-
rary political and economic thought have assumed Promethean
proportions; it would seem that we are living in another, modern tower of Babel. The tongues are many: the Marxism of the
radicals, the socialism of the liberals, big business echoing Adam
Smith, these and many others, and many shades of each. But in
this chorus one dialect dominates, collectivism, whether it be
called centralization, socialism or planned economy. We have
PM, the *New Republic* and the *Nation* to assure us that Europe
is headed for socialism, and it can hardly be doubted that for
some time we have been witnessing a steady drift away from the
conception of society and state taught us by classical liberalism.
The reaction from individualism to a state-dominated policy
and economy was strong, and it has been hastened immeasurably
by the war; under war-time conditions capitalism has almost
ceased to function (planning by the state has displaced it) and
now, at the close of the European war, we see England nearly
socialized, in France we hear of plans for the nationalization
of industry, while Russia, the most gigantic collectivist state
in history, dominates the continent, its influence spreading far
beyond its actual conquests. Then too, at the beginning of the
war we saw the omnipotent statism of Germany and Italy.

But for all that the outcome is far from clear. The liberals are already crying that the peace is being lost to the reactionaries, and certainly we are witnessing a desperate counterattack by the proponents of classical politics and economics, the advocates of free trade and a competitive economy. Capitalism too is not without its able defenders; Frederick Hayek's *The Road to Serfdom*, which has raised such a storm of controversy, both in England where it was first published, and in this country, is a frontal attack on socialistic collectivism. His book may profitably be taken as a focusing point for this discussion, both because it is so well known and because it defends so ably an important position in contemporary political and economic thought. It has frequently been said in recent times that the most important problem to be faced today is the problem of a planned economy.

IT SEEMS CLEAR THAT CAPITALISM WILL NEVER REGAIN ITS FORMER PLACE; WHAT THEN IS TO TAKE ITS PLACE? Liberal thought is unanimous in declaring that socialism provides the only solution. Now the Popes have unequivocally maintained that socialism is totally unacceptable to Catholic thought. Nor did they mean, as some have asserted, that socialism is to be rejected only insofar as it is connected with atheism and the denial of Christian morality, but acceptable in the measure that it is purely economic doctrine. Christian thinkers, then, have a strong obligation to assist in the clarification of thought on this vital problem. In this paper we use Mr. Hayek's book purely as a matter of convenience, as a means of localizing the arguments for and against a planned economy. Our concern is to establish the metaphysical and theological assumptions underlying both the capitalist and socialist positions. In so doing, we shall make clear the metaphysical doctrine underlying the Catholic position. Too often discussions of this economic problem proceed by totally ignoring the doctrinal assumptions which govern conclusions in the fields of economics and politics; this is to be expected in an age which is ignorant of the role of metaphysical and theological wisdom in governing and ordering the lower sciences. We may expect this in those outside the Church. But that there has been no such investigation by Catholics to date is truly an astonishing fact. It is not surprising, then, that Catholic economists have been led to wonder whether socialism as an economic system may not be acceptable to Catholics. We shall attempt to establish that socialism, precisely as a purely economic solution, and considered in abstraction from its denial of morality, rests upon a fundamentally false metaphysical position and consequently cannot lead to a just state. In so doing we will show that the Papal solution is the only solution which will ensure a just social order as it alone is governed by the true metaphysics.

THE CAPITALIST POSITION

The thesis of *The Road to Serfdom* is familiar. Hayek, an Austrian economist who lived through the Nazi rise to power, is convinced that the democracies are traveling along the same road already traversed by the totalitarian states. In his opinion it is the liberals who are unwittingly leading us to totalitarianism. Simply his argument is this: socialism, that is, any sort of central direction or planning, leads inevitably to the tyranny of dictatorship. For practical purposes, he equates socialism with collectivism.

The key to Hayek's thought is his absolute dichotomy between a competitive economy and a centralized dictatorship; in his view there is not middle ground between these two positions, any middle position being merely the first step toward the complete central planning of a dictatorship. Any effort to replace the autonomous controls of a free society by direction from above is bound to lead to tyranny. Thus, he sees but two alternatives: a free competitive economy, or central direction, i.e. planning. (He uses "planning" to mean "planning against competition," or "planning to replace competition" in contradistinction to a type of planning of which he approves, planning to provide the widest scope and most effective field for competition.)

Thus, Hayek's position may be summarized in three points: first, there is his absolute conviction that authority inevitably becomes tyranny; second, and following from the first, an absolute dichotomy between a competitive economy and a central dictatorship; and third, his belief that economic dictatorship brings with it political dictatorship.

This position is a generalization drawn from historical instances, for the most part founded on analysis of modern states. The fact as such is inescapable: modern authoritarian states have for the most part become tyrannies. Political freedom does usually go when the state assumes direct control of the economic system. But does such a generalization have an absolute value? IS THERE A NECESSARY CONNECTION BETWEEN AUTHORITY AND TYRANNY, OR IS THE CONNECTION ONLY CHARACTERISTIC OF MODERN SOCIETY? And if the connection has a certain necessity, either universal or in modern times, what is the reason for it? Most important, we must decide whether Mr. Hayek is right in his contention that authority, in the sense that he objects to it, inevitably becomes tyranny.

WHAT IS AUTHORITY?

To resolve these questions and to judge adequately of this thesis, a somewhat extended analysis of the nature of authority is necessary. In this way Catholic teaching concerning the state will be made manifest in relation to modern theories and the way prepared to judge of them in the light of the Catholic Faith.

In the first place it should be clear that authority can exist only when a group of men are united for a common purpose. Men by their very nature live together in society, since they are not sufficient to themselves, but require the aid of others, not only for physical survival, but above all, for a truly human life. Society, therefore, is formed for the common good, inasmuch as this cooperation is not undertaken for the good of any one of the persons as an ultimate end. Now just as there is a principle in the individual, namely reason, which directs his acts so that he will attain his end in due course, so there must be a directive principle of society, if it is to attain its end; we call this principle the *common good*. The efficient principle is the ruler or government whose work it is to order all things as they are common, that the common good may be attained. It is fitting that there be one person or group of persons to concern itself with the common good, both because men are apt to place their private good above the common good, and because, if strife is to be avoided, it is necessary to have an authority to decide the means which are to be employed to attain the common good. This authority may be one man, a group of men, or the will of the majority of the citizens.

Authority, therefore, follows from the very nature of the common good, and, in like manner, the kind of authority exercised will correspond to the particular nature of the particular common good, for, as we have said, there will be a common good whenever men cooperate for a particular end or purpose. Thus, the authority of the ruler of the family, the father, differs from the authority of the ruler of the state, which in turn differs from the authority of God Who is the Ruler of the universe. By this principle a common good is higher as it is more universal, and the higher the common good the more completely the members of the society depend on it as deriving their good from it. Now, since God is the ultimate of common goods, we may, by analysis of that relation by which the universe depends on Him, arrive at the truth concerning the lesser common goods, such as the common good of the state, provided we are careful to predicate the properties of God as He is seen in this relation only according to proportion in regard the rules of analogy.

SINCE MEN DEPEND ABSOLUTELY AND WITHOUT QUALIFICATION UPON GOD ALONE, IT WOULD FOLLOW THAT ABSOLUTE

AUTHORITY BELONGS ONLY TO GOD. In the state, the personal good does not depend absolutely on the common good, but only in this or that respect; consequently, while authority would thus be attributed to the state, it would be a limited authority and not the absolute authority which is proper to God. It would follow that the authority of the head of the family would be even more limited, for the family is the least universal among common goods, and, furthermore, it depends not only on God, on the state as well; on God in every respect, on the state only in some. Further, since the authority which a given order possesses comes to it in virtue of its rank in the hierarchy of common goods, it follows that, if this hierarchy is perverted or destroyed, the corresponding roles of authority will also be perverted. Thus, when a state, denying that God is the ultimate common good, makes itself ultimate, it becomes man's last end, and it will arrogate to itself the authority that belongs to God alone. Now it is the property of God, as the absolute ruler of all creation, and therefore as its Creator, infallibly to bring about His Will without violating the freedom of His creatures. Thus, when the state attributes to itself the authority proper to God, i.e. an absolute authority, since it in no way possesses the suavity of Divine Omnipotence, it must, if it is to attain its end, violate that freedom which it can no more move freely than it can create a free will in the first place. In short, it will inevitably become tyranny. Such a state, imitating the omniscience and omnipotence of God, would govern its citizens as God governs His creatures; this is the origin of totalitarian violence.

But the analysis must be carried further. The necessary limitations of any created authority are further manifested by the consideration of another property of Divine Rule. We have already seen two such properties: first, that God infallibly attains His will in the creature; second, He attains it without violating such free wills as He has created. From these two a third follows, that God foreknows and causes the minutest happenings of the universe, attaining His Will sometimes through necessary secondary causes, sometimes through free secondary causes. Thus, God governs the universe in every respect, not a leaf falling without His permission, or, as a socialist might put it, He organizes the world absolutely.

It follows that since the state is a society of persons, each being therefore a free agent, the authority exercising the rule for the common good must respect the nature of those agents, even as God Himself respects it. But further, since human authority, unlike the Divine, cannot, as we have seen, determine things absolutely without violence, the authorities of the state must be limited, leaving a measure of autonomy over which it can claim no dominion. This autonomy, further, would be not only personal, but would include the autonomy of the family as well as of smaller political units relative to the ultimate political ruling body. This would seem to be the metaphysical doctrine behind democracy (democracy taken in the sense of freedom and autonomy for inferiors), and it is remarkable how great a synthesis of authority and freedom was achieved when this doctrine was held, e.g. the rule in medieval France and Spain attested by the great autonomy in the Spanish provinces.

We may conclude that the test of a state will lie in its attitude to lower bodies and groups within the state. One which visions itself as God will inevitably tend to absorb the functions of lesser groups and thus destroy them. Virtually or actually, it affirms that there is only one cause, the state, which rules its citizens as Calvin's God rules creation. It will attempt to exercise a central planning authority which will destroy any freedom in its inferiors. Germany and Russia furnish convincing illustrations.

SOCIALISM LEADS TO TYRANNY

We may now return to Mr. Hayek's thesis. I think we must agree with his assertion that *socialism, or collectivism, inevitably leads to some sort of totalitarian tyranny.* Socialism's first principle is the centralization of all authority, planning and organizing the economic life of the state in one governing group; as such, it denies all secondary authority. Thus, the centralized body will organize to an ever-increasing degree the entire state economy. This inevitably, and in proportion as its principle is maintained, annihilates freedom. As Hayek points out, Russian Communism and German National Socialism are merely the logical following out of the tenets of socialism. This is evident in the light of the above analysis, inasmuch as socialism arrogates to the state the kind of authority and organization that belongs properly to God. But in the created order, *absolute planning* and *freedom of action for inferiors* are simply incompatible, and, for this reason, we must accept Hayek's conclusion. There is an interesting corollary anent the liberals' claim that socialism is economic freedom. This is not the place to discuss that, but I think its speciousness is easily detected in the light of the preceding analysis.

We must also agree with Hayek in his conviction that economic and political freedom are necessarily connected. Just as a state that maintains as its right the authority and dominion proper to God alone, will inevitably swallow up all economic control, just as inevitably will it extend its absolute control to political matters. And we may add that absolute authority in political matters is just as incompatible with political freedom as absolute economic authority is with economic freedom. This is an *a priori* argument which is formally metaphysical; many authoritative Catholic writers have manifested it on properly political grounds.

AUTHORITY MUST BE MAINTAINED

We cannot, however, agree with Mr. Hayek's conviction that there is a necessary connection between authority and tyranny, nor with his maintenance of an absolute dichotomy between a competitive economy and collectivism. If, as we indeed agree, the socialist state is to be rejected, it does not follow that the only alternative is an individualistic economy in which there is no con-trol of economic life beyond the impersonal discipline of the mar-ket. Strangely, it would seem, it is because he implicitly accepts a totalitarian doctrine that Mr. Hayek is led to reject author-ity. What is common to both positions is a certain unequivocal notion of authority; either it is denied altogether, or authority is absolute. The Nazis embraced absolute state authority because they saw one truth and were blind to the other. Now it appears Mr. Hayek sees the other side, rejecting authority because it seems it must be absolute, as the Nazis rejected freedom because it appeared absolute. But as St. Thomas repeats again and again, whatever is said analogically, is said according to the more and the less, and BOTH "FREEDOM" AND "AUTHORTIY" ARE, AS WE HAVE SEEN, ANALOGICAL TERMS. Both sides err in this that they fail to see the hierarchy of both freedom and authority. They see no essential difference between a created and uncreated authority, and hence do not see that there is a properly limited authority which specifies political rule. And, as a matter of fact, the individualists make the same mistake about freedom that totalitarians make about authority. They want unlimited freedom for the individual just as the total-itarian wants unlimited authority for the state. For both there is no hierarchy either in the universe or in the state; neither side sees that a perfection is limited according to the limitation of the nature receiving that perfection. The contrary positions have a common metaphysics.

PERVERTED AUTHORITY

Yet, admitting that Hayek is wrong in equating authority with tyranny, there is a further difficulty, for he appears to have the facts on his side, at least the facts of modern history. We have all seen enough of the abuse of authority in our time not to be unaware that, at least practically, it seems to lead to tyranny. And so, Hayek has due cause to hear authority, for only a very thin line separates it from the most outrageous violence. St. Thomas was well aware of this, and in *De Regimine Principum* takes care to impose powerful checks upon the rulers' power. But in our day the danger seems to be even greater, as it is attested by the Holy Father's Christmas message of 1944, in which he asks that a greater role in government be given the people. When we ask why authority should be particularly dangerous in our time, we have not far to seek for the answer. Earlier we pointed out that the authority which a given order possesses is predicated of it in virtue of its place in the hierarchy of common goods, and that, if this hierarchy is perverted or destroyed, the roles of the respective authorities will also be perverted. Thus, when God is denied or ignored, the total hierarchy of things is immediately inverted, and the lower orders lose no time in taking God's place. From all this it is clear that a just state cannot exist as long as God is denied; for the state will never say merely that does not exist, but rather it will, and does, say: "God exists, but I am He." It is therefore not only metaphysically necessary, but profoundly realistic, to maintain that a JUST STATE AND SOCIAL ORDER IS IMPOSSIBLE UNTIL MEN RECOGNIZE THE JUST SUBORDINATION OF ALL THINGS, NATURAL AND POLITICAL, TO GOD. Perhaps this is the providential meaning of our modern Feast of Christ the King.

A MIDDLE ROAD

We may now see that, not only is a position between individualism and collectivism possible, but such an intermediary position provides the only possible just state. Such a state would not arrogate to itself the absolute planning of the economic life of the whole; there would be no central direction which would deny all subordinate direction, an abuse to which Hayek rightly objects for reason we have noted. A just state would recognize that it cannot govern the whole of life, inasmuch as it could not do this without destroying freedom, but neither would it allow a state of society composed of autonomous, competing individuals, each solicitous of himself exclusively. Rather, it would adopt a middle course, and, since God rules the universe through free, secondary agents, the state would in its turn heave the organizing and planning of economic life to those subordinate groups properly engaged in this task, that is, to the employers and workers. In short, there would not be one exclusive cause in the state, but a hierarchy of free causes.

But while we are insistent that the state has not the authority of God, yet we must not on the other hand forget that the state does participate in God's authority, and should exercise, therefore, a real power among the citizens. Solicitous as it is of the common good, IT MUST BE THE FINAL JUDGE WHETHER THE PLANNING OF THE SUBSIDIARY GROUPS FOSTERS OR HINDERS THIS END. In the words of Pius XI: " . . . the state . . . should be the supreme arbiter, ruling in kingly fashion far above all party contention, intent only upon justice and the common good." Elsewhere, he describes the function of the state in regard to these groups as " . . . directing, watching, stimulating and restraining." Thus, there would not be but one cause in the state, but the lower groups would be truly autonomous all the while they were being directed by the higher. This is an application to the state of the hierarchy of authority and freedom as it is found in the universe, and I think it can be readily shown that this is the philosophical doctrine underlying the various social encyclicals of the Popes.[1]

---

1   No attempt has been made to prove in this paper the Aristotelian-Thomistic doctrine of authority and freedom; rather the intention has been to let its truth be manifested by its fruits as applied to the fields of politics and economics. For only if one maintains that authority and freedom are compatible (in theological terms, that there is no incompatibility between Divine Omnipotence and human freedom) can one avoid the trap of the moderns. For if one holds that authority and freedom are incompatible, then a choice must necessarily be made between collectivism and individualism, both of which the Holy Father has told us must be avoided.

It should be made clear that the purpose of this article is not to provide concrete proposals on specific economic issues, nor even to formulate the kind of political economy which seems to be most in harmony with the metaphysical points we have indicated. The purpose here is rather to formulate the philosophical principles underlying any just politic-economic order and thus to provide principles upon which contemporary economic proposals, especially in the controversy between free competition and planning, may be judged. It further proposes to demonstrate the metaphysical doctrines underlying the Papal social encyclicals. To that end a brief analysis of the *Quadragesimo Anno* of Pius XI will be given at this point.

PAPAL MESSAGE

The Holy Father's conception of the state is that of a society organized in an ordered hierarchical fashion in which the state is in somewhat the position of an overseer, seeking always the common good, and respecting always the specific perfections of each level in society, not destroying their proper functions but rather providing any necessary help and protection that they may the better perform their functions:

> . . . just as it is wrong to withdraw from the individual and commit to the community at large what private enterprise and industry can accomplish, so, too, it is an injustice, a grave evil and disturbance of right order for a larger and higher organization to arrogate to itself functions which can be performed efficiently by smaller and lower bodies. This is a fundamental principle of social philosophy, unshaken and unchangeable, and it retains full truth today. Of its very nature the true aim of all social activity should be to help individual members of the social body, but never to destroy and absorb them. The state should

leave to these smaller groups the settlement of business of minor importance. It will this carry out with
greater freedom, power and success, the tasks belonging to it, because it alone can effectively accomplish
these, directing, watching, stimulating and restraining, as circumstances suggest or necessity demands.
Let those in power, therefore, be convinced that
the more faithfully this principle be followed, and
a graded hierarchical order exist between the various
subsidiary organizations, the more excellent will be
both the authority and the efficiency of the social
organization as a whole and the happier and more
prosperous the condition of the state.

This remarkable passage is typical of the Holy Father's care
to maintain at once the authority of the state and the freedom
of the lower groups, or, in terms of our analysis, the autonomy
of the free, secondary causes. In an admirable way, it reconciles
the two in a just mean between the extremes of collectivism and
individualism. In regard to the state taking to itself too much
authority, the Holy Father adds:

We feel bound to add that to Our knowledge there
are some who fear that the state is substituting itself
in the place of private initiative, instead of limiting
itself to necessary and sufficient help and assistance.

On the question of free competition, the Pope adds:

. . . just as the ordering of human society cannot be
built upon class warfare, so the proper ordering of
economic affairs cannot be left to free competition
alone. From this source have proceeded in the past
all the errors of the "Individualistic" school. This

school, ignorant or forgetful of the social or moral aspects of economic matters, teaches that the state should refrain in theory and practice from interfering therein, because these possess in free competition and open markets a principle of self-direction better able to control them than any created intellect. Free competition, however, though within certain limits just and productive of good results, cannot be the ruling principle of the economic world . . .

Thus, while free and unrestrained competition cannot be approved, neither can the control of economic life by a central state authority be justified. It is the task of the individual groups concerned, subject, however, to " . . . the state which should be the supreme arbiter, ruling in fashion far above all party contention, intent only upon justice and the common good . . . " As mentioned above, the state's function would be "directing, watching, stimulating and restraining" and:

. . . true and genuine social order demands various members of society, joined together by a common bond. Such a bond of union is provided on the one hand by the common effort of employers and employees of one and the same group joining forces to produce goods or give service; on the other hand, by the common good which all groups should unite to promote, each in its own sphere, with friendly harmony . . . From this it is easy to conclude that in these associations the common interest of the whole group must predominate: and among these common interests the most important in the directing of the activities of the group to the common good.

THE COMMON GOOD

The so-called classical economics denied the whole concept of the common good, except insofar as it conceived it as the sum of individual goods and having its only reality in the individual goods. Contemporary thought, be it Communism, Fascism, Socialism, attributes great significance to the neglected concept. Common knowledge of totalitarian doctrine will attest to the truth of this assertion. As a classical liberal, Mr. Hayek rejects the doctrine of the common good, and in an interesting passage he explains why:

> The common feature of all collectivist systems may be described, in a phrase dear to socialists of all schools, as the deliberate organization of the labors of society for a definite social goal . . . The social goal, or "common purpose," for which society is to be organized is usually described as the "common good," the "general welfare," or the "general interest." It does not need much reflection to see that these terms have no sufficiently definite meaning to determine a particular course of action. The welfare and happiness of millions cannot be measured on a SINGLE SCALE OF LESS AND MORE. (Capitalization mine)

What Mr. Hayek is objecting to in this passage, is fundamentally the same evil that founds his complaint against authority. The authority he objects to is wrong precisely because it absorbs and thereby destroys the lower orders; it becomes a sort of swollen monster, having, so to speak, devoured its inferiors so that it alone remains to contemplate the desolation it has wrought. SUCH A COMMON GOOD IS A MISNOMER. It is in fact a private good inasmuch as all other goods are denied for its sake, rather than fulfilled in it. Hayek describes this appalling caricature of the common good accurately:

> The German idea of the state, as formulated by Fichte, Lassalle, and Rodbertus, is that the state is neither founded nor formed by individuals, nor an aggregate of individuals, nor is its purpose to serve any interest of individuals. It is a Volkgemeinschaft in which the individual has no rights but only duties . . . There is a life higher than the individual life, the life of the people and the life of the state, and it is the purpose of the individual to sacrifice himself for that higher life.

We have here a clear illustration of the way in which modern totalitarians make the common good a private good, the good of a logical abstraction, a nation conceived as something existing apart from the person who constitutes it.

But we cannot infer, from the fact that the common good has no existence apart from the persons constituting the state, that it is formally identical with the good of those persons taken singularly, i.e. as a sum of personal goods. Rather THE COMMON GOOD IS OF A SPIRITUAL ORDER, at once containing the individual goods and greater than they, as St. Thomas says, more divine because it is more universal. In the state, as in the universe, we may distinguish two principles: the individuals and the order uniting them. Of these, the order is the more perfect and related to the individuals as form to matter. But since order implies a principle, there is necessarily one thing to which the individuals are ordered. In society it is the common good of the nation, in the universe it is God, the absolutely universal common good. Now one may, for one reason or another, consider the individuals in themselves, abstracting from the order of which they are a part, or one may consider solely the order of the individuals to their principle, i.e. the common good, be it the state or God. In so doing one abstracts from the proper difference among things, conceiving them only as they differ in degree, not as they are different in kind. Thus, the person, the family, the various professional groups, the trades, etc., are seen only as *less* than the state and as having no being or perfection which is not to be found in the more universal order as though that could subsist in itself. Even more, the state is conceived as a kind of substance in which alone the perfection is to be found, a sort of self-subsisting form. THIS HAPPENS WHEN WE ATTRIBUTE TO REALITY THE ACTUAL SEPARATIONS WHICH THE MIND MAKES WHEN IT CONSIDERS THINGS. In being, the form depends on the matter, and the matter on the form. The common good, to apply the principle to the point under discussion, depends on the individuals in one way, and the individuals depend on the common good in another. The opposition which is established in a state of abstraction leads to a denial of one or the other of the principles.

THE ROOT OF THE ERROR

The individualists see the perfection of the part, that the perfection of the whole, as a whole of order, presupposes the existence of persons composing the order; the common good, then, is seen as nothing (because it is supposed that the perfection of the person in every way can exist apart from the common good, the individual being a principle in one respect). The totalitarians, on the other hand, see the individuals as nothing because they attribute existence per se to the common good. But the common good so conceived is no longer the common good, because it is not common; it is a good opposed to the private good, and therefore itself a private good. Then the individual "has no rights but only duties"; the "higher life" is now predicated of the state per se, subsisting apart from individuals. But as such it is only a myth and serves to mask the selfish private interests of some special group. IT IS INTERESTING TO OBSERVE THAT BOTH PERSONALISTS AND TOTALITARIANS SINGULARIZE THE COMMON GOOD, AND THUS THEY AGREE THAT THERE

IS NO COMMON GOOD. For both, the good of the individual and the good of the state are private goods.

This reduction of the common good to a private good is, as has been shown, common both to individual (and its contemporary counterpart, personalism) and to totalitarianism. Further, in both doctrines, the private good that is substituted for the common good, and becomes a quasi common good, since it is that for whose sake all else exists, is the good of a person. In individualism, it is the human person and in totalitarianism it is the state erected into a sort of person. Now this identification of the common good with the good of a person can only be understood by an analysis of the perfections proper to God as the exemplar common good. In this ultimate common good, we have the one case where the common good is also a person (excepting, of course, Christ). This union of perfections in God should properly be diversified in the lower orders so that the lesser common goods would not be persons but would, however, both be composed of persons and entrusted to a person, or persons, according to the form of government, having the authority to bring about the common good. Totalitarian states, however, having made themselves the final common good, THEN ASSUMED THAT PERFECTION WHICH BELONGS ONLY TO GOD, to be a personal common good. Individualism or personalism, on the contrary, having substituted the individual person for God MAKES THE PERSON INTO THE ULTIMATE END OF ALL SOCIAL AND POLITICAL LIFE, simply subordinating the state to the person. I think that it is only in this light that the classical liberal doctrine of individual self-interest in economics can be explained. (Interestingly enough this doctrine, although progressively abandoned in economic life in favor of planning, is now being increasingly applied to international affairs, so that it is assumed as a matter of course that each country should adopt the policy of individual self-interest in all matters of international policy.) The doctrine holds that by seeking one's own self-interest the welfare of the whole is infallibly attained. Clearly, it did not work; but it is interesting to understand why men were disposed to believe it. The doctrine of the common good, I believe, gives it its plausibility.

GOD AND MAN

Now God acts always for Himself, nothing outside of Himself is ever the cause of any action of His. But since God is the cause of all that is good in the universe, it happens that in acting for His own glory He has willed to create things outside of Himself and thus in acting for Himself, God communicated His good to others. Since He is the universal common good, it follows that in acting for Himself, He benefits those who are dependent upon that common good and whose private good is derived from that common good. Hence, MODERN LIBERAL SOCIETY HAVING SUBSTITUTED THE INDIVIDUAL PERSON FOR GOD ALSO ATTRIBUTES TO THE HUMAN PERSON THIS QUALITY OF GOD'S, VIZ. TO BE THE CAUSE OF ALL THAT IS GOOD IN THE UNIVERSE. It then follows that in seeking his own good each man will communicate that goodness to others, as God does, and thus by seeking his own interest, be it economic or political, he will automatically procure the good of others. The individuals' personal goodness becomes the principle of the good that others obtain. The order of things has become completely reversed. That is but one example of the inversion of the order of the universe. In knowledge, we have the theory that a thing only exists insofar as it is known; in economics there is the labor value theory which holds that all the value of things men make is derived exclusively from the labor put into them; in mathematics we are told that mathematical objects are created by the mind, reality only furnishing the occasion for our knowing them.

But when we ask why both of these positions singularize the common good, and thus deny it, we are led to an important discovery. For a single error underlies both theories. On natural grounds, the underlying error is a false conception of the nature and purpose of the state. The state is conceived as existing only for the material well-being of the people. It is a victory of Marx since it amounts to a concession to his view that the economic consideration is the only valid one both for the state and for the individual. Since the only common good admitted is the economic one, the notion of the common good as a spiritual reality is clearly precluded. But to make the exclusive end of the state, and therefore its common purpose and goal, economic, is ipso facto to destroy the idea of the common good. FOR ONLY A SPIRITUAL GOOD CAN BE SHARED BY MANY WITHOUT THE GOOD OF ONE NECESSARILY DESTROYING OR LESSENING THE GOOD OF ANOTHER. This truth may be seen most clearly in the Exemplar of all societies, the Most Blessed Trinity. There the common good is the immaterial perfection of the very Deity. In the temporal human order, the state, composed of creatures having body and soul, the purely spiritual common good of the Blessed Trinity is imitated imperfectly; for, while it is primarily spiritual, it relates to material welfare, since men do live in a society in part to supply their material needs. When men denied this spiritual nature of the common good then, it was inevitable that henceforth only mutually exclusive and opposed private goods should exist in the state.

IT IS WORTH NOTING that the distinction, held by many contemporary Catholic writers, between the person and the individual, by which man is subordinated to the state only as he is an individual, and not as he is a person, raises the same difficulties encountered by individualistic and totalitarian doctrines. As a consequence of their views, man would be subordinated to the state only as he is a material being and not according to his proper perfection as a man, i.e. his intellectual nature in virtue of which he is said to be a person. Thus, for them too the common good, as a political reality, is not a spiritual good, nor is society formed for a proper spiritual end. Again, the role of the state being reduced to the economic order, the doctrine entails all the evil consequences of individualism and totalitarianism. This is not to say that such persons in fact hold these views, but rather that these are the logical consequences of the distinction between person and individual. To be consistent they would be constrained to hold these consequences.

In sharp contrast to these materialist views, Aristotle makes it plain that insofar as the good of the citizen is aimed at by the state, that good is happiness which he defines as activity in accordance with perfect and complete virtue. In this relation, the fostering of virtue is the first function of the state; for that reason, education plays an important part in politics. But because man cannot be happy without the physical necessities, his nature being what it is, his material needs must be regulated too. It is significant, however, that Aristotle, and the scholastic tradition, treat of economics as something, like ethics, presupposed by politics rather than included in it. But in so far as the private agencies fail, these things become a burden of the state, as the state must step in to punish young evildoers when their fathers do not exert their authority.

We have seen that the root cause, both of the denial of the common good and the socialist and Marxist misconceptions of it, lies in the denial of the spiritual nature and end of society. The two moments in the genesis of this false doctrine would be, first, the denial of the spiritual nature of society; second, the denial of the common good, or a materialist degradation of it. It is natural to ask, at this point, what it was that disposed men to the conviction that society existed only for economic ends. As it is stated here, this would appear to be an error in the natural order, i.e. an error about the nature of the state, its end as such in relation to its citizens, etc. Yet it seems unreasonable that men as a whole (excepting Catholic thought) should have made so great an error, and for so long, in matter so crucial to human happiness, except under the appearance of a superior truth. The observable facts almost suggest an explanation beyond the merely natural order. But in the light of the Faith it is abundantly evident. The spiritual nature of society was denied because men denied the ordination of the individual (individual and person are used here synonymously) to the state, and the private good to the common good. More precisely, it was claimed that insofar as man is a spiritual being, he is in no way subordinate to the state, but rather, in this order, the state was subordinated to him. BUT WHY SHOULD THE INDIVIDUAL HAVE BEEN MADE THE END OF THE STATE? Because of the alleged superior dignity of the individual as compared with the state, the transcendent dignity of the personal good, which appears private, relative to the common good which is transitory.

THE DIGNITY OF MAN

Now the Greeks, too, were aware of the dignity of man, the dignity of an intellectual nature; but they did not for that reason deny the whole natural ordination of the particular good to the more universal good of the state. And so, we might ask whether the ancient Greeks and the moderns mean the same thing by the "dignity of man." The ancient concept is founded on natural reason alone; but is this true for the moderns? Here we must adduce the fact that the modern world has been profoundly influenced by Christian Revelation; that Revelation tells of a dignity conferred on man, a dignity infinitely higher than the dignity of nature, not something due to man, but a free gift having its principle in the infinite merit of Christ. In this connection it is worth recalling that in his Christmas Message of 1944, the Holy Father spoke of Christmas as the feast of human dignity, and, indeed, a single soul justified through Christ is immeasurably more precious than the whole natural universe.

When the modern liberal speaks of the dignity of man, is he in fact speaking of the natural dignity of a rational creature, the dignity of the person known to the Ancients? Even by natural reason it seems probable, but with the eye of the Faith we know that the moderns, although they deny Christ and the whole order of grace, persist in predicating of man the dignity which is his only by a supernatural gift. *Do not the moderns, in fact, see every man in the likeness of Christ, the very Christ they deny?* How else account for the quasi-mystical exaltation of the human person so prevalent and so powerful in recent times, the crusading zeal of the modern liberal with his desire to redeem man from the burden of poverty, oppression and injustice?

THE DIGNITY OF CHRIST

The truth emerges clearer when we consider Christ as He is King of the universe, its End and Final Cause. As such, He is its Common Good, a Common Good Who is also a Person. More, He is so transcendent a Common Good that He is the Source of all that is good in men, their goodness being but a remote participation in His. With this doctrine in mind, we may attempt to trace the process of secularization, following its two main streams as they take their source in Christ's twofold perfection, as Person and as Common Good. One line of thought, then, started from the doctrine that Christ is a Person and that every man, by participation in the life of Christ through grace, is "another Christ." Proceeding to a more integral secularization, having progressively denied Christ, it predicated the perfection of Christ of every man. Thus, as Christ is the end of the universe, so the individual, in acting for their own self-interest, were thought ipso facto to bring about the good of the whole; as Christ is the Source of all truth as Incarnate Wisdom, so the private opinions of each man became infallible sources of truth, truth became personal and, as another consequences, a multitude of philosophical systems arose, each one peculiar to its creator.

On the other hand, the secularizing of Christ as the Common Good, having denied Christ, predicated His Goodness of the state. Then, just as men derive all their goodness from Christ and are at once totally dependent upon Him and totally subordinate to Him, so it is said that men are totally subordinate to the state, and dependent upon it, in no way escaping its power. Hayek's description of totalitarian doctrine as we have quoted it ("There is a life higher than the individual life, the life of the people and the life of the state, and it is the purpose of the individual to sacrifice himself for the higher life") assumes a heightened intelligibility. Is it not in fact through a perversion of Christ's doctrine that men will sacrifice themselves in the way they do for a totalitarian state? But this is matter for understanding, not for demonstration.

IMPLICATIONS OF THIS ANALYSIS

If this analysis is correct, it has important implications for the resolution of contemporary errors. It would follow that any attempt to treat such errors as individualism, personalism, collectivism, as errors simply in the natural order, must be inadequate. True enough they are errors about natural things, but the natural error is in the nature of a term produced by doctrines outside the natural order. *Hence these economic and political doctrines so vital to contemporary thought and life are ultimately and fully intelligible only in the light of the Faith.* By the light of natural reason, one may see (at least theoretically one is able to see) that those doctrines are irrational; but we fail to see how they exert so profound an influence over men's minds. Even more seriously, not understanding that supernatural truth is the source of their strength, we are helpless to overcome the error.

It was the misinterpretation of the Christian doctrine of the dignity of man, then, which led men to believe that there is no subordination to the state in the personal, i.e. spiritual order. Once this was accepted, it necessarily followed that the only function of the state was in the material welfare of its citizens. (As a matter of fact, it was first denied that the state had any dominion over economic matters, but, as it was progressively realized that subordination in this order was a practical necessity, the state began to assume this role.) Likewise, subordination in the material order being more or less recognized today, it is coming to be realized, particularly in the totalitarian countries, that subordination in the spiritual order is also necessary. Thus, we see in Russia, for example, the organization of the whole life around a common ideology, granted it is in a paradoxical way a materialist spirituality. That is, the whole of life is centered about *ideas* of the economic process.

Further, we may readily see how advantageous it would be to the Enemy of souls to bring about this perverted doctrine of the state. For God ordained men to live in a temporal society by way of attaining their end, the supernatural end as well as the end of natural happiness, to live, that is, under the dominion of a state whose duty it was to foster virtue in its citizens. If this is denied him, therefore, man is deprived of that natural aid to his spiritual good which God had intended for him. Political and economic doctrines, then, most definitely are not matters indifferent to the Faith. But again, neither is the Faith indifferent to politics. The subversion of the political order following the denial of Christ recalls His words: "Do not think I am come to destroy the law or the prophets. I am not come to destroy, but to fulfill." Christ, Our Lord, is the Creator of heaven and earth. Our Redeemer is also the Author of our nature. That is why Holy Mother Church so carefully safeguards the truths of nature, knowing as She does that grace works through nature. By the same reasoning, the Powers of darkness are constrained to undermine nature and to obfuscate the truths of natural reason. Only in the Church, therefore, will the totalitarians, the individualists, the liberals, find the truth they cherish purified of every error and therefore not constraining them to deny another truth. Totalitarians will find themselves subordinated to the common good, liberals will find the true principle of community, and both liberals and individualists will find the justice and freedom of persons which can only be attained when every man is loved as Christ and because of Christ; for only then will the natural law be fulfilled.

WILLIAM DAVEY, T.O.P.

SECURITY

Ah, to be rich,
    Never fretting nor crying,
With nothing to fear,
    But the prospect of dying.

Estranged Bedfellows

MODERN CHRISTIAN REVOLUTIONARIES
Edited by Donald Attwater
Devin-Adair Company

It is hard to believe that a Catholic edited these five little books, here bound in one volume. One has visions of a villainous, greedy publisher forcing upon an unhappy Donald Attwater all sorts of authors and subject likely to catch the attention of this or that buying public. But this thesis breaks down when one reads the introduction, in which the editor professes to be happy about this babel of tongues, this potpourri of truth and error.

Be it on Mr. Attwater's head then. The result of his endeavors is utter chaos. Of his five subjects, only two are Catholic; of his five authors, only one, himself. The one study of a Catholic by a Catholic is the only really commendable section of the book. The subject is Eric Gill, whose very close friend, Donald Attwater, was, and it is admirably done. It is as neat and precise an analysis of Gill's thought as one could wish, and Gill was eminently qualified to be considered a modern Christian revolutionary.

I cannot find the heart to denounce the study of Chesterton with the wrath it deserves because F. A. Lea, who did it seven years or so ago, has already recanted in part, in appended notes, and has no doubt already had the wrath of Catholic England on his head. Suffice it to say that F. A. Lea is not a Catholic (and openly deplores the misfortune of Chesterton's conversion), was only twenty-three years old when the essay was written, and throughout it compares G. K. Chesterton unfavorably with someone named John Middleton Murry, a pantheist and Marxist.

The study of Nicolas Berdyaev is very competently done. Berdyaev is nominally a Russian Orthodox, philosophically really an existentialist. His biographer and critic, Evgveny Lampert, understands Berdyaev, understands Russian, understands the Orthodox Church and knows the position of the Roman Catholic Church, so his study is precise and intelligible. Those who are familiar with Berdyaev only through his study of the bourgeois mind will be surprised to see how far his thinking has strayed from Christianity. He is a revolutionary, in a sense, but is he Christian?

The same question arises in regard to the essay on Kierkegaard, Berdyaev's philosophical forebearer in existentialism. But apart from whether or not Kierkegaard really fits under the heading of a Christian revolutionary, it would have served some purpose to have made a penetrating study of his existentialism in the light of St. Thomas, inasmuch as the doctrine is causing a mild flurry at the moment. But this study by M. S. Chaning-Pearce only adds to the confusion. It is bad enough that a man who does not really understand should try to analyze another man who did not really understand either (and in a different way), but Mr. Chaning-Pearce goes to the trouble of quoting a dozen or so other men who don't really understand (in their diverse fashions) and once in a while suggests a wild parallel between Kierkegaard's philosophical errors and the progress of the soul to God as described by St. John of the Cross. In the end all you can be sure of is that Kierkegaard was a profoundly melancholic man.

There is no point in detailed discussion of the fifth essay, as it is the same story. Nichol Macnicol, a vague Protestant, analyzes Charles Freer Andrews, another vague Protestant, in a wonderful treatise lacking key concrete facts. It is hard to see anything through the haze, but seemingly Andrews was a gentle and winning person who fell into ineffectual sentimentality from which Catholicism would have saved him. He went to India, where he was a friend of Gandhi and Tagore, and where he evidently lost his Christianity in a blur of universal brotherhood. He does not sound (for all that he worked against racial discrimination) either Christian or revolutionary, but he was probably very nice.

CAROL ROBINSON

THE NATURAL LAW
By Heinrich A. Rommen
Trans. By T. R. Hanley
Herder

Any treatment of a fundamental philosophical concept should have the twofold aim of analyzing and exposing the concept and defending its validity against attacks. These two aims guide the author of this book on the natural law.

He has devoted the major portion of the work to an historical survey of the origin and development of the natural law concept from the Greeks to the present day. His most effective defense of the concept is also contained in this section, for he brings out clearly the vitality of the concept, its ineradicability from human thought. He makes excellent defensive use of the horrible effects of a denial of the natural law that all of us have had to witness during the last decade. At present, all serious ethical, juridical and political thinkers are on the spot and the author refuses to let the get off it without acknowledging the need of some fundamental norms that are above the individual and the state.

After tracing the historical fortunes of the natural law concept, the author passes to a consideration of the nature and content of the natural law. Such problems as the relationship of metaphysics and ethics, morality and law, the individual and the community, natural and positive law, come up for discussion. These problems are presented sharply enough, but the author does not penetrate very deeply in giving a solution. Perhaps he is restrained by a consideration of his readers; in some cases, as, for example, in his discussion of the relation of person and the common good, it seems that the author is just not taking sides. At least, that is the impression that is given.

A simple exposition of a traditional doctrine that is under attack is not very helpful either to those who still cling to the doctrine or to those who attack it. A vigorous defense of it must be made. Such a defense may not convince those who deny the doctrine, although they are attacking it on the basis of half-truths and hidden errors. But a complete defense is even more necessary for the benefit of those who still hold the traditional doctrine more from sentiment or an external reason, such as the author develops in his first section, that from deep conviction, and a penetration of the flimsiness of the opposing arguments. This task, which should be expected from a contemporary work on the natural law, is not done with any thoroughness by the author of the present volume.

JAMES M. EGAN, O.P.

"Therefore I say to you, be not solicitous for your life, what you shall eat, nor for your body, what you shall put on. Is not the life more than the meat: and the body more than the raiment? Behold the birds of the air, for they neither sow, nor do they reap, nor do they gather into barns: and your heavenly Father feedeth them. Are not you of much more value than they? And which of you by taking thought, can add to his stature one cubit? And for raiment why are you solicitous? Consider the lilies of the field, how they grow: they labour not, neither do they spin. But I say to you, that not even Solomon in all his glory was arrayed as one of these. And if the grass of the field, which is today, and tomorrow is cast into the oven, God doth so clothe: how much more you, O ye of little faith? Be not solicitous therefore, saying, What shall we eat: or what shall we drink, or wherewith shall we be clothed? For after all these things do the heathens seek. For your Father knoweth that you have need of all these things. Seek ye therefore first the kingdom of God, and his justice, and all these things shall be added unto you. Be not therefore solicitous for tomorrow; for the morrow will be solicitous for itself. Sufficient for the day is the evil thereof." (Mt. 6:25)

INTEGRITY

The Anniversary Issue

October, 1947 ~ Vol. 2, No. 1.   25 cents a copy

SUBJECT ≈ OUR LADY & RUSSIA

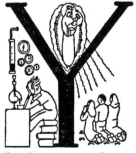

YOU HAVE OFTEN HEARD IT said that God is indifferent to the fortunes of men today. Humanitarians sometimes imply that *they* are the ones who must pity the poor, the prolific and the incurably diseased, because a heartless God only adds to their suffering with a harsh moral law. The Communists have carried this trend even further. What would the world do without their beneficent planning!

This curious view of affairs is only possible because of a secular press which confines itself to "facts." A "fact" is a physical act (that Mrs. A was murdered today by her husband, while at breakfast), or a statistical conjecture (that thirty-five percent of the women in greater New York like to pay $1.10 for their nylons), or an opinion (as long as it is reported second hand — "I have it on the authority of, etc.").

But if God communicates with men (whether interiorly by grace or in a blinding vision) that is not a fact, and so is not reported in the newspapers, or taken seriously in gatherings of learned men.

If *all* the facts (including spiritual ones) are taken into account, God's relationship with the modern world takes on quite a different aspect. Never in Christian history has God revealed His concern, and warned and advised men so publicly and directly as in the last century through the apparitions of His Mother.

We have tried to show in this issue that Our Lady's messages hold the only key to the solution of today's acute and worldwide problem.

We have also included the first of two articles (WHAT IT MEANS TO BE A CATHOLIC) by Father Carr, a Canadian Basilian to whom we owe a long-standing debt of gratitude for light along the way in our search of synthesis. HEAVENLY HOUSTON is another in our cities' series.

THE EDITORS

Open Letter to Comrade Stalin

Give peace to the peoples separated from us by error or by schism, and especially to the one who professes such singular devotion to Thee and in whose homes an honored place was ever accorded Thy venerable icon (today perhaps often hidden to await better days); bring them back to the One True Fold of Christ, under the One True Shepherd. (Act of Consecration of Pope Pius XII.)

THE POPE MOST CERTAINLY DIDN'T ADD TO your pleasure on October 31, 1942, Comrade Stalin, when, without even as much as an approving nod from the Soviet Supreme Council, he dedicated the world to the Immaculate heart of Mary, giving special place of Russia. And just to be sure that no one misunderstood, he repeated those words on December 8 of the same year before some forty thousand people in St. Peter's Basilica. But don't give full credit to His Holiness for the ideas enunciated on those occasions. The Virgin herself had requested such a course of action in her instructions to the children at Fatima.[1] Frankly, she wasn't inclined to consider very favorably your plans to ostracize her. No amount of your present-day decrees and orders can serve to obliterate the glory of her position in Russian history and it would be a difficult matter to convince the Mother of God, in view of the love and devotion heaped upon her in the past by your countrymen, that the people of Russia would not now be delighted were she to return.

Yes, she was the subject of endless flattery from all classes before the days of "classless societies." The names of those who penned her praises in song would read like a list of the great

[1] [Original] Editors' Note: According to Lucy, the surviving Fatima child, Russia has yet to be consecrated alone, in the manner Our Lady wished.

in Russian music. And the outstanding figures in the field of literature seemed never embarrassed at the thought of turning a bright phrase in her honor, even so good a comrade as Alexander Blok having been victim to her charms, leaving us his *verses of a Beautiful Lady.* But were you to destroy all mention of her in the literature of your own country, we would still have the testimony of those from other lands, friend and foe of Russia, believer and unbeliever alike, to bear witness to the devotion she knew from the prince and peasant.

Thus, it is that we read with interest and amusement the comments in the travelogues of that sturdy champion of American low-church Protestantism, Samuel Irenaeus Prime, written in the 1870s. How bewildered he is to discover that in Russia "the Greek religion is like the Romish" for they "pay apparently the same honors to a picture of the Virgin that the Romanist does to a statue." And what is his disgust to discover that women are not alone in this folly for frequently he observed that "in the middle of the day, and on a week-day too, respectably appearing, well-dressed gentlemen were standing or kneeling before the altar offering their devotions. The men, as well as the women, appear to be religious in Russia. And it struck me as very strange to see a fine-looking, full-grown man coming in at noon-day into a church, bringing a little wax candle, walking up to a shrine over which is a picture of the Virgin, kneeling before it, bowing his head to the floor, crossing himself again and again, lightning his candle and sticking it into a hole prepared for the purpose and once more prostrating himself to kiss the pavement, and then retire!"

And there is the witness of an American statesman, Albert J. Beveridge, in his book, *The Russian Advance,* written at the turn of the present century. "It is not for nothing that noble, peasant, prince, criminal, philanthropist, society leader — all classes — make obeisance to the holy images. . . . Granting all their superstition, conceding their ignorance, giving full credit to every unfortunate phase which the Christian religion takes among this peculiar people, he who travels the empire from end to end, with eyes to see and ears to hear, cannot but admit that here is a power in human affairs, blind it may be, cruel oftentimes, no doubt, but still reverent, devotional, and fairly saturated with a faith so deep that it is instinctive, and the like of which may not be witnessed in all the earth.

Furthermore, testimony is contained in the three volumes on Russia written in 1839 by the Marquis de Custine, who considered the peoples of the earth perfect only insofar as they were French. He journeyed to Moscow and visited a shrine of the Virgin where he "observed that everybody who passed this chapel — lords, peasants, tradespeople, ladies, and military men — all bowed and made numerous signs of the cross; many, not satisfied with so humble a homage, stopped, and well-dressed women prostrated themselves to the very earth before the miraculous Virgin, touching even the pavement with their brows; men, also, above the rank of peasants, knelt, and repeated signs of the cross innumerable." And so infectious was this devotion to the Virgin, that the Marquis, seeking relief in the company of non-Russians, discovers to his chagrin that even his coachman, an Italian who has lived some years in Russia, is likewise "an adorer of the Virgin of Vivielski. . . . I risked a few doubts as the authenticity of the miracles of his Virgin of Vivielski; had I denied the spiritual authority of the Pope, my Roman servant could not have been more shocked."

Of course, Comrade Stalin, your propagandists, who know how to turn a phrase to their own benefit, would undoubtedly claim that the proof of her low standing is evident in the fact that her icon was always put away in a corner. But wait just one minute with that line of reasoning! In America being put away in a corner is not exactly a sign of respect, but the Emily Posts of Russia know full well in their country the reverse held true. Yes, it was in that corner where the guest of honor was always seated that they were so proud to exhibit the picture of their Mother and her Divine Son.

The omnipresence of these icons was a source of amazement to the visitor. W. J. Birkbeck, a high-church Anglican who spent much time in Russia, has given us the following picture of the situation: "Novelists and travelers have again and again described the station at Wisballen, from the platform of which at the one end may be seen the red brick church of Edytkuhnen with its characteristic, if rather poor, German gothic spire, and at the other end the blue star-bespangled dome of the first Orthodox church on the Russian side of the frontier. But I think that what strikes the foreigner most, when he emerges from the ordeal of the customhouse, and makes his way into the justly be-lauded buffet where he has to wait until the train is ready to start again, is the presence of a large sacred picture in the corner of the room with a lamp burning in front of it. And from that moment until he re-crosses the frontier, so long as he is under a Russian roof, he will never be out of sight of these visible evidences of the nation's belief in the Christian Faith. In Germany and very often in England, you may enter a strange house, and you may come out again without knowing whether its owner is a Christian or an infidel. In a Russian house, this is impossible. In every room you will find in the corner an icon, either of the Savior or of the Mother of God, or of some one or more of the Saints. And this custom is not confined to private houses. You will find the same thing in the public buildings: in the rooms of the offices of the various government departments, in the shops, in the railway stations, in the cabins and dining saloons of the steamers, in the bazaars, and, in fact, in any place where men meet to transact the ordinary business of life. No foreigner who has traveled in the smaller steamers about the lakes and rivers of the northern part of Russia can have failed to be struck by the manner in which everybody in the cabin, before he settles himself for the night turns to the icon and performs his evening devotions, and the same thing when he rises in the morning. As for private houses, they all, from the palace to the humblest cottage, are provided with them. If you enter a room without an icon, you may be sure that the house belongs to a foreigner.

You know as well as I do, Comrade Stalin, how the natives treasured these icons as signs of their love for her and her protection of her clients. Nor were the people of Russia timid about invoking her aid and expecting her assistance in times of distress, of war and of national calamity. How often, when the enemy threatened, they would gather about one of her icons and would feel prayerfully secure that she would obtain victory for their cause. And when she did, the Russians — being simple and naïve, as the educated Westerner would say — could not understand why they should not give special honor to the pictures of one who had especially honored them. The "civilized" foreigner, often unsympathetic to such ideas concerning the Saints, did sooner judge as scandalous and idolatrous, rather than edifying, these many evidences of the favor of the Mother of God and the manifestations of respect paid her by the people. M. Spinka of the Chicago Theological Seminary gives us a typical observation for one of this class: "The very heart of the Russian peasant's religion was his worship of the images — the icons — and the relics from which he expected relief from his many ills; and next to this was his belief in the magical powers of the sacraments, with which his concept of 'salvation' was identified. There were no less than 241 officially recorded 'miracle-working' sacred icons, among which the various representations of the Mother of God pre-dominated." Spinka would, evidently, set a limit to the Mercy of God and the intercession of His Saints.

It has often been stated that the history of these famous icons of the Mother of God is the history of Russia itself. Such a one is that of the icon of Our Lady of Vladimir which had been brought by Duke Bobolinbski from Constantinople and placed in the Cathedral at Vladimir in the twelfth century. When the hordes of Tamerlane threatened Moscow, the icon was brought to the besieged city and the sparing of the city was credited to the intercession of the Mother of God. In commemoration of this event, the icon was thereafter honored in the Cathedral of the Assumption situated in the Kremlin and before it the tsars crowned themselves and patriarchs were consecrated.

And who is there who has read Tolstoy's *War and Peace* with its account of events in the War of 1812, who can forget the scene on the field of battle when Kutuzoff goes round his troops bearing the icon of Our Lady in order to raise the morale of his men? And one hundred years later, when thanksgiving services were held on the same field, her part in the victory was not overlooked. The icon was carried on foot by detachments from every town and village through which it passed on its eight-day journey, from Smolensk to Borodino and great was the acclaim it received from tsar and peasant and soldier and civilian. This same icon, at a much earlier point of history, had been borne into battle against the Tatars under Baty.

These accounts could be related endlessly, for numerous were the favors granted the land of Russia through the intercession of the Mother of God. But let us consider for a moment what must have been her favorite shrine, situated just outside the Kremlin, and the goal of all the faithful who would not think of entering or leaving the confines of Moscow without calling to pay their respects. We take our accounts from the works of two outstanding American guides.

From Ruth Kedzie Wood's *The Tourist's Russia,* we derive the following: "Returning to the Red Square, the Sunday Gate is to the right. Against its further wall and between two arches stands the Chapel of the Iberian Virgin. The crowd of the faithful often extends to the pavement before the tiny shrine. Dusty pilgrims from far-off provinces lay down their ragged bundles and tea-kettles, and enter to kneel before the wonder-working picture, which flames with gold, pearls, and brilliants. Shopkeepers, maids coming from market, an officer in full accoutrement, a shabby cure, a lady descended from her limousine, make the poklon, and repeatedly bow to the floor in common humility. If the Virgin drives away like the Bambino of Rome, in her own carriage with bare-headed servants, to pay a visit to the ailing, she leaves a substitute, which does not deceive her devotees who know well that the Virgin of Mount Athos bears the mark of a Tatar ball on her cheek. The praying, crossing, bending, is uninterrupted from daybreak to dark. The odor of poverty, of incense, and flowers on the altar is overcoming.

"A young woman turns to kiss the glass which covers the icon. Her way to the door is impeded by a press of old and young. Perhaps she is leaving Moscow or has returned after an absence. At any rate, she has fulfilled the obligation of every Orthodox traveler in Moscow by paying homage before or after a journey at the Chapel of the Iberian Virgin."

In the travelogues of Burton Homes we read: "Her state-carriage is drawn by six horses with driver and postilion in brilliant livery, but bareheaded. Her progress through the streets is like that of an empress. All traffic ceases, every head is bared and bowed, all hands wave the outline of the cross, all lips are moved in prayer; and when, upon arrival, the huge gilded frame is carried from the coach, we see scores of men, women, and children throw themselves upon their knees and crawl frantically toward it."

Whatever else you might care to say, one thing is certain — Mary is definitely not ignored! And we can gather some idea of the difficulties you have had with the persistence of the Iberian Virgin from the following remarks of Will Durant in his book *The Tragedy of Russia:* "In 1932, out of fourteen hundred pre-war churches in Moscow, four hundred were open (including two synagogues), four hundred were shut and barred; the rest had been abandoned, torn down or transformed. Some were changed into theatres, others into store-houses, garages, plumbers' shops, Soviet meeting-rooms, headquarters for the local atheist league, etc. The monasteries were closed, and the monks were put to work. The shrines that had dotted Russia, as the goals of pious pilgrimages, were dismantled, and at last the famous Iberian Virgin, at the approach to the Red Square, was taken down."

"At last," you say, and it sounds like such a complete and final victory. But do you really believe that she will meekly resign herself to exile because you have so decreed? She treasures the loyalty she knew from the people of Russia and if those in high office have tried to take advantage of her favored position, the Mother of God has known better than to blame the people accountable for the present excesses of commissars. So it is that she has seen fit to defy your challenge and, under the circumstances, you would do best to back down from your opposition and set her coach in order for her triumphant return. You should be warned that she has a powerful Son of Whom she is justly proud and Who will see to it that nothing stands in her way. There is no doubt in her mind about the future. She states very definitely, "My Immaculate Heart will finally triumpth." This dedication of Russia to that Immaculate Heart is her own way of doing things. You have been for so long enmeshed in the business of fifth columns and "boring from within" that you fail to comprehend the encircling tactics that she is calling into play. Comrade Stalin, you have refused to open the door like a gentleman to let her into Russia, so she has retaliated by opening the vastness of a mother's heart and taking in all Russia.

PAUL F. ROWAN

THE STATUS QUO DUET

To change our ways,
  We will refuse to,
We like the mess,
  We've gotten used to.

The Pertinence of Penance

EITHER THE U.N. IS WRONG, OR OUR LADY IS wrong. The U.N. (and the League of Nations and the Marshall Plan and the Yalta Agreement and all the rest of them) proposes to remedy the undiagnosed and mortal disease of society with sundry economic and political nostrums. They increasingly favor researches and committees and plans, on the theory that the situation is vastly more complicated than at first was thought, and also on the unconscious pre-supposition that once the facts are known the remedy will be obvious. Our Lady, on the contrary, grossly "oversimplifies" things. Her message is brief, always the same (whether at La Salette, Lourdes, Fatima or Heede), and it is more and more insistent: *Do penance.*

Now as nothing has been said about penance at the U.N., so far as I know, it is possible that men do not think Our Lady's advice is very practical. The purpose of this article is to suggest that maybe it is much more practical than they think.

IRRELEVANT TO WHAT?

What are we trying to do anyhow? Are we trying to save democracy? It isn't very important whether we save democracy or not, except insofar as the existence of democracy conduces to some greater end beyond itself. Men have been happy under kings as well as councils. Democracy is not an end in itself and (being a particularly unromantic form of government really, and not to say, vague, at the moment) there is little likelihood that there will be a successful crusade on behalf of it.

Or are we trying to bring about some sort of materialistic millennium? Obviously, if this is our goal, penance does seem a little absurd. The probability is that most people who are trying to fix up the world have some globular housing project or garden suburb in mind by way of eventual beatitude.

Here is where they break sharply with Our Lady, who says the goal is the salvation of souls and the Beatific Vision. The framework of reference in the two cases is entirely different. If you accept the secular view, which does not look beyond death, or even at death, then penance doesn't pertain. If, however, you accept the Christian structure, which places this life as a time of trial, sees Hell yawning and the sight of God inviting, then it can immediately be seen that penance has some relevance to our present mess. All the materials' and secularists' strength consists in keeping people's eyes focused on their false framework of life. Otherwise, they would have no real power. Doesn't it seem as though some of the credit for our narrowed vision belongs to the Devil? Possibly this is his greatest triumph, that he has set the modern problem in terms which cannot but turn out to his advantage. If people have jam on their bread, and peace in which to pursue their money-making without the hazards of war, they are his. And if they fail of peace and are bombed to death, they are still his, but maybe sooner. How crude of Our Lady to have shown the Fatima children a vision of Hell! It is so obvious then that the real issue is the salvation of souls.

HOW DID WE GET IN THIS MESS?

Here again Our Lady would "oversimplify." She would simply say, in complete disregard of all interesting studies of sociologists, the vast researches of statisticians, and the new discoveries that are being made every day, that we sinned against God. We broke the rules (the moral law, that is) so *of course* everything went wrong, and this is our punishment, which nothing can mitigate, save we are sorry and beseech God to help us.

The only alternative explanation of our predicament is that of our Russian friends, whose theory is that it is the inevitable result of inexorable economic laws, working through increasing chaos to a classless millennium.

Our statesmen in general refuse to accept this determinist

position, and scorn Our Lady's verdict if they have heard of it. This leaves them shaking their heads and saying that the matter is vastly too complex to be understood without vastly more research. Withal, they keep sliding toward the Communist position.

It will be useful to examine Our Lady's hypothesis to see if facts do bear it out.

WHO SINNED AND WHAT SINS?

The hypothesis is that we're in our mess of instability, war and threats of war, famine and all the rest of it, because we have sinned. We certainly must have sinned on a vast scale to have warranted such a vast and tragic disorder. And so it appears.

In the first place, there is a universality about sin which is unprecedented in Christian history. It once was that the poor remained virtuous while the courts disported themselves. Infidelity, immodesty in dress, avarice, love of luxury and all the rest are now nearly as indigenous to the tenements as to Park Avenue. We have really attained a sort of equality, if only an equal guilt.

So it is also with countries. We like to fancy that our American hands are cleaner than some in Europe and Asia, but we committed some of the worst national crimes. Who dropped the atomic bomb? President Truman has not repented, and neither have we. We Americans also were responsible for some of the most ghastly air raids in Europe, not to mention looting, rape and black markets. We are the greatest materialists in the world. We have legalized divorce, are the chief promotors of birth control, increasingly favor euthanasia and conscientiously keep the mention of Christ out of our schools. Need one to go on? The air is heavy with impurity and commercialism, with worse vapors threatening. So, Our Lady is right at least in her diagnosis. Now what about the prescription?

WHAT IS PENANCE?

Penance is sorrow and satisfaction for sins. It means first of all an acknowledgment to God that we have sinned against

Him. That means confession on a personal basis. On a national basis, it would mean something like a day set apart for sackcloth and ashes, or flags at half-mast during congressional beating of breasts, as representing the citizens at large. It would mean in consequence a shift back to the morality economy (where good is done for its own sake) from expediency (where good and bad are done indifferently according to whether or not it will pay).

As for satisfaction for sin, that means simply doing something distasteful to make up for sins, let it be anything from accepting cancer patiently to giving up cigarettes or eating spinach, or going without a new Nash.

WASTED SUFFERING

One of the most ironic things about today is that the amount and degree of suffering is enormous (has it ever been greater?), and it is virtually wasted. It is not wasted in this sense, that it satisfies God's justice (for it is punishment for sin, most of it). It may also serve to show men their folly and cause them to turn again to God and so save their souls. But is this usually the case? The suffering is too severe for the softened and weakened nature on which it falls. Cancer has not provoked a return to religion, nor do the majority of European sufferers seem so much chastened as bitter. But suffering far less than ours, if patiently accepted and offered to God in contrition, could be enormously efficacious.

It is the same way with our good deeds. Just as we have made suffering useless to our salvation because of our impenitence, so even our virtuous acts are unmeritorious because of the movie. Things done for reasons of expediency do not help to win Heaven. If you give a million dollars to the poor out of vainglory, or loan money to Britain in order to save your own economy, or are honest because it is the best policy, there is no virtue in it, nor does much permanent good come of it even here on earth.

MORTIFICATION AND FREEDOM

Now let us look at another aspect of penance, the effect it has on our own spiritual nature. All penance has the indirect effect of mortifying our desires because it involves willingly denying them satisfaction.

The world chaos is miniatured in each of us. There is a certain hierarchical order of our faculties which we only achieve (thanks to original sin) after patient self-discipline and self-denial. If, instead of mortifying ourselves, we go in for self-indulgence, we encourage our passions to revolt against the control of reason. Thus, we become progressively enslaved to our own lower natures and there is neither peace nor order within men. Naturally this is reflected in the condition of the world at large.

We love to exalt freedom from democracy but what good is political freedom to men who already are enslaved to themselves? What good is liberty if we are not masters of ourselves? It is like giving a drunkard the keys to the city.

What good are noble ideals if you can't carry them out? Modern American man is like a general who glibly promises to rush reinforcements into a breach and then finds his troops only laugh at his orders and continue their card playing. Or rather he is like a young man who cannot pass the acid test of manhood in order to wed the fair lady, or save his city, or win the crown of martyrdom, when the acid test consists in going without a cigarette for twenty-four hours. It's not that he prefers a cigarette to a fair lady and the rest, but just that when he comes to give orders to himself, he discovers a mighty insurrection has taken place. Isn't penance relevant to this state of affairs?

PENANCE AND BOURGEOIS SOCIETY

The austerity of life which the spirit of penance fosters has its exact opposite in what is known as bourgeois living. It is the way you and I live. Of its essence are comfort, ease, mediocrity, labor-saving devices, pretension. It is the social ideal of an all-pervading commercialism, the beatitude reflected by the advertisements. It used to be rare and limited to the comfortable, merchant middle class, but now bourgeois living has spread over all, especially in America.

The way you incite a Communist against the Western democracies is to point with scorn at our bourgeois softness. It can almost be said that the strength of the dictators, whether Communist or Fascist, lies in their fairly accurate condemnation of our vulnerable softness. They sometimes lie and often exaggerate, but the basis is really there.

The paradox of the situation is that our Fascist and Communist enemies really cherish the ideal they pretend to scorn. Karl Marx had enormous respect and admiration for the achievements of bourgeois capitalist society. The real grievance is that the Communists do not share in our luxurious living and they hold it out as a goal to their subjects, while asking them to despise it meanwhile in the interests of sacrifice to the state. One of the most pitiful aspects of Hitler was revealed after his death. He was a not a fanatic, tragic, selfless madman. He was a petty bourgeois man who loved overstuffed furniture and geegaws in too great abundance and deplorable taste.

So, our bourgeois living both attracts and repels our Communist enemies who are, in a sense, comrades behind the imitation-oriental-rug-beside-the-Bendix-automatic-washing-machine façade. As long as we cherish comfort and ease and pretension we are at their mercy. If they do not win us by force, they will win us by peaceful suasion. Is penance pertinent?

OUR LADY AND PENANCE

What has penance to do with Our Lady, why is she God's emissary in this crisis? Well, it appears to be because of her role as Mediatrix of All Graces. That explains the apparitions. "I can scarcely restrain the arm of my Son," she said at La Salette, weeping. She is interceding for mercy for us and to get us a little more time to repent, whereas we have long since deserved complete disaster for our sins against God. If we had listened at Fatima, and done penance, we would have staved off the recent war and the terrible suffering continuing from it. We were warned of this at Fatima and reminded of it at Heede.

As Mediatrix of Graces, Mary has the power to increase the merit of voluntary sufferings and to distribute the graces that are earned by them. This is the burden of De Montfort's teaching, that we should give to Mary all our satisfactions to distribute as she will. This is what she asked of the children of Fatima, that they make sacrifices for sinners, so that she would have more graces to distribute. The advantage of having Mary distribute the graces is not only that they are increased through her mediation, but also because she knows, as we cannot, how best to use them to avert universal disaster, and she has made it clear that her use of them will be, in a way she alone knows, conducive to the conversion of Russia, which will in turn stop the propagation of errors which cause the loss of very many souls.

THE UNEQUAL BURDEN

In a world of dog-eat-dog and eye-for-a-eye, we have forgotten the sacrificial nature of Christianity. Who is to do penance? Is each man to do it in proportion to his sins? Or are only the evil to do penance? Of course not! It is almost the other way around. Those who are the most pure and the least sinful are to do the most penance. "Make sacrifices for sinners," Our Lady demanded of three innocent little children at Fatima. Christianity has always been an "unfair" arrangement in this regard, ever since the Sinless One offered up His life for all of us who sin from the beginning to the end of the world.

OUR LADY AND RUSSIA

Mary specifically mentioned Russia at Fatima. Why is Russia so crucially important? The fate of the world doesn't hang on what happens in Holland and Greece, so why Russia? Obviously, this mystery is bound up with the fact that Russia is the seat and source of Communism. In fact, Our Lady's appearances at Fatima coincided with the Marxist coup d'état in Russia and she knew it for the menace it was, before the world even took the matter very seriously.

There is something unique about Communism in comparison with other ills which beset mankind. Is it possibly this, that it represents the Devil's fully organized attack on what was once Christendom? The advent of Communism was preceded by several hundred years in which manifold errors increasingly coalesced into systems. In the last century there arose Freemasonry, a secret society which gave form to the errors of the rationalists, and was a medium for an organized and seemingly diabolical attack on the Church. Indeed, this was the setting of the apparitions both at Fatima and at Lourdes. Communism seems to have superseded Freemasonry as an instrument of occult powers. Now it is in the open, has absolute political power, which is at the same time complete economic control. It is highly organized and persistently universal. Its propaganda tenacles are everywhere, and everywhere also antithetical to the Faith.

If this thesis is correct, and Communism does represent a major foothold of the Devil in world affairs, then Our Lady's intercession is vitally necessary for it is she who will crush the Serpent (that is to say, the Devil), to whom she was never subject because she was immaculately conceived.

If our struggle is against preternatural powers, then the U. N. is going to be pretty impotent, and we are going to need Mary's help badly. It is also obvious, if this is the case, why Russia will have to be converted. You can defeat a nation, but the Devil you can only exorcise. Once he has got this far, he will take advantage of our every weakness (and certainly he can outsmart us, for he has an angelic intellect) to spread his influence everywhere for his own ends. The naivete of statesmen will but play into the hands of the enemy.

From the secular point of view Russia doesn't seem at all consistent, and even the wisest among us cannot predict her next move. Now she tells the truth, now she doesn't. One minute she is conciliatory, the next obstinate. Why? What is Russia driving at? The whole thing makes sense only in the light of one end, and that is the destruction of souls. Only Lucifer, Our Lady and the Church understand the real issue of our times.

"This kind can be cast out only by prayer and fasting." Again, our role becomes clear. Penance is of the essence.

RUSSIA WILL BE CONVERTED

Our Lady of Fatima said that in the end Russia will be converted. If we do not do penance the errors of Communism will spread to every country in the world, but in the end, Russia will be converted. How that will be if we don't do penance, has not been revealed. Obviously, it will only come about after terrible suffering.

But there is no reason why we shouldn't do penance. If our Lady chooses to use the graces that way, the sufferings of one cancer victim lovingly accepted might mean the conversion and salvation of Stalin. And heaven knows what might happen if Catholic office girls dressed poorly for Our Lady's sake and for the sake of the salvation of souls ("Christians ought not to follow the fashions," said Jacinta shortly before her death).

To those who believe, it should be obvious that the burden of righting the world situation lies chiefly with them.

CAROL ROBINSON

BENDING THE SAPLING

Eye to the future! Ear to the ground!
    Nose to the grindstone, my lad!
And you'll have the happiest future, my son,
    A contortionist ever had!

Bogoroditza

THE SUN WAS SHINING BRIGHTLY. THE crowds moved in well-controlled patterns to and fro, from the Peace Chapel of Our Lady of the Cape to the exhibits, and back again. The Marian Congress was in full swing. Dominating the whole scene, the immense statue of the Virgin with arms outstretched seemed to embrace the whole world, and lift it up...up to her Son's pierced feet.

Suddenly the whole picture faded . . . and I was back in Russia, the Russia of my childhood and youth. Recently, it seems, I have been making this journey into my past more and more frequently, and from the oddest starting points too, such as busy New York streets, restaurants, the South Side of Chicago, the rolling green hills of Wisconsin, and now from the Marian Congress in Ottawa, Canada!

It is early September. My unruly blonde hair is neatly combed in two pigtails. My brown dress and black apron (the uniform of all high-school students in Russia) are without stains or tears. I am ready for the first fall day of school.

My mother and father are waiting to bid me Godspeed on this my new year of study. Slowly I walk up to them and kneel before them. They lift high the icon of the Blessed Mother (a holy picture painted in oils on wood and encased in silver and gold), making the sign of the cross with it. Father in ringing tones begins: "Suffer little children to come unto me." Mother answers: "For theirs is the Kingdom of Heaven." Then together they pray: "Defend, O Lord, Thy children from every adversity, Mary ever Virgin Blessed interceding for them. We pray Thee to regard with tenderness this Thy little one. Pour into her soul the grace of the Holy Spirit, that through Him she might be enlightened and instructed for all times in that which is pleasing to Thee, and may the *Bogoroditza* (She-who-gave-birth-to-God) guide her always to Thee!" Thus, yearly I am speeded to school, realizing early in life that learning is *learning* only if through it I become more pleasing to God. So did with me millions of other Russian children and youths.

Years, months and days merge into moments on this pilgrimage of mine into my past. . . . And it is summer again, with school far behind me. Mother and I are gathering herbs, medicinal and savory ones. Herbs are either food or medicine and, as such, come under the blessed and competent eyes of the *Bogoroditza*. Had she not been a housewife too? Had she not prepared meals and nursed kin and friends? Of course she had! And so, laden with the fragrant load, mother and I stop at the Church. The priest comes out smiling and intones the *Blessing of Herbs*. It is long and beautiful. I remember but part of it: "may these blessed objects act as a protection against the mockery and deception of the devil, wherever they are kept or carried, or other disposition made of them. And through the disposition of the Blessed Virgin, may we, likewise laden with sheaves of good works, deserve to be lifted up to heaven. . . . "

Herbs first, the fruits of the orchards next. These are blessed while yet on the tress, just before harvesting, and always on her Assumption day. Again, lovely litanies are chanted to her, and long blessings said with repeated requests to her to take them and all our petitions to her Son. . . . And then the harvest. . . . Then the seeds are blessed on her birthday.

Another summer comes and goes in a twinkling of an eye. It is my betrothal. Again, the heirloom icon is brought out of my parents' bedroom and my fiancé and I are blessed. After the blessing, it is installed in an outdoor shrine, surrounded by the loveliest flowers of our garden. Before it the solemn ceremony of pledging our troth is performed by a priest, the wedding ring is blessed and put on my right-hand finger, to be transferred during the Nuptial Mass to the left-hand finger.

The bridal room after the nuptials. Already "She-who-gave-birth-to-God" is installed there. The vigil light that is to burn night and day until our death flickers slowly, throwing deep shadows on her face, making it come to life.

So it is before her that bride and groom kneel, asking her blessing once more on their wedded life and their fertility, which is viewed in Russia as the infinitely great and awesome privilege of being co-creators with God in bringing souls into this world. To her they turn once again in this their first night of love, when their spiritual pledge of one-ness will be consummated in the flesh, thanking her by slowly and devoutly reciting the Magnificat!

It is she who, by her presence, gives strength to the young wife when, her time having come, her bed of love for a moment becomes her bed of pain. It is to her that the young mother or father lifts their newborn child. It is to this shrine, this center of the household, that the child is brought every morning and every night to learn his or her prayers and to be blessed, for the night or the day, by the parents and by the *Bogoroditza*. Here, too, are held all the family counsels, for isn't she the Mother of Good Counsel? **To her, Mother of Sorrow,** are brought all the family burdens, pains and griefs. To her, the Mother of Perfect Joy, they come with their joys. From her, the Spouse of Divine Wisdom, each and all ask for wisdom is the hour of need. It is she again who receives the dying prayers of those whose lives she shares and has blessed from birth to their last moments. *Bogoroditza Mater Bohia spasi nass!* This is the constant prayer of Russia, today, yesterday and, I firmly believe, unto the end of time. "You who have given birth to God — Mother of God — save us!" . . . and she will!

It's fall again, in this strange, dreamy journey of mine into my past. We are making ready for our annual pilgrimage to one of her innumerable shrines that dot Russia like an immense rosary — the *Bogoroditza* of Kiev, the fair city on the river Knepr, of Kazan on the Volga, of Tver in the very heart of Russia. In big cities, marvelous are her churches; in little villages, infinite is the number of her chapels. On all roads from north to south, from east to west, through that vast land of Russia, she waits in her wayside shrines for the pilgrim, the traveler, the beggar.

There wasn't a palace, house or a hovel that did not have her holy icon. It may have been a priceless gem of art incrusted in silver, gold and precious stones. It may have been just a cheap chromo. But always the vigil lights burned before her, and always she was the center of the household. Even the Communists have been powerless against her. For people still have her icon. It may be hidden well, but it is there and, as of old, it is brought out in moments of need, joy and sorrow. The present Russian government was compelled by common sense to keep her (icons) in its museums, for some are priceless works of old Byzantine art. For it was from the Greeks that the first Russian monks learned the difficult art of painting icons. What matters where she is placed? Whether in a museum or a house, the fact remains that she *is* in Russia, enshrined forever in the heart of her people.

I collided rather violently with a dark-robed figure, who suddenly called out my name. I looked up. There was the crowd. It was Ottawa, Canada, again. But the *Bogoroditza* was there too, standing high up in the sky, dominating the city, the world—with arms outstretched, calling her children to her! I was no longer in Russia, but what did it matter. She was here! I had come back from my pilgrimage into my distant past to find her who shared my whole life, and that of my people, right beside me!

O Bogoroditza, bring your own beloved Russia that loved you so much and I am sure still does, even though in secret, back to your Son, back to your Spouse the Holy Ghost, back to your Father and mine Who art in Heaven. Bogoroditza — Mater Bojia — Spassi Rossiu!

CATHERINE DE HUECK

All the News
"Fit" to Print

ON OCTOBER 13, 1917, THE WEATHER IN NEW York City was fair, and the forecast was colder that day and the next, with fresh northwest winds. (In certain parts of Portugal, it was raining.) There was much happening in the world to interest the press of the United States, especially the New York papers which cover European news quite thoroughly, and specifically the *New York Times,* with "all the news that's fit to print."

The Chicago White Sox and the New York Giants were fighting through the World Series. The *Times* gave the fifth game all the space it could, a column on the front page and a full page inside, with all the facts, figures and phantasies of the 8 to 5 White Sox victory.

The war, the first World War, took a lot of space, too. In Germany the prestige of Chancellor Michaelis was reported as shattered, and his position so shaken that his deposition was considered imperative. One of his difficulties was the German inability to stop American transport.

On the fighting fronts, the Germans had landed detachments on the Riga Islands, and in France and Belgium the British army under Haig was slowly moving forward.

The United States was in the midst of the second Liberty Loan drive, and everyone was pushing so the set quota would be met. On October 13, 1917, a total of $525,000,000 had been subscribed, and (as more recently) all the advertisements carried bond slogans. Another popular slogan was: "Everyone can help win the war by conserving food — eat all you want but don't waste an ounce."

Over the Top, by Arthur Guy Empey, was advertised as "the most widely read and talked over book in the country," and Sergeant Empey himself was in New York City lecturing (a favorite pastime of authors) and giving an authentic demonstration of trench warfare.

There was much other entertainment in New York City. In the motion pictures, Theda Bara (the vamp) was appearing in *Cleopatra.* Another prominent movie was *Fall of the Romanoffs.* On the stage, Billie Burke was in *The Rescuing Angel,* David Belasco was producing *Tiger Rose,* John Philip Sousa was at the Hippodrome, and Fred Stone was preparing a new play, *Jack O'Lantern.*

Among the books, Joseph C. Lincoln had a new Cape Cod Story, *Extricating Obadiah,* and Winston Churchill (not the former Prime Minister) had a new book, *The Dwelling Place of Light,* which was reviewed on the first page of the *Times Book Review Section.*

That radical movement for woman's suffrage was also in the news, and the National American Suffrage Association had issued a call for its forty-ninth annual convention, which was to urge Congress to pass the federal woman suffrage amendment without further delay.

These were the more important items that filled the papers that day.

But over in Portugal, in the hill country called the Serra da Aire, in the geographical center of Portugal, a dramatic scene was being enacted before seventy thousand people (more than attended the World Series) — seventy thousand people who had tramped to this isolated section through mud and rain, standing for hours in the thick slime, waiting, waiting, waiting… waiting until the Blessed Virgin appeared to three little shepherd children, and the sun danced wand whirled in the sky, and all who saw it shouted that it was a miracle, confirming the story of Fatima.

October 13, 1917, was the culminating day in the series of events that year, when Our Lady appeared to these little children, and through them sent her message to the world, asking the consecration of Russia to her Immaculate Heart, promising that if this were done Russia would be converted and there would be peace. If not, however, Russia would scatter her errors throughout the world, provoking wars and persecutions of the Church. And people (and that means us) must pray the rosary, perform sacrifices, make the five first Saturday Communions, pray for the Holy Father, and after each mystery of the rosary say, "O my Jesus, pardon us and deliver us from the fire of hell. Draw all souls to heaven, especially those in most need,"

The newspapers in Portugal carried many accounts of the strange happenings of October 13, 1917 — even the most anti-clerical papers. But not the press of the United States. The only mention of Fatima to be found was in the advertisements — for Fatima, "the sensible cigarette."

In fact, it is almost unbelievable to see how little an impression the tremendous story of Fatima has made on the general press of the United States. *Time,* in a feature on Salazar and Portugal a little over a year ago, was so little concerned with the vital fact of Fatima that its name did not even appear on the map, and the article carried no mention of it. Natural resources were carefully delineated on the map, but not supernatural ones. *Time,* with its then two editors, its managing editor, its two assistant managing editors, its nine senior editors, its thirty-nine contributing editors, and its forty-seven editorial researchers — not to mention its domestic and foreign news staff — must have known the story of Fatima. The only possible conclusion is that *Time* did not think it very important. But then, what happened at Fatima was only the Mother of God warning the world of the inevitable results of its sins.

FLOYD ANDERSON

On Pilgrimage To Fatima

BY A SERIES OF CIRCUMSTANCES THAT I LIKE
to consider near-miraculous, I found myself flying to Portugal
to attend the First International Pilgrimage of Catholic Action
Girls to Fatima from May 3 to 5, 1947. The pilgrimage was organized by the Catholic girls of Portugal as a thanksgiving to Our
Lady for having kept their country out of the war, to thank her
for the present peace, and to beg for a true and lasting peace.

It was during the first World War that the Blessed Mother
honored Portugal by appearing to three little shepherds near the
village of Fatima and gave them messages on which the future of
our world now hangs. Our Lady appeared every month for six
months. At the last apparition, in October, 1917, she performed
the miracle she had promised, in the presence of seventy thousand Portuguese; at which time the sun appeared to dance and
spin and to fall from the sky. Some of the messages given to the
children are still unknown; they are to be kept secret until some
time in the future. Others have unfortunately been fulfilled; I
say unfortunately because Our Lady foretold the occurrence of
World War II, the starvation and suffering of the people, the rise
of Soviet Russia. She requested that we turn from sin and make
sacrifices for sinners and showed the children a vision of hell.
She also requested that Russia be dedicated to her Immaculate
Heart, that we say the rosary often, that we keep the five first
Saturdays, (that is to receive Communion, to say the rosary and
meditate for 15 minutes on the first Saturday of each month).
Two of the little shepherds, Jacinta and Francisco, died shortly
after the apparitions; Lucy, the eldest, is still living and is now a
Sister of St. Dorothy in Portugal.

I was met at Lisbon by a Portuguese girl I had met in New
York and at whose home I was to live during my stay. Right outside the airport, a little girl about three years of age came running

up to me, hands outstretched, barefooted, speaking rapidly in Portuguese. Although I didn't have the slightest idea of what she was saying, her attitude was obvious — she was begging, whether money for candy or essentials, I didn't know, but she was the first of many beggars I was to come across in Portugal. Maria, my friend, told me she was a gypsy and as different from the ordinary Portuguese as a gypsy in America is to the ordinary American. A short distance from the airport were many rows of houses. Maria told me that they were homes for the workers built by the government and then proceeded to give me details about them: only young married workers can rent them; rental is about twenty dollars a month; size of house depends on size of family; in thirty years the man owns the house outright; in case of his death, it is given to his wife without further payment. Most of the houses had small gardens around them and seemed as attractive as many of the homes now being built in America; and much nicer than our government housing.

Soon we were driving down the Avenida da Liberdade, Lisbon's most beautiful avenue, the sidewalks of which are made of small pieces of stone with intricate designs of black and white, laid by hand. There seemed to be building going on all over the city, new apartment houses, new hospitals; and, besides all these, the city was preparing for the eighth centenary of its founding with many monuments, lighting, grandstands, and flagpoles. There seemed to be no shortage of building materials. I saw many men repairing the streets and sidewalks by hand, putting the pieces of stone in place and pounding them down with heavy wooden weights. These streets wear much better than most of our modern streets.

Lisbon is a beautiful city of pale yellow, green, blue, pink, and other pastel-colored houses, sometimes with colored tile. Many of the houses in the city, and the majority in the country, have a picture of the Blessed Mother or Saint Joseph, or some other Saint, on the front of the house in tile. There are many mountains throughout the city, numerous small parks, fountains, and in general appearance it is a well-kept city. Jacinta, one of the little shepherds, shortly before her death foretold that Lisbon would be visited with great devastation and destruction. Whether this prophecy is yet to be fulfilled or whether the penances and sacrifices of the Portuguese people have withdrawn this penalty, I do not know, although one of my friends told me something about having heard that the sacrifices of the people had saved Lisbon.

On May 3 we took part in a dialogue Mass at the National Catholic Action Girls' headquarters in Lisbon and then buses left from the headquarters with the foreign delegates for Fatima. There were representatives from Brazil, United States and Canada (me), France, England, Belgium, Poland, Russia, Italy, Spain, Ireland, Portuguese India, Portuguese Africa, and elsewhere. The pilgrimage was run by the Portuguese J.O.C.F., J.I.C.F., J.A.C.F., and J.U.C.F. (Young Christian Workers, Independents, Students, Farmers, and University Students). It was excellently organized, with certain of the groups in charge of the transportation, housing, food, sightseeing, etc. on the road to Fatima we visited Alcobaca and Batalha, two of the ancient, massive, beautiful monasteries in Portugal — there is nothing in the United States to compare with them. At both historic places, the people of the villages came out to greet us; they seemed particularly enthusiastic to hear that I was from America. (It would seem that they still believed the streets of New York are paved with gold.) At Batalha, the Bishop of Helenopole, the Hierarchical Director of Portuguese Catholic Action, spoke to the crows and officially welcomed us.

Finally, around 5:00 p.m., the buses began to ascend the mountains around the Cova de Iria. It seemed as though we were going up and around, up and up, until finally we could go up no farther. The scenery was beautiful. We were at the top of the mountain, at the Cova de Iria, the place where the Blessed

Mother appeared. All along the road were stone crosses to mark barefooted. A small chapel is built on the exact spot where Our Lady appeared; some distance away, a tall, straight, pure white basilica is being built. There is a large hospital for the sick and another new hospital being built. There are many new convents recently built in the neighborhood, including the Dominicans and the Carmelites. There are no hotels; only a few *pensions* where some of the people might get beds. The vast majority of the thousands simply curl up in blankets and sleep on the ground, or in their wagons and cars. Hundreds do not sleep at all but stay up all night praying before the Blessed Sacrament exposed on an outdoor altar in front of the basilica. Guida, another of my Portuguese friends, told me that the Bishop of Leiria will not permit hotels to be built in order to carry out more exactly the Blessed Mother's desire of sacrifice and penance, and also to keep the shrine from becoming too commercial. Nevertheless, there were many small stands selling religious articles that reminded me (oh, blasphemous thought!) somewhat of Coney Island, with their loud vendors and persistent sales talk.

The evening started off with a procession at about 10:00 p.m. Everyone had a candle with a paper guard around it that gave a lantern effect. There were about thirty thousand people present of whom twenty thousand or twenty-five thousand must have been the Catholic Action girls. (At some times there are as many as one hundred thousand to three hundred thousand and in May, 1946 at the crowning of the statue, there were present seven hundred thousand.) At midnight, we had Benediction and then the Blessed Sacrament was exposed all night. The rosary was recited and hymns were sung. At the stroke of every hour, the chimes of the basilica ring out with the favorite song of Fatima, which tells about the apparition and Our Lady's kindness to Portugal; it is similar to the hymn sung at Lourdes, and the chorus is the same, *Ave, Ave, Ave, Maria.* At about 2:00 a.m. the foreign delegates went to tents that had been prepared for them for a little rest.

Most of the Portuguese girls remained awake all night. However, sleep was impossible for us; it was one of the coldest nights that I remember in my life -- besides the cold, the rosary was recited and hymns sung all night with a priest leading the prayers and the songs over a microphone.

At 6:00 a.m., Mass was celebrated and thousands of us knelt in the dirt to receive Communion. About thirty priests went among the people distributing the Hosts; about twenty-five thousand Holy Communions were given out that morning. At noon, the statue of Our Lady was carried in triumphal procession from the little chapel to the altar of the basilica. The foreign representatives were all given a chance to carry the litter on their shoulders. The people were very demonstrative and threw flowers that had been sent from Holland for the occasion. High Mass was celebrated; at the offertory the delegates went up to the altar with various gifts (candlesticks, chalices, candles, etc.). During this Mass all the sick, about two hundred that day, were individually blessed with the Sacred Host. After the Mass, the statue of Our Lady was carried back to the little chapel, this time carried by the Portuguese girls. Everyone had out white handkerchiefs and waved them as the statue passed. By now it was about 2:00 p.m. and many of the people began to make their way home, on foot, on donkeys and carts, bicycles, cars, buses. Many of the Portuguese girls left this day, but a number of them and all the delegates remained overnight, sleeping in the hospitals and convents. The following morning, we visited Fatima, and the graveyard where the bodies of Jacinta and Francisco now rest, the place of the apparition of the angel, the pond where Jacinta once requested the frogs to be silent because she had a headache, and other places dear to those familiar with the story of Fatima. We also had the honor of meeting the mother and father of Jacinta and Francisco. They were very simple people and I was amazed that they did not get annoyed with the mob that surrounded them with all sorts of questions and requests. At 5:00 p.m. we left Fatima and returned to Lisbon.

Two weeks later I visited the convent near Porto where Lucy, now Sister Mary das Dores, lives. However, because I did not have permission from the Bishop, I was not permitted to see her. I was told by my friends that the Blessed Mother still visits her. In 1946 Lucy visited Fatima — the first time since she left there about twenty-five years before.

There have been hundreds and hundreds of cures recorded at Fatima, both spiritual and temporal; yet one cannot help but realize that the "message" of Fatima has gone *unheeded*. We have not mended our ways, we do not make sacrifices for sinners, we do not do penance, we do not pray the rosary often. How then can we avoid the penalty that has been foretold us? — that unless we do these things the errors of Communism will sweep the world, bringing devastation and destruction. But there is one bright spot on the horizon: ultimately, Our Lady promised, her Immaculate Heart will triumph and we will have peace.

MURIEL DONNELLY

The Crass Struggle

Shut the Doors, They're Coming Through the Windows!

FAILURE TO NOTE THE BEAM IN THE EYE OF the bourgeois American has made us incapable of either diagnosing or treating the mote in the eye of the Russian Communist. Consequently, much of the present anti-Communist journalism is obviously a case of the coffee pot calling the samovar black. Christianity and Catholicism are being brought in on a string to bolster the position of the self-seekers who find the native technique of economic extortion more to their liking than the imported variety. As the plot thickness, we may find Catholic Americans forced to sandwich the task of restoring a Christian social order between atomic forages against the Russians, just as they now feel compelled to confine their apostolic activities to hours sublet from mammon. All of which sounds like a Hearst editorial with reverse English, unless, of course, it can be substantiated by common sense. The common sense follows:

Communism is as incalculable as a New Englander's rheumatism. It reacts in response to a change in weather, but, in New England, as in the climate that generates Communism, the weather is constantly changing. It is important to bear this in mind whenever Communism is being discussed. Any calculation we may make is only as dependable as the momentary view through the periscope of an attacking submarine. Even while the readings are being charted, the enemy may have reversed his course.

The modern crusaders for the Faith are encountering the same difficulty their more warlike ancestors met when dealing with the Huns. The formal, ponderous, and calculated maneuvers of the armored crusaders made them as easy prey for the little dark men who rode in, high on their horses' necks, let fly their arrows, and then retreated. The crusaders were so weighed down by the impedimenta of tradition and self-importance, more concerned with the techniques of battle than the cause for which they fought, that the naked barbarian found them a simple target. The modern Communist is unimpeded by any formal tradition. He is naked of any loyalty to principles. He is free to attack or retreat with any weapon or motive he chooses. Against him, the lightest weapon, the most unhampered stroke, the simplest maneuver of which Christianity is capable, will be victorious. And these, the appropriate instruments, are the things of the spirit: purity, poverty, faith, charity and justice.

The unfamiliarity of the bourgeois American with these weapons of the spirit, as well as his proneness to adopt the weapon and motive of the Communist, makes him not only a prey for the Communist, but also a victim to the same disease from which the Communist suffers. To prove this point is the purpose of this article.

COMMUNISM IS NOT A FOREIGN "ISM"

Communism is only accidentally Russian. It is essentially a universal trend of modern times. No immigration restrictions can keep it out of this or any other country. Possibly the Russian brand, which is the most fashionable right now, can be isolated and controlled, but the native facsimile will grow where Moscow or Marx are unheard of. Our own country has its common garden variety of Communism. Curiously enough, it is being peddled as an antidote for the Russian disease. This medicine which we Americans have been taking in large doses for the last few generations, has produced an illness, which when it reaches the critical stage will be indistinguishable from the disease that plagues the Volga shores.

The American trend which now parallels the course of Marxist Communism, and which will eventually arrive at the same destination, has as its propaganda organs the common daily newspapers and the over-subscribed national periodicals. There is a substantial and formal similarity between *The Saturday Evening Post* and *The Red Star,* between the Detroit assembly line and the Leningrad work shop, between Coney Island and the Moscow Park of Culture and Rest. This similarity explains why Marx danced with delight when he read of capitalistic technological advancement, not because he was against it, but *for it.* Like Eric Johnson, Marx felt that the blessings of industrial capitalism were not universal enough. To make them so, Marx devised Communism.

THE PRIMACY OF ECONOMICS

The first point of agreement between the bourgeois American and the Marxist Communist is that economic values take precedence over and determine all other values. Thus, economic gain, the law of supply and demand, free enterprise, all of which are economic terms, are used as points of departure in deciding the worth of all personal, institutional, and political policies. It pays; therefore, it's good. The job pays more; therefore, it's a good school. In common opinion and public parlance, the economic yardstick has become the sole universal and unquestioned measuring instrument, so much so that it is unnecessary to press the point.

Many people who resent the ruthless invasion of economics into the domain of education, religion, and human relations, none-the-less concede the pre-eminence of economics over politics. Here they go along with their bourgeois or Marxist neighbors, agreeing that the task of government is strictly in regard to the citizens' economic welfare. Consequently, temporal affairs that *merely* dispose men to or away from virtue, are no longer considered the concern of government. The government, they say, administrates for men's bodies, not for their souls.

Although it is the task of the Catholic Church to administer to men's spiritual needs, she cannot exercise authority over temporal affairs which are the occasion for vice or virtue. If the state refuses to administrate in this regard, then men's souls are left prey to educational and emotional assaults, which, were they directed against their bodies, would be prosecuted as criminal. Unless the government sees to it that temporal affairs are toward men's spiritual good, then there is no authority answerable for the moral state of the nation.

Contrary to Christian tradition, the common good (which it is the task of government to achieve) is no longer considered a *spiritual* good, but a *material* good. This, of course, makes politics the handmaid of economics, appoint of agreement between the bourgeois American and the Marxist Communist.

RELIGION IS AN OPIATE

When Marx declared that "religion is the opium of the people," he did not mean what the Marxist usually claim he meant. He did not mean that the privileged classes were using religion as a drug to keep the underprivileged anesthetized. No, he meant that religion is a *consolation* for the injustices and burdens of life in a capitalistic world. When the classless society emerges, then there will be no more human suffering and no need for the consolation of religion.

The bourgeois American subscribes to the same definition of religion as Marx. In America, religion is generally cherished merely for its *consolation* value. A tremolo on the organ, a theologically inaccurate sermon full of sweetness and light, a studious avoidance of the ghastly details of the Passion and our contribution to it, a sentimental misinterpretation of the Sermon on the Mount, the presentation of a god who always *understands,* demanding no greater retribution than a few coins dropped in the collection box: *this* is the psychological haircut, shave, and massage which the average American erroneously call "religion."

When one goes to the movies, one wishes to be entertained. When one goes to the doctor, one wishes to be cured. When one goes to church, one wishes to be consoled. Failing to satisfy these various desires, the patron abandons the movie and the doctor for another, while the church is abandoned for the psychiatrist's couch.

Just a small charge of militant atheism could blow this parody of religion into the oblivion it deserves, leaving the road clear for Communism. We can expect no martyrs for so shallow a faith, and, besides, there is no *consolation* in martyrdom.

THE MYTH OF PROGRESS

The student of Marx cannot help but notice the contrast in attitudes as Karl proceeds from a discussion of the world as it is to be the condition of man in the eventual classless society. A fairly keen social analyst suddenly becomes a dewy-eyed mystic who attributes to future men superhuman virtues, simply because beeves will be butchered and jams potted in a new and different way. This expected metamorphosis proceeds from a messianic hope, for nowhere is any cause predicted which would warrant so remarkable an effect on human nature.

This false messianism is not a new phenomenon in America. It has its counterpart in the philosophy cherished by hard-headed business men, and also by "starry-eyed idealists" like Henry Wallace. Both Mr. Wallace and his enemies on Wall Street have great hopes for the future. This hope is unrelated to any particular thing that now exists. It is aptly called a "*faith* in the future of America."

With a disintegrating and uncooperative economic machine, the Wall Street mystics each morning set their course for some golden shore. Errors, blunders, unemployment, waste, housing shortages, depressions, inflations, and deflations receive neither a shameful blush nor a repentant sigh. Those things were yesterday, or this morning, but just around the corner a new era of prosperity is waiting. Some morning's sun will paint the windows of the Stock Exchange a golden hue. *The Times* will speak in glowing terms of workers satisfied at their work and insatiable at the store counters. All mankind will have become charitably competitive and courteously acquisitive. Dog will no longer eat dog, nor will the devil take the hindmost. Why? Progress of course! Things always get better, inevitably!

Mr. Wallace has a different but not a dissimilar mystical hope. He believes in the *Common Man,* a man no longer prone to greed or concupiscence. This specie is remarkably unlike anything we (or Mr. Wallace) have ever met, but is apparently to be sired and suckled by the same imaginary parents as Marx's Perfect Proletarian. Upon the arrival of these twins, we are assured that both the state and *The New Republic* will wither away for lack of anything to do.

Unfortunately, the bourgeois American has accepted the pleasanter aspect of Christian hope without accepting Christ, His suffering, and the theological virtue which gives it validity. Their very unwillingness to confess past sins, is the guarantee of future disaster. The most hopeful prescription that they could hear would be, "Go, and sin no more!" but forgiveness (as God designed things) must wait upon repentance.

MASS PRODUCTION

The bourgeois American and the Marxist Communist are pledged to mass production. Every curve and angle on their blueprints for the future presupposes assembly lines and subdivided work. Peter F. Drucker, in an article on the late Henry Ford (*Harper's,* July 1947), with no derogatory intent gave this definition of mass production. "… mass production is not, fundamentally, a mechanical principle but *principle of social organization.* It does not co-ordinate machines or the flow of parts; it organizes men and their work."

In making this clear, Drucker does no more than admit calmly the fact that has been hurled accusingly at the factory system for many years by both Catholic and non-Catholic thinkers. The fact that it is an organization of men moves it out of the sphere of expediency into the sphere of morality. Careful consideration of the entire problem has convinced some Catholic social think-ers that such a system of social organization is fundamentally immoral. It is against the nature of man. Mere preoccupation with the question of wages, hours, and working conditions will do nothing to remove the innate evils of the system itself. More than that, an increase in wages and leisure to men accustomed to the degradation of mechanical slavery tends, if anything, to corrupt them more. Mass production breeds irresponsibility; increased income and leisure broadens the area over which the irresponsibility can be spread.

As Ducker points out, this social organization is not at all confined to the factory. The Luce publications use an assem-bly line technique in editing their magazines. The Army used it extensively for logistic purposes. Office forces have become an assembly line experience. Its effect upon Catholic religious worship would make an interesting and appalling study for any liturgist, and might at the same time make clearer the need for social reform as well as liturgical reform.

Getting used to mass production, physically and psycholog-ically disposes men to Communism. What had to be accom-plished by revolution in Russia, a country hardly touched by mechanization, could be conceived undetected and mature rap-idly in a society already accustomed to regimented irresponsibility.

A MASS MENTALITY

It is the end of industrial capitalism and the end of Marxist Communism to reduce society to a mob of co-ordinated automa-tons. The men who devised both schemes were sufficiently pene-trating to see that men will use their minds, inconvenient though it might be. They discovered, however, that mental preoccupation with *particular* things only slightly impaired the mechanical pre-cision of the man-tool. In addition, this concern with particulars had the twofold advantage of creating initiative (desire to *have* par-ticular things) and keeping men from thinking about universals.

You see, thinking about universals means to be philosophic and "such men (says Shakespeare) are dangerous." An automaton may safely ask "What, where, when, or how many," but for him to ask "Why," would mark him out as a radical and disgruntled automaton.

Advertising has succeeded in keeping the bourgeois American mentally concerned with particular things, preserving him on ice until some demagogue may find it useful to thaw him out. Each new gadget, soup, or best seller postpones the day when he might ask the questions, "Why am I here? Where am I going? What is the purpose of life?" in answering these questions men would differ one from other, each finding a peculiar distinctions men would differ one from the other, each finding a peculiar distinction in a specific calling. Concern with particular things on the part of the individual produces in the collectivity a mass mentality.

For example, a political leader might say, "we are entering an era of prosperity." Each man concerned about particular things will feel that "prosperity means more particular things to be concerned about. Hurrah!" this is the mass-mentality reaction. But the philosophic mind will ask. "What *is* prosperity? Is it a quantitative or qualitative condition? What has it to do with happiness which is a spiritual thing?" You can see that that kind of reasoning is ill-adapted to a society of automatons.

CONCLUSION

Communism is a universal idea. Its roots lie in too great a concern for the things of this world. Bourgeois Americanism is rooted in the same oil, and unless it is transplanted, the fruit it bears will be the same. The representative of the F.B.I. fingerprinting Communist party members may wake up to discover that he himself subscribes to the same errors. In our anxiety and vigilance to barricade the door against Communist infiltration, we may have left open the windows of our hearts and minds to the same enemy.

ED WILLOCK

What It Means
To Be a Catholic

EACH AGE HAS ITS SPECIAL DOCTRINES OF the Church that are paramount for it. In the first centuries, they were the Unity and Trinity of God, the Divinity and Humanity of Christ; at the time of the Reformation, they were Grace and the Sacraments, and so on. These doctrines were studied and debated by the great minds of the times. It is not easy to preserve purity of doctrine. From the very first, men went astray. It is remarkable, when one thinks of it, that right in the time of the Apostles themselves, among their own disciples, false teachers arose. The Epistle of Saints Peter, Paul, John and James battle against deviations from Divine Truth. It is the great prerogative of the Church that she is the depository of Divine Truth.

What is the doctrine that is the center and core of Divine Truth today? Maybe there is more than one. If so, there is probably one that is principal. What is it? Divine Truth is not simple arithmetic or geometry, which can be learned, remembered, and handed on to others. The long history of error reveals that quite plainly.

What is the most important doctrine of the Church for our day? It goes without saying that this is a very serious matter. We cannot go into this from all angles; there is one phase well worth our study. For some years past, a wonderful fire of zeal has come into being. It has spread widely, and continues to grow. This apostolic zeal, this flaming thirst for the spread of God's kingdom on earth will be satisfied with nothing short of the universal reign of Christ and God. The numbers, everywhere, the devotion, enthusiasm, work, sacrifice in all classes, clergy, religious, laity, must gratify the Holy Father and warm his heart.

Now here is where doctrine comes in. People cannot preach the truth and spread it unless they know the truth. If they are going to spread the Gospel to those outside the Church, they must know the truth themselves, and know the minds of those whom they instruct.

Again, let us insist, this is not at all easy. They may have the Faith, they may be sincere. That is not enough. They must have an understanding of the precise doctrine or doctrines that will convince others.

Not only is it difficult to present doctrine pure, taken by itself. This difficulty is aggravated and intensified by association with those outside the Church and breathing the same air, seeing things in the same light. This can happen to the very ablest and best. It can happen to a whole community, a whole country, and, of course, without the Catholics knowing it. They think they are all right. No matter how good a Catholic a man is, no matter how pious, how hard a worker for the conversion of souls, for Catholic action in any of its branches, he cannot ignore doctrine. His mind, his life, his work, must be firmly grounded in a clear intellectual grasp of fundamental truths. After all, what makes a man a man is his reason.

This whole matter was brought forcibly home to me when I came to my position here in the University of Saskatchewan, and had the responsibility for the Catholic students here. The trouble was not on the social side. That could be handled in a fairly satisfactory way. What should be given them by way of instruction? The time available for it was very limited. The students are all sorts, women and men, old and young, country and urban, single and married, some educated in Catholic schools, others in public schools, with little or no religious instruction. Outside of philosophy classes (and there it was only a small proportion of them), the only opportunity for instruction in religion was in the sermon at Mass on Sundays. Fifteen or twenty minutes was all that could be allowed.

That does not seem much. Still, twenty-eight sermons each year for three years, eighty-four sermons; and one hundred and twelve for four years — that is a lot of talking, quite a chance for instruction.

But what to give them? There was no time to be wasted, every minute had to be utilized. It had to be really and truly streamlined.

If you think I sat down one evening in the quiet of my room and planned it all out, you would be all wrong. It has taken me five years. I think I have it now, and that is why I am writing this article. If I can do so, I should like to help others.

The germ of a right idea came early. The students lived among Protestants (by Protestants I mean all outside the Church). Their friends were Protestants. Why were they Catholics? What did it mean to be a Catholic? If their friends did not ask them that day, they would ask themselves, almost unconsciously, thinking what they would say if they were asked. There was no point in giving the answers to the ten thousand questions which Protestants could ask about the Church; fortunately, there was no time to try, although that is what the students like. Even the great dogmas — how could one attempt to deal with them?

But that one question: Why are you a Catholic? If you have that, is not that enough? What answer would I give myself?

I conducted a meeting of a group of men for an hour each Sunday. They called it a forum. It was a Catholic discussion group. There were thirty to forty men in it, of all classes: teachers, lawyers, doctors, business men, workmen, mostly well educated and of a quite high intellectual average. I would place them against any similar group anywhere in America for intelligence, and for the knowledge and practice of their religion. This last year the group discussed three questions: why Protestant do not come into the Church; why Protestants do come into the Church; and lastly, why Protestants should come into the Church, or what does it mean to be a Catholic? I will not go through the answers given. I let them do all the talking. It all boiled down to this: Catholics have a better chance to save their souls than Protestants; the Catholic Church is a better church than a Protestant church; we are all trying for the same place, only by different roads, and our road is better.

These were not the only ones from whom I sought the answer. I have talked with any number of people. It is always the same. The Catholic Church is better, a Catholic with the aid of the Sacraments stands a better chance. It is a difference in degree. There is no yawning gulf between them.

To understand the difference between Christianity, that is the Catholicity, and anything else, it would be hard to find a better way than to look at St. Augustine's experience as he described it in *The Confessions*. One day he was a pagan; the next day he was a Christian. It was more gradual than that but the contrast was as great. In his search for Truth, he found many good things among the pagans, especially among the Platonists. In them he found "though in the very words, yet the thing itself . . . that in the beginning was the Word and the Word was with God and the Word was God. . . . But I did not find that the Word became flesh. . . . I did not read that in due time He died for the ungodly."

It is the Incarnation that makes Christianity, and makes the Catholic Church of God. To know what it means to be a Catholic, a man must understand what took place when the Son of God took human flesh. In learning about the nature and life of the Christian man he must constantly come back and look at *that* Man that was Christ, and then turning again to the Christian man he will see what he is from his likeness to the Word made Flesh. It would be difficult to insist on this too strongly. Man is made up of body and soul. When an individual body and an individual soul come together in union there is a human being, a man. In all cases other than that of Our Lord there is a human person. The Church teaches that in Christ there was present a human soul and a human body but not a human person. When we say a person, we mean a being endowed with intellect and will, capable of knowledge and love, and able to live its own life of freedom within self, without being forced by something from without. Personality is the final perfection of human nature. Intellect and will exist in the soul. We can imagine a soul and a body coming together; until they actually come in contact, they do not possess the perfection of human personality; neither of them is a human person. Once they meet to form a human being the added perfection of personality appears. When the soul of Christ came into union with the body, in that case and in that case only, the human personality did not appear. There was no need for it. The Divine Personality of the Word was there. Never forgetting this difference in Christ, we can now turn to what is called the supernatural life in man, to the Christian soul.

When the Word became flesh, of course, the Father and the Holy Ghost were there too; they are never separated, wherever one is there the others are also. In human language, we attribute the Incarnation to the Son.

At Baptism, God comes into the soul of the one baptized, whether it be a little baby or an adult. Something takes place that is similar to what took place when Christ was conceived. The Three Divine Persons are there, as really and truly and sub-stantially as they were and are in Christ. The new Christian is a son of God, as Christ was; not completely the same, because in this last case the human person was there before Baptism, and continues afterward. Redemption is attributed to the word, so we would seem to be justified in attributing to the Word a place in each baptized soul similar to His position in Our Lord. The Father and the Holy Ghost are there too.

So, in thought we can contemplate the world of Christian souls, we can see them all, and see Christ at their head. In each soul the Word is there, united with the soul. In Christ there is one personality, that of the Divine Son; in the others the two personalities are present, the human as well as the Divine. All the others are sons of God too, because the Son of God has taken each of them over to Himself and made it His own. They are brothers of Christ, and his co-heirs.

The baptized becomes divine. It remains human, but God dwells in it. Nor does He merely abide there. It is a union of the soul with God. God works through the soul. All the good the soul does is done by God; all, every bit of it, is God's work. Every good act of the baptized soul is God's work. It is not a case of being shared by God and the soul, part God's work, part the soul's. No matter how little you make the soul's work, if you take it away from God you are in error; all good is from God, all. The paradox is that every act of the man is the soul's too. The two work together, they both do the work, but they don't divide in between them. We must hold firmly to this truth, paradox as it may seem. This will have to suffice for now. Baptism is a great work of God. St. Thomas Aquinas asks whether the justification of the ungodly is God's greatest work. The ungodly are all who are not baptized or who are in the state of sin. If we asked if justification of the unbaptized through Baptism were God's greatest work, it would be included in the question of St. Thomas. He answered, "The justification of the ungodly, which terminates at the eternal good of a share in the Godhead, is greater than the creation of heaven and earth, which terminates at a mutable good." He goes on to quote St. Augustine, "for a just man to be made from a sinner is greater than to create heaven and earth . . . for heaven and earth shall pass away, but the justification of the ungodly shall endure." Again, St. Augustine: "Let him that can, judge whether it is greater to create the angels just, than to justify the ungodly. Certainly, if they both betoken equal power, one betokens greater mercy."

In *The City of God,* one of the greatest books of all time, St. Augustine describes the Christian Church in the world. To do this, he has to describe another city, the city of the world. Good men and bad are mixed together, and often indistinguishable to the outer view. The city of God is composed of good men, the sons of God, scattered among the others. It is the same in our day. All that has been said so far holds good, for all baptized man have not fallen into grievous sin. It is not a question of good, pious people who are very devout, attend daily Mass, go to Confession and Communion often. It is true for them, of course. No, it is for all baptized souls who have not fallen into serious sin, or if they have sinned grievously and been reconciled to God. Once God enters the soul in Baptism, He remains there and works there unless the soul turns from Him in sin.

So, the strange fact offers itself of men working together, talking together; God is in one and He is not in the other. Another man cannot notice any difference between them. The God-like man himself does not know that God dwells in him and works in him, that the good deeds he does, the good thoughts he thinks, are God's work in him. His every action is different from the same action of the other man. Whether he does a kindness for a friend, refrains from some impulse to anger, or other temptation, any good he does, any evil he avoids, is infinitely more different from the same acts of the other man than day is from night. This is because he is like Jesus. Every simple act of Our Lord was different from similar acts of other men, because He was God; and the Catholic man is like Him. God works in him. He cannot glory in it; he had nothing to do with God's bestowing this sublime privilege on him. It is God's free gift to him and why God chose him is His secret.

God is in all things, and everywhere. It is a way quite different from the way He was present in Our Lord from the way He is present in Christian souls. He is present in all things by His immensity and His power. He made all things, so He present in them as their cause, as Shakespeare is in his works. Further, God maintains things in existence, so He is present in all things, by His power keeping them in being. His presence in the Catholic soul is entirely different. There He enters as a friend, in person, a loving friend, resembling the loving presence of God in Christ. There is mutual knowledge and love, as between friends. It always comes back to this. God would like each man's knowledge and love of Him to grow to perfection, and quickly; He would like all men to come to perfect knowledge and love of Him here on earth. But He will not force the soul, not as a rule. He is patient, and not displeased with the average Christian who does not advance far on the way to perfect union with God in knowledge and love. The average Christian may not say many prayers, he may be very ordinary in his life, yes, less than ordinary. As long as he obeys the law of God and so does no serious evil, God continues to abide in him. It is an interesting speculation to consider a baby baptized, then brought up outside the Church and growing to manhood, a maturity, without ever knowing that he had been baptized, or had anything to do with the Catholic Church. Suppose he never commits a grave sin? Once God comes to the soul in that personal way, when the Three Divine Persons enter and unite with it, only sin turns them out. Naturally, such things cannot be examined empirically! Still, striking instances such as this do occur.

The Catholic Church is not just one among a number of churches, even if it were reckoned the best of them; nor is it one among a number of religions. It stands alone. Between it and anything else there is an immeasurable abyss. The Pope did not arrange things this way, neither did the Bishops or the priests who so ordained things. It was Christ in His inscrutable wisdom who taught this, and founded His Church. Why He did it thus and not otherwise, only He knows. God is above all laws, and can make exceptions to His own regulations. He laid down Baptism as the normal entrance into the Church. He can come to men and sanctify them without formal Baptism. On occasions He has made exceptions like that, but Baptism is the normal way for God to come into the soul and make it holy. We have good reason to think that such special cases are rare.

The Catholic does not wait until he dies to be united with God. That union takes place immediately at Baptism. It continues on all through life, and after death still continues on into the Beatific Vision. It is the self-same life with God; it is eternal life, and it begins here at Baptism. It is like a plant. The seed is planted in Baptism and it grows and develops during earthly life. In some it grows very fast, in rarer cases it reaches the stage of perfect union with God as far as is possible in this life. In others the growth is slower, and the flower and the fruit do not come until the next life. But it is the same eternal life with God.

And this is what it means to be a Catholic. This is the central doctrine to teach students, or anyone else. It does not mean the end of learning. That will never come to an end. Even the angels in heaven will never plumb the depths of the riches of the wisdom and the knowledge of God. But an adequate grasp of the meaning of the Incarnation and its reflection in the souls of men will throw a light on things human and divine and will guide men in union of knowledge and love with God.

HENRY CARR, C.S.B.

THE LATEST SENSATION

Isn't it nice to be able to sit
　　At home and watch the batters,
And see Joe DiMaggio get a hit,
　　And pretend that it actually matters?

The Blessed Virgin Is Mother to the Russians, Too

It is not enough to gather in great numbers around the altars the Blessed Virgin, there to lay offerings, flowers and petitions. That is even more need to renew our moral conduct in public and private life, for thereby we lay that solid foundation on which alone rests the structure of domestic and civil life, a structure of domestic and civil life, a structure not fragile and tottering but homogeneous and endurable. (Pope Pius XII)

NOTHING GREATER HAPPENED ON MAY 13, 1917, than the visit of the Queen of Peace to three ordinary children at Fatima, Portugal, yet it made no news flash, no headline—just as unheralded as a Boy's birth at Bethlehem, yet the world records its time from the birth. Generations to come (if we let them come, for between birth control and the atom bomb, human life is worth little) will recall that day with great joy. Our Lady came to remind us like the kind of Mother she is, to pray, to ask God's help to be good for it is not easy to be good unaided. Then she asked us to offer up our sufferings to her Immaculate Heart in reparation for our sins. How inadequate our penance seems when confessing our sins! The saints were compelled to great austerities and penances to quiet their consciences which made vivid the enormity of their sins and God's Mercy to them. Our Lady asked, "Do you wish to offer yourselves to God in order to bear the sufferings He wants to send you as a means of reparation for the sins which offend Him as a means of supplication for the conversion of sinners?" It is only the old "deny yourself daily"—"Take up your cross and follow Me."

We have to be reminded that we are baptized and are now children of God, for our memories are dull. We are materialists. We do not live by our Faith, nor are we faithful to our duties, nor do we love God or our neighbor. Talk about washing dirty linen in public! Don't you think we Catholics ought to blush with shame, knowing that our sins stink to high heaven so that His Spotless Mother has had to come down, first at La Salette in 1846, at Lourdes in 1858 and at Fatima in 1917? St. [Louis] Grignion de Montfort has said that if Mary were better known, Her Son would be known and loved. If this is so, and the Church approves his writings, let us hasten Mary by reading of these many apparitions.

The prayer the Blessed Mother asks for is the rosary said daily by families, all together. Just imagine everyone meditating — perhaps on the Holy Family begging for a place to stay December 24 and, quite weary from house hunting, being given a stable. Could anyone who meditated on the mystery leave an extra bedroom go unused or a ten-room house empty when there are so many in need of a home? Imagine the revolution that would take place if Christians prayed with the mind and heart and not only with the lips. Most of us have lost the knowledge of sin, we live soaked in it. It screams from billboards, subways, newsstands, front pages, radios — till it no longer shocks. We grow smug because we think that what we do is little compared to another's sin.

By prayer and penance, we shall draw God's Mercy for our own and our neighbor's sins. Our neighbor is he who is most in need of our mercy. Are not the Russians in need of our mercy? Do you recall the city of Sodom, in the Old Testament, that was about to be destroyed but Abraham intervened? He begged God to spare the city if fifty just men could be found. And the Good and Merciful Lord of the Universe willingly replied that He would (as if He delighted to be saved from carrying out His Justice). After feverishly searching everywhere, the Holy Prophet sheepishly admitted that he couldn't find fifty, would forty do? Again, it was accepted and the conversation continued in like vein till the number was ten. What a hard time Abraham had searching for ten just men! (So many of us think sin is of the twentieth century, even thinking it was easier to be good years ago.) Abraham held his breath while God, Who made man in His own Image and Likeness and gave him Paradise to enjoy, graciously admitted that yes, if only ten just men were found, He would save the city and restrain His just anger. In 1846 at La Salette, France, Our Lady said it was her constant prayers that held back God's Avenging Arm and It was very heavy. It is one hundred years that she has been begging us. At Lourdes and at Fatima the message is the same: *Pray and do penance for sinners.* And here is her glorious promise: "If my requests are heard, Russia will be converted, and there will be peace." Since Russia is not yet converted, we know "ten just men" have not been found to pray and do penance. How admirable is the awe-ful patience of God! How long will He wait?

War is the result of sin. Only one is without sin — Mary Immaculate. We are weak but she is strong as an army set in battle array and unlike all other armies cannot be vanquished. De Montfort says, "It is with the Heart of Mary that the New City will be built in truth, justice and charity." Mary must rule all hearts, then Jesus will rule. If each Catholic in America consecrated himself to Mary and *lived* the consecration, America would be a Christian nation, Russia would be converted, and then we would have peace. Don't be afraid of the seeming hopelessness of such a big job. We must pray for big-things for the needs of individual souls, for the community, for the nation, for the whole Church. What greater need is there than conversion of Catholics to "live as sincere, convinced, integral Catholics" (Pope Pius XII)? The world has tried conscription, conferences, atom bombs, spent billions, killed and ruined millions, but it has not tried Christianity! And it is our fault, we Catholics, that the world is not Christian. Not just the priest but every lay person is obliged to be apostolic. We are like Lot's wife. We want to be saved but we look back to sin and then we cannot move.

Let us renew our moral conduct in private and public life and thus build a solid foundation for domestic and civil life. Picture families at peace. Husbands and wives being patient, never speaking sharply, being considerate, each outdoing the other in sacrifice for their children who are obedient and respectful. And at night all pray together, thanking God for their blessings. But what do we see in the average family? Husbands and wives quarrel, children selfishly think only of their own desires — one to a move, one to a dance, one at the radio, one not talking to another in the family.

I have my own life to lead! . . . He is lazy. . . . I am not going to be a slave to my family. . . . He can't hold a job, just a bum. . . . . Why did he get married if he can't afford a baby? . . . That's his worry, not mine. . . . Give them the rent? — why? I was going to buy a new dress. . . . He doesn't like me, why should I help him? . . . Their house is always a mess and there is so much to do when you visit them. . . . I know children mess up a house but I want a real vacation. . . . I must save for my old age. . . . Who will take care of me if is got sick? . . . Charity begins at home (and you can be sure it is rarely in the home of a person who utters it). . . . I don't want to be poor and go to a charity ward. . . . Can't send food to Europe. . . . Should eat leftovers — economize — are you kidding? . . . I work hard and I need the best. . . . I eat what I please. . . . It's my money. . . . Pay more money to my workers? . . . I pay all my competitor is paying. . . . Share the profits! . . . They're mine. . . . Let the workers become owners. . . . You're a radical. . . . I don't care what the Pope said. . . .

Love the Communists? . . . Don't you know they killed the priests and nuns and hate the Church? . . . They should be shipped to sea and drowned. . . . I'll go to war any day against Russia. . . . Convert them? . . . They are hardhearted like the Jews. . . . Sure, I know Christ was a Jew but you know what they did to Him. . . . I am not prejudiced — one of my best friends is a Jew, but she's different. . . . If you worked with them, you'd hate them too. . . . Pray for them like St. Stephen whose prayers converted to St. Paul? . . . You're a fool! . . . Bet you even think the colored can be civilized. . . . I know they have a few good scientists, musicians, dancers, singers, but they're the exception. . . . They shouldn't be lynched for raping a white woman? . . . They deserve it. . . . It isn't justice? . . . . Look what they did to Archbishop Stepinac . . . It's worse when we are unjust for Tito does not pretend to be Christian, but we say we are, then we allow our colored brother to be murdered. . . . Is it rape or the color of the woman that you're thinking of? . . . You're too idealistic. . . . Do unto others as you want them to do to you? . . . Be practical!

Yet the beatitudes were given to the ordinary crowd as a practical guide to holiness by the God who made us and knows of what we are capable with *His help*.

All things we want done to us we must do to others and can with God's help. Peace on earth was promised to men of good will, which means God's Will. Most of us live by what we desire at the moment, but God wants us to live by His will. The trouble is we don't ask — that is, pray fervently enough. A New York subway ad last Advent pictured a man of "good will" because he had the "good taste" to buy the company's product. This is as bad as people saying daily, "I had a good time," when they mean "I enjoyed myself because I did what I wanted" or "doing bad things because I wanted to do them." If we don't want an atom bomb used against us, we shouldn't use it against any other country. We should protest our country's doing so and feel called to do penance for this national sin.

The children of Fatima had this vision of hell where sinners go who do not repent: "Our Lord showed us a great sea of fire which seemed under the earth. Immersed in those flames were the devils and the damned. They were like transparent furnaces floating in this fire and carried about by the flames which came from them. Clouds of smoke were falling on all sides like sparks from a great fire; the cries and signs of sorrow and of despair were horrifying and awful. The devils were distinguished by the horrible and repulsive shapes of animals terrifying and unknown, but transparent and black."

The sight lasted only a moment and the children said they would have died of horror but they knew the Blessed Mother had told them they would go to heaven. Scenes from battles, the atom bomb, the horrible Texas City disaster sound very much like hell. It is the Devil's job to make us feel there is no hell, that, that he isn't tempting us. How can we resist a temptation if we are unaware it is a temptation? The Blessed Virgin complained that more would go to hell because of the sins of the flesh. Boldly *Life* printed recently that "no fashion is ever successful unless it can be used as an instrument of seduction," and then had pages of the fashionable, immodest styles our Catholic women will be seen wearing.

Mary, the Blessed Virgin, is Mother to the Russians, too. And she is the truest Mother that ever lived! Not till all her children are happy, till she has formed perfectly all parts of the Mystical Body of Christ, will she be happy. The Blessed Mother desired Russia to be consecrated to her Immaculate Heart. Now Mary is speaking to us. You have the Mass, the sacraments to be holy. My children in Russia are suffering and are misled to hell. Their souls are starving. Their government has taken away their priests so they have no Mass and no Sacraments. Could you not pray for them? Could you not make a sacrifice and offer up the Mass and Holy Communion the first Saturday of every month in reparation to my Immaculate Heart? Say the rosary that Saturday too, and meditate at least fifteen minutes on one or all of the mysteries. Is this too much to ask of you busy people?

Nothing you do, no sacrifice is so little that it will not help souls in need of mercy. Don't wait till the Church is persecuted everywhere and in the catacombs before you start filling the churches, your hearts with God, your days with prayer. Do your duty, whatever it may be, teaching, being a mother, a nurse. Perform all your actions from a motive of pure love of God and ever to see God in your neighbor. Your daily prayers will save souls, especially your Russian brothers and sisters. Be not hard-hearted. Pray also for Joseph Stalin (how unlike his namesake, yet grace changed the prosecutor Saul into the Apostle Paul), for Gromyko, Molotov, for the millions in Russia who want peace as much as you, nay more than you. I know! I see their hearts. And they are suffering. Can you not have mercy and pray for them? Sacrifice a little of yourself for them. Do not eat That Body and drink That Blood and then close your heart to your Russian neighbor.

Let us pray with the Pope. "Give peace to those peoples separated (from the Church by error and discord, particularly those who have professed a special devotion to God so that no house was without its venerated icon — now put away in hiding against a better day); give them peace and bring them back to the one fold of Christ, under the one true shepherd." Baroness de Hueck Doherty once told how, in Russia, upon entering a home, a visitor always greeted the icon, representing God and His Mother, then turned to his host. This was in the days of Holy Russia. We could imitate the Faith they had. How many of us would take time out to greet Christ, when we enter a home, instead of not even noticing a crucifix on the wall — if we are lucky enough to find one prominently displayed at the entrance. Don't we hide our crucifixes in a dark corner of the bedroom? Are we ashamed of Christ?

Mary is the Mediatrix of All Graces. She will not distribute all these ample graces until we, her children, cooperate by prayer and penance. Russia will be converted, she promises, and there will be peace if we do all that she asks. There are some who say all this talk of Fatima is overrated, that this devotion to Mary detracts from God, but do not be misled. De Montfort's canonization last July 20 holds up his teaching, the *True Devotion to the Blessed Virgin Mary*. That is it. The more we know and love Mary, the more Her son Christ is loved.

JULIA PORCELLI

Heavenly Houston:
Hub of the Hemisphere

"PAPER, MISTER?" THE TIMID NEWSBOY WAS
making just enough noise to sell his papers, but not enough to
disturb the cop on the beat.

"Paper, Mister?" A man in rancher's clothes emerged from the
swinging doors of the Opera House Bar and said, "Here, boy!"

Running up eagerly, the boy handed him a paper and saw him
reach for a nickel. Then a shot rang out from across the street
and the man gasped as he quietly wilted to the sidewalk at the
newsboy's feet, clutching the paper in his left hand and a nickel
between the thumb and forefinger of his right.

Glancing across the street, the newsboy saw a tall man leisurely
descending the courthouse steps and adjusting his hip equipment.
The boy's eyes returned to the lifeless form at his feet and saw a
rivulet of blood trickle across the newspaper and underscore a
headline: HOUSTON HAS FORGOTTEN GOD, SAYS
EVANGELIST.

Thoughts tumbled into the boy's mind as the bystanders
silently collected. That's my nickel, thought he, and this is a
big opportunity for me. If I loudly and persistently demand
my nickel I will make a hit with the local bigwigs always on
the lookout for a youngster with a tough appreciation of the
business-usual angle. There will be publicity and a good connection for me.

Then he heard the witticisms of the bystanders. "A good hundred yards," said one, "And smack dab in the heart — damn good
shootin'." "I saw him reach for his rod," said another. "He was
only reaching for a nickel," laughed a third.

But I just can't do it, decided the boy, I feel too sorry for God.
He must be awfully ashamed of us all. So he stood silent and

pondered the headline as the corpse was carried away — nickel, newspaper and all.

IN THE BEGINNING, GOODS

My early recollections of Houston are clustered around that incident. It may serve to show how business, finance, marksmanship and murder, grim humor, grim preaching and a deep sorrow for God have all worked together to make Houston what it is today: a metropolitan area with over a half-million people thoroughly regimented to the requirements of a republic under capitalism, and with no culture that cannot be measured in dollars and cents.

Just as a physician may diagnose smallpox by scrutinizing one of the festering pockmarks on a human body, so may a Christian diagnose the illness of the national body politic by examining any one of our metropolitan pockmarks, such as Houston. But that has been done many times before, so we shall not go into it here.

Instead, let us take a glance at Houston's beginnings. To do that we dash out to Harrisburg, mother of Houston, now a one-street business section just within the southern limits. There, a little over a century ago, the Allen brothers, realtors of that day, named their new sub-division after General Sam Houston, hero of the shortest revolution on record and first man to be duly elected President of the Texas Republic.

It seems that historians are not in full agreement as to the why and the wherefore of the Texas revolution. They are divided in regard to one version, which is the most realistic and unpopular. It does not detract from the glory of the august personages involved, but it does serve to show the influences of business on Houston's very beginnings.

According to this version, the chief characters — Sam Houston, Santa Anna and Andrew Jackson — were all Masons. Mexico's Antonio Lopez de Santa Anna was an unsuccessful revolutionist who had been encouraged in the belief that the Texans would help him unseat the Catholic Mexican government. When he

marched into Texas with his army, he didn't get the cooperation he expected, and he started shooting people right and left.
This was just the opportunity Sam Houston had been expecting,
so he ran Santa Anna down at San Jacinto — a few miles from
Harrisburg — and captured him. (The monument that stands
there today in honor of Houston's victory is one of the many
architectural erections of Jesse Jones, Rajah of Houston. It is a
few feet taller than the Washington Monument.)

But to get back to the brother-Masons who figured in this version. Nearly everyone wanted to execute the captured Santa Anna
for his extreme cruelty. Perhaps Sam Houston wanted that, too,
but, after all, they were brother-Masons. So, Houston appealed
to another brother-Mason, his good friend Andrew Jackson,
that great exponent of the famous humanitarian slogan, "To
the victor belongs the spoils." They managed to get Santa Anna
safely out of Texas and gave him a start in the chewing gum
business in New York. There were signs of money in chicle even
at that early date. Of course, this version is not covered in the
orthodox history books, but it serves to show that the economic
angle — always sub rosa but uppermost in Houston's currency
culture — was on the job at the very beginning.

THE TRINITY OF SPIRITUAL HOUSTON

Perhaps no American city has outgrown more slogans than
has Houston. Her remarkable industrial growth has rapidly rendered them obsolete. Back in the roaring twenties the slogan
changed from "Where 17 railroads meet the sea" to one of greater
scope: "Where 18 railroads meet 30 steamship lines." Later on,
this became entirely inadequate and the slogan "Gateway to the
Americas" was adopted. At present the opinion is divided as the
most appropriate slogan. Some like "Gateway to Latin America,"
while some prefer "hub of the Hemisphere."

For a spiritual picture of Houston, we must first take a look
at her impressive skyline, then put a clothespin on our nose and

take a trip down the ship channel to inspect a half-billion dollar's worth of industrial installations — all the while listening to the endless legends of the fabulous Jesse Jones. The skyline, the ship channel and Jesse Jones; they compose the trinity of spiritual Houston — and there's not any mystery about. We wonder what would happen in the world if each Catholic had half the faith of the Jesse Joneses.

SEEK YE FIRST THE KINGDOM OF GREED

It has been often repeated that there's nothing the matter with the world — it's just the people in it. As the next brush-stroke in this spiritual picture, let us reverse the old saw and pin it on the people of Houston. There is doubtless plenty the matter with the city's physique, but there is not much the matter with the half-million people who live here. It would be hard to find a more loyal and lovable half-million anywhere on the planet. In fact, their loyalty has reached the proportions of a vice. The average Houstonian cannot so much as join a labor union without feeling uncertain about whether he is violating the principle of "don't bite the hand that's feeding you.' The feeling he has when listening to a labor export clashes sharply with the feeling he has when buying his groceries on payday. The payday feeling nearly always wins. That's why unions have had no bed of roses in Houston.

There are many other things, however, which do receive plenty of support. The chief of these is the list of religious cults and sects found in small type in the Texas Almanac. Perhaps no city in the country is a better hunting ground for this list of greedy heresies than is the city of Houston. The bait used is common to most; it is almost invariably as awesome and terrifying a perversion of Apocalyptic eschatology. But it seems to get the recruits. There are almost a hundred different sects and cults waxing fat in this city on the fear and ignorance of their fellows. Sometimes we wonder if it isn't simply Protestantism going through the process of destroying itself.

These people cannot compare in zeal with the fanatics of early American sectarianism. Today, they are loyal, in a large degree, to our national religion: indifferentism. One may work for months in office or factory and then discover by chance that one's fellow-worker devotes his spare time to the unobtrusive propagation of one of the myriad forms of modern Gnosticism. Each of these sects claims a corner on all truth. As one jovial Irish priest recently pointed out: St. Paul found in ancient Greece an altar to an unknown god. There may be one in Houston, but I doubt it. Every sect I've seen claims the only leased wire to Heaven.

CLASS LINES AND TYCOON CULTURE

The next brush-stroke in this spiritual sketch requires us to divide the half-million into three classes — along the usual economic lines — in order to get them into the picture. First, we have the class that revolves around the group of oil tycoons, sundry other millionaires, and their sycophants. Politically, they support a staunch republicanism that insists upon being called democratic. They have carefully schooled themselves in the art of taking everything for granted. With the help of Dale Carnegie, they have learned to conceal the crudities of snobbery and we are very good at winning friends and influencing people.

The citizens in this class, who are masters in the use of slightly bored expression and the tilted eyebrow, perhaps deserve the most credit for Houston's big-name status. (The city ranked tenth in building construction during the first six months of 1947.) To them, many things are a bit naïve, including practical Catholics, whom they place in the same category with small boys preoccupied with Mother Goose. Nothing upsets them but a rubber check.

Next, we have the management class. This includes corporation executives, small business men, professional people, white collar workers and others of the well-known bourgeoisie. In Houston, this class has been, during the past half-century, the poorest boring ground for Communists in the entire United

States. They little dream, however, of the great success the fellow-travelers have achieved through them in accentuating the class lines. Upon them the timeclock, the hourly wage and other implements of the divide-and-conquer technique — spawned in underground Russia during the last century — have not been lost.

These people like to point with pride to the city's educational rather than to its industrial growth. Rice Institute, University of Houston, St. Thomas University, St. Anthony's Home, and many other cultural mileposts make them feel that we are getting somewhere. Most of them believe that something is wrong with our whole educational system, but it is more of a vague feeling than a conscious criticism, and so does not interfere with the time-honored practice of muddling through.

Others of this class feel very good, not so much about what Houston is doing as about the things Houston has quit doing. They will remind you that the city's one-time notorious red-light district has long since been gone and forgotten, and that public morals have consequently improved. In a sense, this is true. Sex immorality is not advertised as it once was; it is more genteel, more sophisticated, more involved with marriage and divorce, and it is much more sanitary. Moral improvement seems to have little to do with these changes. Expediency appears to be the motive involved. To those who still yearn for the "good old days" of blatant debauchery, there is Galveston, fifty miles away, beckoning to the sporting element.

These people will likewise point out that men are no longer shot down in cold blood on our streets, simply because the police department is efficient and free of graft. They skip the fact, meanwhile, that the Houston policeman is perhaps the most overworked and underpaid in the country.

They will admit that we used to have a lot of religious bigotry here, but they are quick to remind you that no such condition exists today — that Catholic, Protestant, Jew and pagan all live together harmoniously and put their shoulders to the wheel.

True, but we are silently mindful of the fact that Catholicism gained a bit of respectability only when there arose in its ranks at least one oil millionaire to vie with the others — who like to parcel out culture with plenty of strings attached.

A considerable number of this class insist upon referring to the thirty-odd thousand Mexican inhabitants as Latin-Americans. They do so, of course, through a false sense of charity, little dreaming that the Houston citizen of Mexican extraction is not a bit ashamed of his ancestry. Mexicans are considered in the same dark, Jim-Crow light with the Negroes. One way in which this is evidenced is the daily list of marriage licenses in the newspapers: the bride is never a "Miss" if she is a Mexican or a Negro, she is just plain Juanita Gomez or Sally Washington. Even Catholics have been known to miss Mass rather than attend it in a Mexican parish when time would not permit them to pass through the slum to a more distant and a more acceptable church.

Now let us take a glance at the third class, the click-punchers and hourly wage earners. If I give more space to this class, it is because I am a member of this class myself, and also because this class is perhaps of more importance to the future. The orchardist gives more thought to seedlings than to large trees — though laden with fruit — whose seasons are numbered. Everyone knows what a banker thinks about, or what a business man or a doctor thinks about; and it is not hard to detect the mental processes of a professor or a shipping clerk or any others of the two foregoing classes. But what does the assembly line worker think about as he puts on bolt number 9,999? What does the turret-lathe operator think about as he turns out hundreds of little metal gadgets with the monotony of a robot? We know that thought is always the forerunner of action. The answer to this question may be an important key to the future. Mr. Joseph Stalin seems to think so.

When I became a clock-puncher six years ago, I was amazed to discover that our system offers no pipeline for the utilization of the vast amount of wasted mental energy of industrialism and no safety valve for the release of the pressure it generates. I devoted considerable time trying to find out what this thinking was all about.

Of course, I have no statistics regarding the morals of workers; but from observation alone, it seems certain that there is very little heavy drinking among the workers — especially since reconversion and the stabilization of industrial personnel by the weeding out of undesirables. The average clock-puncher has apparently given up drinking for more and better thinking, if the subjects of his conversation are any criteria. Some of them work thirty-nine hours per week and go to college at Uncle Sam's expense, as a result of their military experience. This affects their conversation and the thinking of the other workers. The subject of religion, however, is rarely discussed because it always gives rise to violent prejudices. There are a few exceptions, however, for in every shop may be found a very slight sprinkling of Christian-minded men — but slight!

Although my clock-punching experience includes immense shops employing thirty thousand men, I am at present working in a small twenty-five-man shop which turns out an apparatus for impregnating the drinking water of cattle with the necessary chemicals not found in the vegetation of the locality.

Once I asked my co-workers, "What is the purpose of life?" Although in the group were two "born" Catholics, no one got the right answer. Robert, the Negro janitor, and a good Christian (Protestant), was the nearest with the following reply: "To answer that we have to go back to the beginning — God. Didn't He make man for the purpose of beautifying the Garden of Eden?" One of the Catholics, well educated and a student at the University of Houston, illustrated the modern type of hedonism with his reply: "The pursuit of happiness." Another summed up his reply — and the basic dogma of modern creedless idealism — with one word: "service."

As on the other classes, the atomic age has had a sobering effect upon the clock-punchers; but they are keeping their feet on the ground. They haven't forgotten that Nobel claimed the basic power of the universe when he discovered dynamite and then dashed madly around the planet trying to prevent its destruction by war. They haven't forgotten that the ancient Chinese had the same dire thoughts about gunpowder and used it for fire crackers only. And the more Christian-minded of the workers — like Robert — know that the basic power of the universe is not nuclear fission but moral fission, a power given to us in the revealed truth of Jesus Christ, a power that will work for us or against us, in reverse, if we spurn it.

THE HOPE OF HOUSTON

Well, this is the spiritual atmosphere in which the Catholic Church finds itself in Houston. Its sixty thousand members (many of them Mexican and enough of them Negro to keep two Josephite high schools going full blast in the colored section) are still less than one-sixth of the population. Nor have they dented the prevailing non-Catholic atmosphere yet, although the annual Christ the King parade does bring the Faith into public view, as do also the many works of mercy in which the Church is engaged.

The Church so far has been laying its foundations and making a steady gain. But the field is more than ripe for the harvest and all Catholics will have to become laborers. That means especially the laity. The sort of apostolic zeal that would raise eyebrows in the East is familiar religiosity to the inhabitants of Houston. Jocism wouldn't have to work under cover. And Jocism is just the sort of movement that could start a chain of moral fission in the dying embers of Protestantism here, that would transform the city before it is too late.

Houston — the Hub of the Hemisphere — affords many opportunities. The Chamber of Commerce is right!

GEORGE R. VAUGHAN
Houston, Texas
Feast of St. Dominic, 1947

DELIGHTFUL IMAGINARY SAINT

The adventures of St. Imaginus, holy monk of the Order of St. Simplicitas, are fascinating and delightful reading. The good Saint approaches material and spiritual problems with humility and unusual sagacity. To solve the financial difficulties of the Astonished Stockbroker, St. Imaginus takes up a collection from the poor of the parish, with happy results for all. The Obstinate Cow, which refused to give milk, was given into the hands of a group of Sisters where the good Saint hoped, "their modesty and the gentle discipline of conventual life might have a salutary effect on one of so wayward a temper." The most significant accomplishment of the holy man was the invention of a game whereby a group of wicked young men in the Saint's parish lent themselves to some virtuous exercise. The Saint's superior, the Parish Priest, was so moved by the remarkable change that he suggested, "Let's have a cricket match and take up a collection for the church debt."

There are twelve tales in this volume. Mrs. McGuire ought to write some more stories about St. Imaginus. He's very instructive in his whimsical way and highly entertaining. There are very good illustrations by Betty Arnott.

JOHN MURPHY

BOOK NOTES

Margaret Munro, who integrates her saints' lives with the Christian view of history, has a new study out of *Blessed Clitherow*, an English Reformation martyr. It's excellent. Especially recommended for mothers.

J. F. Powers' *Prince of Darkness* is the best book of modern short stories we know. The characters are moral men and dramatically authentic. His measurement of their goodness and badness is made by the compassionate yardstick of human experience warmed in the heat of God's Mercy. As befits the times, the author has a chip on his shoulder, but a close look reveals that it is a chip from the True Cross.

A new book on the liturgy is *With Christ Through the Year*, by Father Bernard Strasser, a Benedictine. It's especially good and interesting because of the wealth of liturgical symbols used to illustrate. The subject matter is the Church Year. A little heavy going for the casual layman, but good for liturgists and indispensable for any good Catholic library.

Lord give us always this Bread. St. John C. 6: v. 34

Lord
give us always
this Bread
which is yourself.
To check in us
our greed for
Earthly things.
Madly we crave
for power and possessions
and selfish play and gain
on which we starve to death
and know it not.

Lord
make us like to
this Bread
which is yourself.
That we be
strong,
courageous,
other Christs.
Make us go forth
unselfish, Christ-filled vessels
to let our brothers share
of Your great plenitude.

Lord give us always this Bread.

*O Savior,
through the prayers of
the Mother of God,
save us!*

—Prayer from the Russian Liturgy

INTEGRITY

November, 1947~Vol.2, No.2   25 cents a copy

Subject: Death

DEATH IS, AS IT ALWAYS WAS, the focal point of Christian teaching. If Christ be not risen from the dead, all our hope is vain. Isn't it odd, then, that we continue to wrangle with factions of various shades of pink over who can provide the best housing project?

It would be better to take a stand on "pie in the sky when you die." It's pretty obvious now that this generation is not going to get much justice or peace or continued comfort in this life and that the prospects for future generations are dim. Maybe there is much more of a market for eternal life than we suspect. Why not let the pagans meet us on our own ground for a change? Even communists and millionaires die — and are afraid to die.

As our society sinks lower and lower into despair, it can't help riveting its attention on death. Suicide evidences this is one way, the false gaiety of the night clubs in another, mass escapism in still a third. Hollywood keeps putting out movies dealing with the hereafter — all vague and reassuring. But still men sink themselves in luxury and superficialities to keep from thinking of the inevitable conclusion of their plans, and insofar as it is possible by words and wealth and stealth, the fact of death is hidden from the public eye. The tension is relieved by a mania for murder stories, in which death is amusing or puzzling, life cheap and never very life-like.

It's time the entire subject was brought into the open. The whole enormous contrast between Catholicism and paganism then stands out. We have tried to show it in two descriptive articles (THE DEATH OF A TRAPPIST and DEATH IN A

MODERN HOSPITAL) by a monk and a nurse respectively. Or again it can be seen in the degradation of the burial of the dead from a work of mercy to glaring and vulgar commercialism (THE CASE OF THE PAINTED CORPSE) and in the half-embarrassed awkward atmosphere of a modern wake (THE UNWISE).

The second of Father Carr's two articles on the spiritual life appears in this issue (THE CHRISTIAN LIFE). It reminds us of what the world is tempting us to forget — that in the spiritual life too, we must die to ourselves in order to live.

It is even possible to carry the analogy of death into a consideration of modern society, as Peter Michaels shows in THE DEATH OF WESTERN SOCIETY.

Death is morbid only in the absence of Christ. But without the Hope of Him Who rose again from the dead, and promised that would also. The world can only offer such feeble assurance as that Rabbi Liebman in *Peace of Mind,* to the effect that death isn't so bad because most people are unconscious at the time.

By contrast we can say to our bewildered and disheartened brethren: "We will show you that death is the entrance to a much better life. We will teach you how to live so as to die well. We will give you reason for clinging to your unloved husband, for bearing with your querulous, aged mother, for refusing to bend to dishonesty in your business, for holding to truth to the loss of a college degree, for enduring poverty and popularity and heartbreak and war and famine and cancer, and even martyrdom."

The reason is Christ, Who said, "He who believes in Me, although he be dead, shall live; and everyone that liveth and believeth in Me shall not die forever."

THE EDITORS

DEPART O CHRISTIAN SOUL

Out of this sinful world, in the name of God, the Father Almighty who created thee; in the name of Jesus Christ, the Son of the living God, who suffered and died for thee; in the name of the Holy Ghost who sanctified thee; in the name of the glorious and blessed Virgin Mary, Mother of God; in the name of blessed Joseph, the illustrious Spouse of the same Virgin; in the name of the Angels, Archangels, Thrones, Dominations, Virtues, Cherubim and Seraphim; in the name of the Patriarchs and Prophets, of the holy Apostles and Evangelist of the holy Martyrs and Confessors, of the holy Monks and Hermit this day, and let thy abode be in holy Sion:

Through the same Christ our Lord.

Death of a Trappist

ANYONE WHO WANTS TO KNOW SOMETHING about the death of Trappist must first have a reasonably clear idea of how a Trappist lives. Unfortunately, too many have (at the back of their minds) a completely impossible conception of the Trappist monk dwelling in the semi-darkness.

The monk who abides in these uneasy shadows is a lanky ghost of a man, half starved and not a little frantic with too much concentration on the skull he always has before him. His hands are calloused, but not with useful labor, only with digging his own grave. He digs a little bit out of that grave each day, heaving profound sighs and crooning over and over to himself "*Memento mori! Memento mori!* Remember that thou shalt die." As he is by now getting on in years, his grave is well over a hundred and fifty feet deep and he wears himself out climbing in and out of the thing on moss-covered ladders. When he finally emerges at the top he fumbles around for his discipline and begins beating himself on the shoulders with it, doubtless in an honest effort to speed the coming of the day when he can stay in the earth for good and all.

It is extremely fortunate that such people never existed. But the mere fact that the legend of their existence is so tenacious is something that makes Trappists insist on being called by their true name. The word "Trappist" is an outmoded nickname for the Cistercian Order of the Strict Observance. It comes from La Trappe, an important monastery of the Order in Normandy, where the famous Abbé De Rance instituted a reform of the Cistercian Order in the seventeenth century. The Cistercian life is nothing but the Rule of St. Benedict in the strict interpretation that was given to it by the founders of the Abbey of Cîteaux, in France, in the twelfth century. Penance plays a great part in the life, but only as means to an end. The Cistercian is a contemplative monk, and the fullness of the contemplative vocation is an intimate knowledge of God experienced, as it were, in the darkness of faith and in the contact that is established by a pure and supernatural love. The chief aim of the monk is to empty himself of all the trivial and accidental concerns of worldly existence in order to live for one thing necessary, *frui Deo,* the perfect love that draws us into such close likeness to God that we are said to be transformed into Him, lost in His infinite perfections as a drop of water is lost in a galloon of wine.

Obviously, a lugubrious and monomaniacal insistence on the physical aspects of deaths to the exclusion of everything else would be fatal to such a vocation, because it would be almost entirely irrelevant.

If Trappists have been accused in the past of creating an almost entirely mortuary ideal of the spiritual life, it is the fault of the romantic and pre-romantic movements in French Literature. Poets like Chateaubriand got hold of De Rance and his Trappists and turned the whole thing into a macabre grand-opera according to the taste of his day. But Chateaubriand is one of the most completely unreliable writers that ever existed. He wrote a novel called "René," part to which is laid in the United States. He shows us, for instance, his hero meditating on the brink of Niagara Falls and listening to the "roaring of the crocodiles" on the rocks below. So don't believe anything Chateaubriand tells you about Trappists.

Last year, Father Anselme Dimier, a Cistercian monk of the Abbey of Tamié in the Alps, brought out an interesting little book called *La Sombre Trappe* to trace all these absurdities to their source.

Once all this has been said, to clear the air, we may consider how a Cistercian monk looks at death, how his life prepares him to meet death.

There is no need for a man to make his drinking cup of a skull in order to remind himself of the elementary fact that he will not live forever. But, nevertheless, we all need to be reminded of it. It is one thing to admit, intellectually, the obvious truth that the world can never offer us satisfactions that cannot be taken away; but it is quite another thing to live in practice as if temporal things were not ends in themselves and worldly pleasures were not destined to last forever. Scripture reminds us, "In all thy works remember thy last end and thou shalt never sin." (Eccli. vii, 40.) The implication is that this is one of the things we most easily forget — otherwise there would not be so much sin.

People who have the misfortune to live outside of monasteries, in a world that seeks only to enrich itself by the exploitation of every appetite that can be forced beyond the limits of order, really need some systematic method of reminding themselves of death. One might think that the spectacle of a society that is in its last agony ought to be a forceful enough reminder. The smell of decay that comes out to every movie-theatre and night club ought to be enough to keep on thinking of the grave. But it takes grace to detect these things and too many people have lost their spiritual sense of smell. . . .

Inside monasteries, above all contemplative monasteries, it is different matter. Once he is out of the novitiate, the Cistercian monk seldom needs to make a systematic meditation on death, although discursive reflection on the "last things" is such a fundamental weapon in the spiritual life that everyone will keep it in reserve against an emergency. But a contemplative who forced himself, with too much of a stubborn insistence, to keep picturing decaying bodies and so forth, would certainly ruin his spiritual life. The aim of all discursive meditations is to convince us of our need of God and of God's power to help us. When these convictions bear fruit, as they soon do, in a permanent affective "thirst" for the presence and contact of God, meditation is absorbed into a fundamentally simple and uniform interior "attitude" which accompanies the monk everywhere. His soul becomes like a sunflower that follows the Divine source of all light and warmth wherever it goes. *Oculi mei semper and Dominum.* Its eyes find rest only in constant, silent looking towards God. That is the essence of its prayer.

More than by any system of meditations, this "attitude," this permanent spirit of prayer, in which prayer becomes as natural and easy and as simple as breathing, is nourished by the liturgy and by spiritual reading.

A Cistercian could really afford to dispense with formal mediations on death altogether if he follows the liturgy. The Cistercians recite the Office of the Dead on an average six times a month, and there are four "solemn anniversaries" during the year, when the Office of the Dead and a Pontifical Requiem are sung. The monks know the principal parts of that office by heart, and could sing whole passages of the chant without need of a book. Consequently, it may often happen when one is out at work in the woods and fields that some snatch of chant from one of the responsories of the Office of the Dead may start going in the monk's mind. There is a peculiar pathos in the sober and austere Gregorian melodies of that office, and it brings out all the humility and helplessness that pleads to God in the tremendous words: *Libera me Domine de morte aeterna. . . .*

What is much more fruitful for the soul is a Cistercian funeral. Hardly a year goes by in which someone in the community does not at least receive the Last Sacraments. In fact, Cistercians are much more often anointed than buried. The grace of the Sacrament may keep an old Brother going for another year or two. But in any case, the whole community assists at the ceremony, praying and chanting psalms. You learn more about death by coming face to face with it, through liturgical prayer, than you would get out of books and meditations if you plugged at then for a hundred years.

When a Cistercian actually does die, he is taken down to the monastic church in procession, in an open bier, dressed in his religious habit. He is placed in the middle of the choir with a candle and crucifix at his head and a stoup of holy water at his feet, and until he is buried, two monks will always be sitting by the body, day and night, reciting psalms alternatively in a low voice. They take turns to perform this office of charity. At night, they take long two-hours shifts, so that the constant going and coming may not wake up the others in the common dormitory.

Sometimes these night wakes fall to the lot of a couple of novices and there is no question that it makes a deep impression. The huge, empty church becomes very dark and very silent, and the body in the open bier does not seem to lie as still as it ought to, in the flickering candle light; but you are also very much aware of another presence — when the sanctuary lamp also flickers before the tabernacle — and taking your courage in both hands, you start murmuring the Latin words of the psalms. It is strange how quickly the time goes, and when you suddenly realize that your watch is over and that you must return to your straw mattress and bed of planks, you are somehow unwilling to leave. While you were praying there, a deep and sane and vivifying sense of fellowship was growing up that linked you in some mysterious way with the soul to which that body once belonged and to which it will one day be returned. And as you walk through the dark echoed cloister you are no longer afraid of death or of dead bodies, but you see them as they are — sad, inevitable things whose sorrow is not without an infinitely merciful remedy.

Praying for the dead in this real and down-earth fashion brings you an almost experimental appreciation of the doctrine of the Communion of Saints. One really feels bound in a mysterious and powerful solidarity with these souls, a solidarity that will last forever and which is rich and fruitful in its exchange of graces. The souls of the monks who have died before us come constantly back to our minds and we offer the thought to God in the chalice of some Mass that is being celebrated somewhere in the world at that moment; and in return we feel that many favors have come to us from those who have been grateful for our prayers.

Perhaps the most dramatic thing of all is the way the monk is buried. He is lowered into the ground without a coffin, without a bier. The monastery infirmarian goes down into the grave and covers the face of the corpse and as soon as he climbs out again the earth begins to fall and the dead Cistercian disappears. And yet to many this simplicity and poverty have something about them that is immensely clean in comparison with the nightmare of fake luxury and flowers with which the world tries to disguise the fact of death. It is not the burial of the monk, wrapped in no other shroud than the clothes he always wore that is frightening; no, it is those embalmed corpses, roughed up to look like wax-works and couched in satin cushions, that terrify the heart and make even the healthy smell of flowers horrible by the association they contract with undertakers and funerals.

But the most important thing is not how the body of a Cistercian is buried; that is trivial. The real question is: how does such a soul enter into the presence of God?

The death of a true contemplative is inevitably the crown of a life contemplation. It is the final liberation of a soul from all that impeded it, prevented it from seeing God, held it back from the perfect possession of God and restrained its swift flight to the center towards which it has tended with the almost irresistible gravitation of pure love. At last, the body breaks like a web and the soul leaps out, exulting like a flame into the blinding glory of God.

There is no purgatory for the perfect contemplative, because there is nothing left; his liberation is complete. He has had his purgatory on earth, in years of searing, scorching interior trials, years of charity and humility and poverty and obscure labor that have stripped him of layer after layer of selfishness and imperfection, and reduced him to nothing in his own eyes. He has been delivered from his own selfishness and his own callousness and hardness of heart by years of sacrifice. The penetrating fire of infused love has made all selfishness intolerable for him, and it has purged him slowly and inexorably of every desire for created pleasure, every ambition, every hope of fame or power; for years, all these things have been intolerable to him. The things that cause other men pleasure have caused him nothing but pain, because of the agonizing sense of their insufficiency they brought with them. The things that seem to slake other men's thirst only increase his to a burning torture, and he has long since learned to refuse them all, as Christ refused the vinegar on the Cross. He has long since acquired that wisdom which is best recognized, according to St. Bernard, by the ability to rejoice in suffering because then we truly know we are rejoicing for no selfish motive, but only in the will of God. He has now arrived at that perfection of love which seeks nothing for itself and yet even loves itself perfectly in God, seeing itself as God sees it, loving itself because it holds within itself the perfect reflection of God, cleaned of every stain of selfishness that makes one different from God.

When the last shred of that self-love which constituted a barrier, a difference between the soul and God, has fallen away, the likeness of the soul to its Creator and Exemplar is now perfectly restored; nothing remains but the confirmation and sealing of this union in the glory of an everlasting vision, an everlastingly perfect mutual giving of the soul to God and of God to the soul.

There has never been written anywhere a better description of such a death than that which St. John of the Cross gives us in his *Living Flame of Love.*

> The death of such souls is very sweet and gentle, more so than was their spiritual life all their life long, for they die amid the delectable encounters and sublimest impulses of love.... For this reason, David said that the death of saints in the fear of God was precious for at such a time all the riches of the soul come to unite together *and the rivers of love of the soul are about to enter the sea, and there are so broad that they seem to be seas already.* (Peers trans. Iii, 135)

That is the way the saints, the contemplatives die. Does that mean that such perfection and such a going forth to God is reserved only for those who have lived all their lives in a cloister? Far from it. It may well happen that a Cistercian monk, by failing to make the proper use of the means God has put at his disposal, may be far less perfect than some poor housewife, some laborer in the world. But the secret of that sanctity is the same: the perfection of charity which is most easily and quickly reached by union with God in contemplation. Is this an extraordinary grace that is reserved only for special souls? No! Perfection and the means to perfection are accessible to all, and those who want to travel the road that ends with such an entrance into the glory of heaven have only to set foot on the road by praying to Him Who said ask and you shall receive. They have only to begin leading an interior life and the rest of the way will be made plain.

THOMAS MERTON
Abbey of Our Lady of Gethsemani
Trappist, Kentucky

A POOR FINISH

John Algernon Abbott, had made it a habit,
    To plan every thing in advance.
He properly bathed, and carefully shaved,
    When asked to a tea or a dance.

How sad to relate, that prudence so great,
    Should fail when 'twas needed the most.
He died on fine morning, without any warnings,
    And gave up an unprepared ghost.

The Death of Western Society

IT IS ONLY WHEN YOU SEE OUR WESTERN society as dying that you can make any sense of it. If the contemporary scene is viewed as a deathbed scene, things fall into their right perspective, all the way down to the death rattle contributed by the ignorant but voluble optimists.

This is not an original idea, of course. The obsequies of the West have been celebrated by many a modern thinker. The trouble with most of the learned diagnosticians is the same as the trouble which affects many a medical doctor these days — they do not realize that they are in on the death of what has been redeemed by Christ. They are always comparing ours with the dead civilizations of the modern world, which inevitably corrupted and died, inevitably and mysteriously. Much of the mystery and all of the inevitableness of our plight vanishes if you see that we are attending the last hours, not just of a splendid civilization, but of *Christendom*. The proper comparison is not with Rome or Egypt or even Babylon (despite many a similarity); it is with the Christian man. Societies are not men, and they don't have immortal souls; they will not go to heaven or hell. Nevertheless, a striking analogy can be seen between the death of a Christian and the death of Christendom.

THE ALL-IMPORTANT MOMENT

The most important thing about death is that it is the final decisive moment of a man's life. Our life-paths are marked by temptations to mortal sin (the only real crises), at each of which a man turns decisively toward God or away from God. At death, he has the final choice and so, no matter how the world may choose to gloss over the end of a man, that moment is not ignored by those who know its true significance. God and the Devil contend then for a man's soul. The Devil puts up quite a fight, unless he has long had the case sewed up. But God provides special graces that are even more powerful. In the natural order, God has provided the "fear of death" which comes over a man in his last illness, presaging the end. It brings even the most superficial and worldly people (indeed, especially these people) sharply to the consideration of eternal things and moral judgment. It is a last-ditch opportunity to turn to God's mercy through fear, if one has failed heretofore to seek Him through love. For many, it is the last opportunity to save their souls.

Quite different and far greater is the supernatural help Christ has provided in the Sacrament of Extreme Unction, which, along with Confession and Viaticum, prepare a person for a holy departure from this life, and give graces to resist the Devil's temptations. The last anointing also restores health if it is for the good of the soul.

There is one other Christian aid to dying and that is, as traditionally taught by the Church, that Our Lady intercedes especially at that time — "Holy Mary, Mother of God, pray for us sinners now and *at the hour of our death.*"

THE DEVIL AND MODERN DEATH

In view of all the assistance God gives the dying man, the Devil is relatively powerless because all he can do is present temptations to the imagination. Yet working subtly (when will we learn that the Devil is much cleverer than we are?) and indirectly, Satan has arranged to win the deathbed battle without even bothering to be present. This is how it is done. First of all, he has arranged for a conspiracy of silence about the impending death, under the guise of virtue. Produced as we all are today of a sentimental, residual humanitarianism, it is almost universally considered dastardly to allow a person to prepare to meet God. You must not tell him he's dying because it might kill him, is the curious line of reasoning that is taken. Yet for millions of materialists sodden with self-indulgence, what could be more salutary in the light of eternity than to spend several weeks contemplating the certainty of dying (provided, of course, that the love of God and the prospect of heaven are also made known). It would be enough to sanctify very mediocre material. As long, however, as hospitals and doctors and families continue dogmatically to hold their secular views, the Devil can take a vacation.

There is also the little matter of sudden death. The chances of a man's dying in an automobile accident or an airplane crash or by bombing, atomic or otherwise, are very good today — vastly greater than ever before. If we were all holy people it wouldn't matter if we were caught unawares, but the likelihood is that some of us could use a few minutes for an act of contrition, and so, at present, sudden death plays into the Devil's hands. Indeed, he may have helped invent some of the instruments thereof.

Finally, we find modern man lavishly provided with opiates to ease the pain of dying. This is no simple situation. There appears to be a great increase in suffering (notably cancer) combined with a loss of the ability, physical and spiritual, to accept it. It would indeed be cruel to take away a cancer patient's morphine.

Yet morphine, besides killing pain, gives people a false sense of well-being. A man who is, in fact, about to die feels that his demise is remote. That "fear of death" which God provided in our very nature, as a last salutary warning, just doesn't operate. Does it make very much difference? I have heard of a nurse whose cancer patient was in great physical anguish and even greater moral peril, highly unrepentant and openly contemptuous of God. There was no way of reaching the woman through the pleasant haze of morphine, so the nurse stopped giving morphine, merely going through the motions as larger and larger doses were ordered by the doctor in response to the woman's complaints. As soon as the morphine wore off, the fear of death penetrated even the pain. The patient repented, made her peace with God, and then was given morphine again to ease the last few hours. What this nurse did (her moral duty) would be considered a shockingly cruel and professionally unethical thing. To allow pain for the salvation of a soul is considered immoral — by people who are beginning to commit murder as the latest in pain-killers.

THE MISSPENT LATTER DAYS OF WESTERN SOCIETY

Let us now get to our analogy. Like men, societies die; also like men, they sin mortally (that is, men collectively turn against God). Our society has committed more and more serious sins. There was a terrible break with God when Christendom split and half of it fell into heresy. But a sort of recovery was made. There was another bad break following the Industrial Revolution when men turned their hearts to the accumulation of wealth. But we marched on down the wrong road, still far from its dead end, still able to turn back. Then we turned God out of peace conferences and we turned fervently nationalistic. Again and again, we drove out the religious, confiscating their monasteries. The going got tougher, what with a succession of wars. And we got desperate in sinning, using incendiary and finally atomic bombs. All along the way until now, there has been the possibility of repentance and recovery. But nothing is different. Christendom is dying.

The patient has cancer. It is riddled with it. It is diseased in almost every cell. This being so, the disease may be studied locally. An X-ray of the local cancers of Kansas City or Miami would be almost as revealing as one done in Budapest or Chicago or Moscow. The remedy can also be applied locally — but we'll come to that. Our society is dying and is in a state of mortal sin.

OUR LADY

That's why Our Lady keeps appearing. It is the hour of our death, so she comes to tell us that she is interceding for us, and pouring graces upon us. She says what you say to a dying man: Repent, do penance, pray, turn again to God. You don't approach a dying banker with a new loan system or a dying mayor with plans for a housing project. You don't suggest to a dying not-so-good housewife that she try a new vacuum cleaner, or approach the dying drunk for membership in AA. It is too late for new beginnings in the temporal order. Nothing remains except to repent and make your peace with God. The Blessed Virgin is the only one giving sensible advice these days.

THE FEAR OF DEATH

God is trying to give us the fear of death too, by showing us as clearly as possible that we are dying and that we have sinned. Everything men touch fails these days. Men can't make peace. Men can't stop divorce. Men can't cure or prevent insanity. Men can't distribute the world's goods properly. The financial world is a mess; the economic world is a mess; the political world is a mess. And the atom bomb hovers over us. But why go on? Our heart is failing; our lungs are almost finished. Everywhere there are aches and sores.

God's mercy in our days wears a disguise to the ordinary man. Just as the fear of death is merciful in the case of the dying man (because it is a help to salvation), even if it isn't pleasant, so God is gracious now in allowing our plans to fail. Were we only sick, or even healthy, He would show His love in good harvests and soft rain. But in the hour of death, supreme mercy is to defeat man's hope whenever he seeks it where there is no hope; so that in the end he may turn to his Only Hope.

US AND THE DEVIL

What's happened to the Devil? He's taking a vacation some-place, because he has everyone working for him.

First, he has all the doctors and relatives around to assure us we'll be up and about in a week or two. All those newspaper men, teachers, public officials and professional statesmen who make a life work of reassuring us, belong in this group.

Then the Devil is tempting us to sins of the flesh and unbelief on a colossal scale. His major helpers here are the advertising men who thrust upon us a multiplicity of luxuries to tempt us to sins of the flesh. As long as we are drowned in the comforts and gadgets of materialism, we will be too stupid to see how late it is. But should we try to rise to the intellectual level, we shall only encounter the stupidities and inanities of a decadent and diseased liberalism, calculated to drive us all into the oblivion of dementia.

But the Devil's big work is in opiates. We are doped with spiritual morphine until we have developed a shocking unconcern, a false sense of security. It is done with movies, radio, mass circulation magazines, comic strips. A man need never think, be silent, come face to face with the God Who will so soon judge him.

HYPODERMIC NEEDLES

When a man is dying a nurse will often startle him back into a few minutes of life with a hypodermic needle. In a way, fascism and communism are like hypodermic needles. In a dying, lethargic people they stimulate momentarily a little life through force and emotional fervor. It looks strong, but it can't last because it is an artificial stimulation. Yet we who hate these tyrannic movements had better see them for what they are — an unlovely alternative to death. What have we to offer in their place?

THE LAST SACRAMENTS

It is too late for any purely economic or political nostrum, even a good one. It is interesting to speculate as to whether Belloc's and Chesterton's Distributism (which was essentially an economic scheme) might have saved England and possibly Europe, if it had been applied in, say the 1920s. One wonders if some correction of the ills of usury wouldn't have mended many matters once. Quite possibly so. While we were still suffering from acute mortal sin, there was the possibility of turning back, and whereas it would have to be accompanied by a turning back to God also, it could possibly have started with economic reform. Chesterton's insistence that we go back to where we took the wrong road, and his insistence also that it had to be done very quickly, were probably quite correct at that time. It was the eleventh hour. We didn't turn back. Now it is midnight and we are dying!

There is only one hope for society now, and that is hope in the supernatural. The doctors have failed. Let the priests take over, including the lay priesthood of Catholic Action.

First of all, there must be penance, as is beginning to happen as men are turned by grace from sinning and worldliness to beg for forgiveness. This includes the converts, and the cradle Catholics who are being converted from mediocrity to some comprehension of the meaning of their Faith.

After the turning away from evil to God comes the strengthening of the Eucharist, which more and more people are receiving daily.

And finally, then, these people who have turned away from a corrupt world to purify themselves by the Sacraments, administer to our dying society a sort of Extreme Unction in the form of Catholic Action. Whether it uses the Jocist technique or some other integrating form, this Catholic action must have the effect of dynamically restoring supernatural grace to our dying world. Therefore, all purely natural efforts will fall infinitely short of the vitality necessary. When a billing machine operator invites the engaged girl at the next desk to an explanation of the Sacrament of Matrimony, she is applying a bit of the holy unction, as is the contemplative nun doing penance for the world, and the Belgian Jocist restoring purity to a factory, and the Mexican Catholic Action girl teaching catechism in a remote, priest-less province, and the Hungarian martyr before the forces of communism, and the mother who starts the family rosary.

But the man, whoever he may be, who goes all out for the Republican Party, or rests his hope in a planned society or in our banks, or International Business Machines, or free milk at ten o'clock in the morning, or the Marshall Plan, or what not, is impotent to help dying Christendom and probably will hasten its corruption. And Grover Whalen, with his plan for New York City's Golden Jubilee, is only fiddling while Rome burns.

All men ought to love God with their whole hearts, but at this crucial point no one ought to make his religion a subsidiary or part-time occupation. The only people who can save society are those who give their whole lives to doing so. In the midst of secular occupations, the prime concern will be to speak of God to those with whom they are associated and to try to turn the institutions of society once more Christ-ward.

IF IT IS FOR THE GOOD OF THE SOUL

If our analogy holds, that something like Extreme Unction is being applied to our dying society by Catholic Action and other vital movements, then the patient should recover its health, *if it is for the good of its soul.* That must mean that if the effect is strong enough and successful enough and soon enough to turn men and institutions decisively Godward, we shall be spared. There would be no point in saving Western society if it only meant a continued increase in the population of hell — just as there is no point in having children if they are to lose their souls.

How much has to be done to make it worthwhile to save us? No one knows, but it isn't just a matter of numbers — one person in a state of grace plus another person in a state of grace, etc. There is also the matter of re-directing society, which means reintegrating life with religious principles. If then, health is restored, it will come about naturally, as in Extreme Unction, and naturally in this case means through a new synthesis.

Let us therefore make haste, using all our energy to restore things in Christ. Let those who think we are not in a final crisis consider if they are not enjoying a false peace, opium induced. And let us not be like the social workers and nurses (whom may heaven help) who hide the fact of impending death because the patient is "psychologically unprepared" to face it. God does not wait on our good pleasure, let alone our folly.

CAROL ROBINSON

The Case of the Painted Corpse

WHEN HISTORY HAS RECORDED THE STORY OF these times, and seen it all in the context of past and future, one of the noteworthy peculiarities of the age will be the fact that seeking money as an end in itself was regarded socially as something perfectly respectable. The Christian era had its profiteers, but they were recognized for what they were—outlaws. In the era which follows this one, whether it be Christian (as we hope it will), or communist totalitarian (which seems to be the alternative), social activity toward the end of self-aggrandizement, will once again be regarded as unlawful. One of the few remaining traces of the contempt bestowed upon self-seeking in an earlier and more enlightened age, is the current designation of such practices as "rackets,"

Although the universal conscience of our society accepts profit-seeking as respectable, the individual conscience still, to some extent, rejects it. That is why a man may refer to his business while among friends as a "racket," and yet be angry if the same term is assigned to his occupation by a stranger. Taking unfair advantage of one's fellowmen is sometimes applauded as good salesmanship and sometimes condemned as poor sportsmanship. This is the dual morality of the times.

The most remarkable example of commercialization today is the manner in which we dispose of our dead. In this we have the strange juxtaposition of hard-headed business with bewildered grief. No one in society seems to have an answer for the enigma of death except the undertaker, and his answer is a tally sheet edged in black. The cause and the blame for this accepted practice is what we intend to explore in this article. Why has burying the dead (a corporal work of mercy) become a "racket" (an occupation directed to profit)?

THE GRAND FINALE

We choose as a case in point a typical urban Catholic post-mortem ceremony. In this ritual, we see the magnificent and beautiful send-off extended to a child of God by his mother the Church interspersed with the secular ritual of modern burial practices. Like two slender candles of virginal beeswax, the two acts of the Church burn at the head and foot of the deserted temple of the Holy Ghost: Extreme Unction, the oils of salvation, and the Requiem Mass, the offering of Christ's Body and Blood for a soul seeking peace. Banked around these candles, almost hiding them from view, are the garlands and festoons of an age that has failed to see beyond the door of death into the eternal garden of union with God.

In this dramatic finale to the drama of life, there are three leading characters, the undertaker, the bereaved, and the deceased. As death raises the curtain, we see them together. The undertaker is in control. Upon his face we see, mixed in proper proportion, solemn sympathy and resolute purpose. As the first act of the ritual, he extends his condolences; the second act is a tactful but careful perusal of insurance policies. The information he gleans there is his clue. The estate from which his bill must be paid, is the first determining factor in the choice of props. Later, after he has groomed the corpse for its role, his salesmanship will be the second determining factor. The casket will be chosen under his guidance. When that matter is settled, he can proceed, attentive to his trade, unburdened with financial matters.

When we see the corpse and bereaved again, a strange change will have taken place. Both will have undergone a charm school treatment. New clothes will have been purchased and donned. The hair of the living and of the dead will be waved and set. The cosmetician will have tried to produce in one case a spirit of dignified mourning and in the other a spirit of healthful slumber. The corpse, in posture and mien, will portray a man (or woman) sartorially draped for a convention or ball, who has momentarily decided to take a dignified nap in a sort of elaborately quilted and satinized, over-sized and overdressed bassinette.

Usually, the living room of the deceased, unless it were completely overhauled, would serve as poor background for so elaborate a deceit. For this esthetic, as well as for more practical reasons, the glamorized corpse, the bereaved, relatives, and friends, have all been transported to new quarters. This is called a funeral parlor (home, or chapel). The architecture varies according to the artistic imagination of the funeral director. A Catholic clientele seems to prefer "period" furnishings rather than the nude plastic modernity of their more progressive non-Catholic neighbors. The general impression is that of a man who has done pretty well for himself and "passed away" under enviable circumstances.

The customary practice during the hours when the funeral parlor is open to the public is to exchange muttered sympathies with the near relatives, the more common of which are, "He (or she) is better off", "I'm very sorry," "He (or she) lived a full life," "Doesn't he (or she) look natural?" This embarrassing obligation fulfilled, attention is immediately drawn (to everyone's satisfaction) to the temporal and transient affairs of the living. A determined relative may violate the atmosphere by inciting the gathering to prayer. Some resolute parochial organizations have grimly set to work to restore this archaic practice. When it does occur, the embarrassed piety clashes discordantly with the smoothly rendered "Panis Angelicus" disk-jockeyed from some hidden corner by the busy funeral director.

After the "memory picture" has been painted in unforgettable strokes, Mother Church is permitted to intercede on behalf of her departed child. How good God is to have designed the Church as a perpetual guardian of reality! The prayers of the Mass for the Dead cut cleanly through the curtain of unreality spun by the ingenious funeral director. When the Mass is over, hired flunkies carry the casket away. The weight of the modern casket relieves the friends of the burden and the grace which

313

proceeds from carrying the body of a saint to his last resting place.

At the grave the web of unreality is spun again. An artificial carpet of grass hides the newly dug earth. The casket is hidden behind mountains of flowers. As a reluctant concession to Christian symbolism, a clod of dirt is delicately dropped on the casket with a silver-plated trowel. The great fact of death that might, were it embraced as an inevitable and merciful act of Providence, lead to a conversion of the mourners to a more penetrating understanding of eternal verities, is instead treated like an unclean creature to be hidden behind the tails of a morning suit.

THE HIGH COST OF DYING

Every year in the United States some 1,500,000 dead bodies must be disposed of somehow. Every family in the United States, on an average, has a funeral every twelve years. Every year the nation spends from $350,000,000 to $500,000,000 on funeral expenses.

Every year some 1,500,000 families are subjected to super-salesmanship in their hours of grief, when their defenses are down, when their "sales resistance" is most low, and when they are least able to think objectively and reason logically. Then it is that sales-minded funeral directors point out expensive, metal-lined caskets, bedecked with satin and all the other fancy fixings that add nothing but to the price of the funeral. That is why, though coffins or caskets may be obtained for as little as $30, that fact will be news to most people.

Nowadays most funerals fall into the $300 to $399 bracket, and the $400 to $499 bracket is the next most frequent. At the Centralia mine disaster, to quote a specific case, the funeral costs ranged from $233 to $1,178.50, with the average $732.78. The United Mine Workers protested bitterly at these high costs, but the funeral trade journals felt the charges were well justified in view of the high wages earned by miners. They apparently feel justified in charging all the traffic will bear.

It is only in our generation that burying the dead has become such a costly and sometimes lucrative occupation. As a result, the number of funeral directors has increased tremendously. The problem facing the funeral industry was one that other industries have faced. Their volume of business (i.e., number of funerals) was more or less fixed; their only solution was to sell more goods. And of course, more and higher priced goods would be an even better solution. This seems to have been a uniform decision of manufacturers, distributors, and everyone in the business. And judging from the advertisements in the funeral trade magazines, the trend is still upward. Apparently, the point of diminishing returns has not yet been reached.

Undertaking generally shares the viewpoint of all big business that service is for profit. This is rarely stated as bluntly as it was by one funeral director recently. His firm had changed its method of charging for funerals. It had been based on a high charge for the casket, which represented the total cost of the funeral. They were worried because the public had become more critical of casket costs and values, comparing them with other merchandise and commodities. They were afraid the casket companies would not continue "providing high and unequitable mark-ups to help the funeral director cover up service charges in the retail prices of caskets." Therefore, he wrote, we changed our way of pricing. The first reason he cited was: "For the very good for which we are all engaged in the business and profession, to make more money."

At the 1947 convention of Pennsylvania funeral directors, a certified public accountant cited some cost figures for a small establishment with about 70 funerals a year. His figures were purely imaginary, he said; but out of his experience they certainly had basis in fact. The average sale, he estimated, would be $335. This would be allocated as follows: Merchandise and supplies, $109; wages $77 (including the owner's salary or replacement cost); and overhead expense $105. This totaled $292, leaving a profit of $42 per "case." On the basis of 70 funerals or "cases" per year, this gave a profit of $2,940 for this small establishments, plus the owner's salary, already included.

It is interesting to study figures quoted by the undertaking business. The cost figures include everything that one can imagine especially the owner's salary. There is cost of "merchandise and supplies," allowance for bad debts, depreciation on buildings, equipment and motor vehicles; insurance, interest on debts, other salaries, etc. There is usually a small profit left, with a footnote reminding one that all "cases" do not afford a profit. The figures carefully ignore the fact that the owner has already taken out his own salary, usually a comfortable living, and the "profit" shown is over, above and in addition to this comfortable living.

THE CASKET CARRY-ALL

Up till fairly recently, the casket carried the entire cost of the funeral. Its cost to the undertaker usually represented about 20% of the retail price quoted the bereaved; the remainder of 80% was supposed to carry all other costs of the funeral — representing embalming use of funeral home and all other services.

This is now a trend away from this, to one of selling the "complete funeral" at whatever the family may feel able or willing to pay. This package buying seems to be the sales plan for the future.

All the technique of modern super-salesmanship is put into the sale of the casket. The other "services" generally fall in line with it. It is not today as it was with the ancient Egyptians, when there were three principal types of "cases," depending upon the type of preservatives, spices, and ointments used. Today embalming is but a minor cost, roughly $30 to $35 of the total, or approximately 10%.

The casket companies advertise on a national scale, plugging their product both with the retailer (the undertaker) and the ultimate consumer. They furnish the funeral director with selling points so he may say the right thing at the right time, and make the best possible sale. To the national audience they offer booklets, so they may do the right thing when the time comes, always featuring fear, always stressing water proof, element proof, moisture proof. Delicate and not so delicate hints are made in the casket salesroom about how unfortunate it would be if Aunt Adelaide were allowed to be exposed to er — ah — worms. So ignorant are many moderns of the facts of death that they do not know that after the soul has left the body, the body naturally corrupts, whether a little sooner or a little later being a matter of indifference to its former tenant.

"THE SIZZLE SELLS THE STEAK"

More and more people are disgusted with the super-sales technique to which they succumbed at one time or another, in the fog of grief and shock. "But you want the best for your dear mother, of course," the routine goes, "and I think I have just the thing here in our special padded-silk bronze casket, with a special price on the Class A weather-defying concrete vault." There is often the veiled implication that unless one is willing to put out all the money possible on such accoutrements, the grief isn't genuine, the tears aren't truthful and love is centered more on the insurance money than the late departed.

This sales technique is carefully fostered by the trade journals of the industry, and by the so-called leaders in it. For instance, one of the feature speakers at the 1946 convention of the National Funeral Directors Association was Elmer ("the sizzle sells the steak") Wheeler, a well-known peddler of ideas on a high-pressure salesmanship. No one attempted to hide the fact that a highly competitive business put a premium on salesmanship.

Some years ago, one of the business trade journals featured an article exemplifying this idea. It was amusingly written, but basically the problem was one of selling higher priced coffins so as to make more money. The answer was a simple one: display only higher-priced coffins. Stock the cheaper ones, because occasionally you may be called upon to furnish a cheap funeral by clients who can afford no better; but make it very difficult for them to ask for a less expensive casket. And the tip-off of the callous, unprincipled attitude of the writer of the article (who thoughtfully did not provide his name) was in reply to a bit of dialogue:

After being urged not to display cheaper caskets, the funeral director said, "but if I don't give my clients what they want they will go elsewhere."

"What," said our hero, "after you have the body?"

Another instance is that of the head of one of our American embalming schools. He was in England some years ago, and was shocked almost beyond words by the deplorable state of the English undertaking enterprise. He decried the old-type coffins they still carried and what he considered their unbusinesslike way of doing business. He made it clear that their aim should be to increase funeral expenditure. It was, he declared, a "merchandising" proposition, and he wished people to "buy a better grade coffin."

COSMETOLOGY AND RESTORATIVE ART

With the emphasis on "display," cosmetology and restorative art are among the most important courses in the modern embalming school, and many other courses are co-related to them. Embalming of itself, for instance, is relatively simple; but when considered in relation to display it becomes more complicated and exacting.

Cosmetology is the important factor. As one embalming fluid manufacturer advertises, "your prestige and your income are determined by the appearances of your cases," and of course that's why you should use their embalming fluid — "to gain greater prestige and increased income."

The purposes of cosmetics in embalming have been listed are follows by one authority:

1. Psychological effect upon the bereaved.
2. To afford a well-groomed appearance to the subject.
3. Retain or develop personality of the deceased.
4. Conceal discoloration
5. To emphasize or diminish certain facial features or prominences.
6. Counteract adverse effects of daylight or artificial illumination.
7. Correction of restorative deficiencies of embalming fluid.
8. As a corrective measure for results of incompetent or indifferent operative technique.

All this gives plausibility to the following, which one author has quoted as an advertisement by a London undertaker:

For composing features — $1.

For giving the features a look of quiet resignation — $2.

For giving the features the appearance of Christian hope and contentment — $5.

FASHIONABLE, EVEN THOUGH DEAD

Together with caskets, there has grown up a whole series of transactions in which the undertaker purportedly is rendering a service, but often service with a profit. This is recognized candidly by the trade journals of the business. Speaking of burial garments, one authority advises funeral directors that the original impression of the body reposing is the slumber room before the casket is selected has much to do with that selection. The better the original impression, he continues, the more a family is willing to spend for a casket, a vault, and for a burial garment. The "memory picture" created by the funeral director becomes a strong influence in the choice of funeral merchandise. The article concludes with this touching thought:

"That there are vast profit possibilities in the proper merchandising of burial dresses is evident by our own success and that of many funeral directors throughout the country, whose experiences served to convince us that burial garments do help sell better caskets."

The national Casket Company, ever aware of the possibility of the bigger and better funerals, prepared a booklet, *Funeral Facts,* for general distribution in 1930. It carried this pertinent advice for the general public when time comes:

"The funeral director generally carries a carefully selected assortment of women's dresses and men's suits . . . They are patterned closely after the garments worn by the living . . . The funeral director is also prepared to match the outer garments with appropriate slips, stocking, shoes or slippers. Because of the increasing use of color in caskets and other funeral furnishings, this ability to carry out color harmony is most important. It gives an absolute assurance that the dictates of good taste and personal preference will be followed in every detail."

THE INSURANCE ASPECT

Costly funerals, as we have them today, are a product of the last century. And during the last century there has been a tremendous growth in the coverage of insurance, so that hardly a family today is without insurance of some sort. The connection between these two facts is not an obscure one, for the modern undertaking business would be impossible without the modern insurance business.

The connection is so complete that many Catholics today consider it a disgrace and a shameful act, almost a sinful act, to make no provision for their burial — financial provision, that is. Thus, they lay by money, through insurance policies, so their families may squander it on $500 funerals. The corporal work of mercy known as burying the dead has been effectively eliminated in practice and despised in theory.

When one considers the degree to which insurance institutions depend upon life insurance for their income, and then cast a glance at the institution of the "memorial industry" which it has sired, we can see how modern institutions fatten upon a kind of sentimental superstition that would shame a primitive savage. The hollow "security" which is the insurance companies' stock in trade is epitomized by a concrete-bedded, bronze-encased, satin-covered corpse, which will soon corrupt as completely and as fully as though it were surrounded by nothing by God's good earth.

Without insurance, does anyone believe it would be possible to have such a tremendous increase in funeral costs as we have had in the past century? A funeral in Boston in 1829, for instance, cost a total of $8, without the coffin. A funeral in New York City a hundred years later cost nearly a thousand dollars, not including $750 for the coffin — excuse, please, the casket, for coffin now has a derogatory cheap meaning.

Within the memory of the present generation, undertaking has developed from an adjunct of local furniture dealers to pretentious funeral homes, in the style of Colonial or Southern mansions, replete, undenominational, and about as religious as a movie theater.

Generally speaking, all this has been financed by small policy insurance — the policies having a face value of less than $500, and on which premiums are paid each week. After all, anyone can afford 25¢ a week, is the reasoning, and you wouldn't want your parents to have to provide the money to bury you, would you? Thus, this type insurance is generally considered burying money, and undertakers are happy to concur.

WHO IS TO BLAME?

The memorial industry and the industry of funeral directing do not exercise a tyranny over the people. The high cost of funerals is not imposed. As a matter of fact, cooperative funeral organizations which cut the costs to a fraction, have not been popularly received. Funeral directors who have tried to discourage inordinate generosity to unappreciative corpses have often met with rebuffs. The case is one of corruption not tyranny.

Burying the dead would not have shifted over from a corporal work of mercy to a business unless the Christian concept of death had become perverted. We do not know how to care for the dead because we have forgotten the lessons of Calvary and the Resurrection. We have become so enamoured of temporal life that we cannot graciously bid Godspeed to a soul bound for eternity. We have not lived in sufficient awe of that God-made image composed of body and soul, to approach with respect the occasion of its temporary disintegration. Most of the blame can be socially distributed. The institution is built by common consent.

THE VIRTUOUS UNDERTAKER

Many an undertaker has earned the reputation of being an exemplary member of his parish and community. Compared with men in other occupations, the function of the undertaker has been generally exercised in a praiseworthy fashion. The point we would like to make here is that the standard of measurement is not adequate. Undertaking is in no way comparable to a business, and it is only similar to a profession by proximity. The corporal work of mercy of burying the dead is essentially a religious act, and the undertaker is the celebrant. This is where his dignity resides. This is the measure of the goodness or badness of his work.

Some undertakers with obvious good will have tried to instigate minor reforms within their field. They have discouraged ostentation. They have displayed true sympathy toward the bereaved, advising economy, and not infrequently giving their services *gratis* when the family was poor. They have been of service in cutting the political red tape so confusing to a bereaved family. They have supported their parish church financially and energetically. This is work well done and meritorious, but it is not a reorientation of undertaking to the position of a corporal work of mercy. It is merely the application of Christian trimmings to a secularized institution.

The responsibility for restoring burial practices to their proper dignity lies chiefly with undertakers. The policy of the customer always being right cannot apply to a work of mercy. If indeed undertaking were a profession, as many of its members claim it to be, it would have to be a profession of Faith. The members of Christ are bound together by Charity, not dollars bills, consequently the measure of their service one to the other should be prescribed by God who is the source of Charity, and not by the man who holds the purse strings. It is sad when a man looks upon a brother in Christ and sees only a customer.

As long as the burial of the dead falls under the authority of the undertaker, he must consider it his apostolic duty to bring it into conformity with the spirit of the Faith. His work is essentially an honorable and holy one. If it has degenerated to a kind of macabre stage performance, only he can restore it. Responsibility and authority go hand in hand.

Because it is truly a *good work,* and because Catholic undertakers are far from unaware of the dignity of their work, a few reforms, a few new customs, would go far toward remedying the situation. For example, if the undertaker and his family assumed as their obligation, a special apostolate toward the dead, daily saying special prayers for the souls of those whose bodies they have cared for, a peace and dignity would soon characterize their lives and works. Were the funeral director to make a habit of his and his assistants devoutly participating in the Requiem Mass, a new integration between the Faith and the vocation would be achieved.

Flowing from this would come greater insight into the social significance of decent dying. Perhaps pious associations of Catholic undertakers could be formed designed to sanctify their calling. Such associations might effectively influence the memorial industry reminding the merchants that dollars and cents are no more than accidental consideration in a work of mercy.

When the undertaker assumes the initiatives, his success will rest in the amount of cooperation he gets from his fellow parishioners and from all those who help him in his work. Assistants, hack-drivers, grave-diggers, must realize the source of their dignity. Local gossip might do well to mediate upon death before they criticize any deviation from the absurd conventions of the times.

Perhaps organized Catholic Action can throw its weight in the direction of decent dying just as it is now active in restoring matrimony to its proper position. Insurance salesmen should not perpetuate the myth that it is a disgrace not to provide for one's own burial Christian tradition sets this up as an honor and privilege for the friends of the deceased to care for his remains, which need not, incidentally, require the huge sums which insurance companies have made possible.

There is a hallowed tradition among Christians that last things shall be first. The apostolic undertaker might be the man to dignify the way we die, as a constant reminder of the undignified way which we live. With such examples being shown, perhaps the customer would, for a change, be right, at least about last things.

FLOYD ANDERSON AND ED WILLOCK

HOT TIP

If you should ever chance to go,
    To those dark regions down below,
You'd find the place with people
        cluttered,
    Who knew which side their bread
        was buttered.

Death in a Modern Hospital

HAVING WORKED FOR OVER NINE YEARS IN A modern American hospital, I have seen it in all its sadness, knowing that it could and should be much more consoling than it is, even to those not of the Faint.

It matters little whether the dying are in a luxurious private room, a semi-private room, or a ward — death when it strikes finds them almost always alone. I remember a world-famous pianist dying with no one near him. The newspapers told of his family's being present, but they did not arrive until long after his demise, and he had feared death and most of those who do think this life is the most important. When the patient is dying the nurse on duty calls the doctor, gives what emergency treatment she can, and then goes on with her other duties, looking in on the patient from time to time to see if life still lingers on.

Patients with chronic and incurable diseases often ask about the true state of their health, but no doctor tells them the truth, in all the years I have spent in hospital work I can only remember one case of a patient being told outright that she was dying, her subsequent hysteria and attempted suicide were a good example for the other interns not to repeat the mistake. It is true, as the doctors claim, that not very many are able to take it.

The average person today, even though he has faith of sorts has been absorbed all his life with the things of this world, without any thought for the hereafter. Consequently, when he feels material is slipping from his grasp and realizes that money is not able to buy what he most wants — health — he inevitably loses his balance. Most doctors are no more spiritually minded than the patients and, since they are unable to furnish patients with hope in everlasting life, they hesitate, out of kindness, to plunge them into despair in the face of death. It is that many die without ever really knowing that they are doomed and thus without putting their houses in order.

When a student approaches the final examination for a degree, he invariably crams and studies to prepare himself for it. His family wouldn't think much of him if he were to forget all about it and get out to have fun just before rushing in to face the examiners, yet that is exactly what families force upon those they love when they permit them to rush unprepared and without forewarning toward the one great examination that no one can escape.

Probably most dying people remember long forgotten bits about God, and fragments of prayers, but unfortunately no one is nearby to whom they can mention such things, and so their loneliness is even greater than it would be if people were able to talk to them of God and religion. Catholics receive the last Sacraments, often belatedly, but rabbis and ministers seldom visit their sick flocks. Evidently, their presence is considered unnecessary until the funeral. So it is that many a human slips into the final coma without help, ignorant of the unknown he must face. In the light of eternity, it might be better to die by electrocution in Sing Sing than of natural causes in the best hospital. No one pretends that the condemned man has led an unblemished life, no one kids him about his expectations in regard to longevity, and the consolations of religion are at hand by law.

Modern man, like his ancestors in the Middle Ages, is still composed of body and soul, but unlike those ancients he pays little heed to the soul. The cult of the body, its comfort, well-being and adornment take up most of his waking hours. Death and decay are never thought of, and when death approaches, it is ignored until too late. How little the soul of man is considered, when such specialized attention or no faith, customarily see only the exterior, only the deceased body. They do not allow the patient to face reality. In their great humanitarian efforts, they do not permit the patient to suffer and, if there is no hope for recovery, they would like to permit mercy killing as the ease-all of pain.

On the list of the Euthanasia Society in New York City are thousands of names of reputable physicians and surgeons, and new names are constantly being added. A list of these names can be obtained, and it is surprising how many well-known men subscribe to this modern Murder Incorporated. What escapes the minds of these men is this: the knowledge of whence they themselves have come, why they are here and, most important of all, whither they are going. They cannot see that euthanasia is the most horrible of all practices society has invented to date, and might well kill the very ones who thought of it as a cure for the sufferings of their fellow men. What is an incurable disease? Many years ago, tuberculosis killed almost all who contracted it, yet today very few ever die of it. The same is true of many other illnesses which no longer take their toll of human lives. Killing the patients takes away the means of studying diseases, thus retarding science, and, if ever permitted legally, will be the death of the nation.

Euthanasia is sometimes practiced in hospitals. A doctor will make use of his knowledge in order to destroy life, and sometimes a family will even ask this of the doctor.

Strange as it may seem, many Catholic nurses, while not outrightly in favor of euthanasia, see its usefulness in cases of agonizing suffering. Living as they do in a pagan atmosphere, their thinking becomes tarnished. Above all, they do not realize the reason for suffering and the uses to which it can be turned.

Families at the bedside of the dying are often very awkward. They do not know how to act in the face of death (they rarely pray or they become so hysterical that they are a great trial to those present). It is their ignorance of all matters pertaining to death that is to blame. In this class, some Catholics can be included, especially those who will not permit their loved ones to receive the last rites for fear of alarming them, forgetting in their false solicitude that Extreme Unction is also a healing Sacrament, and has been known to restore health in grave illnesses.

God is the important goal toward which men should travel — all men, of all creeds and colors and nationalities. Catholic doctors and nurses have a serious moral obligation to help even our separated brethren, and those of no particular religion, to reach that goal. In our pagan age, it is almost impossible for those out of the fold not to commit mortal sin. To let them die without giving them a chance to acknowledge their guilt and to say they are sorry is a grave offence.

In our crowded and under-staffed modern hospitals time is rather scarce and many tasks clamor to be done every minute. This is, perhaps, one reason why Catholic nurses do not get around to giving the dying some of the help they need for the last journey. It is sad that no one ever prays at the deathbed of a non-Catholic. For that matter, many Catholic have died in my hospital without a prayer being said. Only once in the nine years I have been in this place can I remember having seen a Catholic nurse kneel and pray at a deathbed.

The need for integral Catholic doctors, interns, and nurses is great. We need them to teach those around us the true values of life, but especially the reason for man's being and his goal. We need constant reminding that the best way to get to the goal is not by the extermination of suffering, but by extermination of sin. It is not by killing the patient that he is helped, but rather by teaching him to use his pain as reparation for his own guilt and that of others, who through this aid may receive the grace to turn to God.

In our prayers, we all ought to include those dying alone and loose in our over-efficient centers of healing, asking that God may grant them the grace of true contrition.

LEONA M. SEGEBRACHT

The Christian Life

OUR LORD CAME TO CAST FIRE UPON THE earth, which was the love of God, and it was His intention and desire that this fire should catch and spread like a forest fire. In our day, despite the dreadful extent of the ravages of evil, the fire that Christ cast has caught in countless souls. These souls, many thousands right here in America, burn with the love of God; they thirst to grow in His love, to be united to Him in complete and perfect union, and to spread His kingdom everywhere. Only they do not know how to go about it, what to do themselves, that they may grow in holiness and love, and so too, how they can help others. This is a good and sufficient reason for trying, with God's help, to explain how souls can live the Christian life in its fullness, how they can grow in the knowledge and the love of God, and be united with Him as perfectly as is possible in this life.

There are ever so many ways of doing this. It would be difficult to find a better teacher than St. John of the Cross. He stands out, without anyone questioning it, as one of the great spiritual authorities in the history of the Church. His doctrine is in complete accord with St. Thomas Aquinas. It is hardly going too far to say that his doctrine of the spiritual life is the official doctrine of the Church. Pope Pius XI made him a Doctor of the Church because of his doctrine, and so gave him the stamp of official approval.

St. John of the Cross was a Carmelite and, working with St. Teresa of Avila in Spain in the second half of the sixteenth century, was instrumental in founding the Discalced Carmelites. Under the figure of climbing a mountain, he teaches the doctrine of the progress of the Christian soul from the beginning to final perfection in complete union with God. He calls this mountain Carmel, because tradition taught that the Carmelites were originally founded by the prophet Elias on Mount Carmel in Palestine. The doctrine is contained in four great works, each of which marks a stage in the advance up the mountain to perfect union with God at the top. These works are, in order: *The Ascent of Mount Carmel, The Dark Night of the Soul, The Spiritual Canticle* and *The Living Flame of Love.*

Very few souls attain to the perfection of the last stage of complete union with God. Nevertheless, the doctrine is the same, and true for all who are blessed with the love of God, and are advancing in it, no matter how far they have progressed. We shall give the substance of his doctrine, sufficient for the guidance of all souls, so they will know what the way is, whether they are on the right track, and what to do, no matter where they stand.

The whole doctrine can be summed up quite simply, and in very few words. Perfection in the Christian life is to become like Christ. We can never become exactly like Christ. Our Lord was a man and He was the Son of God. In Him the human nature was united to the Divine nature and the Divine Person. Other men cannot share a union with God exactly like that. In the case of other men, human nature is united to human personality. So, with them, the human nature and the human person, for perfect union, are united to God, the Second Person of the Blessed Trinity. Keeping this carefully in mind we can say that for union with God here on earth (and it will be the same in heaven) every man must be as nearly as possible like Christ was a man. Every thought, word and deed of man must be what Christ would think, say or do.

This brings us to the first great principle which covers everything. Every man who wants to travel the road toward union with God must cast forth out of his mind and soul everything that is not God. This is the way it was with Our Lord, and that is the way it must be with other men. A reader should stop here, and lay this aside for awhile and allow the tremendous import of that statement to sink in. no one can come to complete union with God until he has rooted up and expelled from his soul everything that is not God!

This is so primary and fundamental that it is best to give the words of St. John himself:

> These counsels for conquering the desires, which now follow, although few and brief, I believe to be as profitable and efficacious as they are concise; so that one who sincerely desires to practice them will need no others, but will find them all included in these.

> First, let him have an habitual desire to imitate Christ in everything that he does, conforming himself to His life.

> Secondly, in order to do this well, every pleasure that presents itself to the senses, if it be not purely for the honor and glory of God, must be renounced and completely rejected for the honor and glory of God....

> Strive always to choose, not that which is easiest, but that which is most difficult;

> not that which gives most pleasure, but rather that which gives least;

> not that which is restful, but that which is wearisome;

> not that which gives consolation, but rather that which makes disconsolate;

> not that which is greatest, but that which is least;

> not that which is loftiest and most precious, but that which is lowest and most despised;

> not that which is a desire for anything, but that which is a desire for nothing;

> Strive not to go about seeking the best of temporal things, but the worst.

> All this is for beginners, and at the very beginning. These counsels are to enable the soul to know how to start.

It is not a pleasant prospect; nor should it be. The soul that wants to be like Christ must expect dreadful sufferings; he must be prepared to face those last dark moments on the cross. Nor is it only that he may meet them. They are as certain as death. One who follows Christ must meet them; his life must be a continual crucifixion. It is not a life of ease and complacency.

St. John of the Cross wrote primarily for certain chosen souls of his own holy order of Carmel. But he tells us himself that it is for anyone who wants to take it. Anyone in the Church, everyone could take that doctrine, accept it, and follow it, and God would be pleased.

Before close union with God can take place, the soul must be purified from all defilement and imperfection. He does not speak of turning from mortal sin. Those he addresses have turned away from grievous sin, and want to come to close to God. The whole question now is that of purifying the soul. Complete union cannot take place as long as there is the least imperfection in the soul. Our Lord had a human soul like ours, and our soul must become pure like His.

The first two of the four works are devoted to describing how this purification of the soul is wrought to prepare it for perfect union with God. God does part of it, the soul does part. Of course, even in the part the soul does, God works with it, because all good that man does comes from God, and God does it. But in this part, there is a very definite work that the soul has to do for itself, and this then is wholly man's, but because it is good it is wholly God's too. This is a great mystery into which we cannot go any further now. Suffice it to say that man has a part to play in the purification of his own soul. This part of his consists in removing all obstacles, so that God can work in the soul. Man must cut out ruthlessly everything that is not God.

The soul must deprive itself of its desire for all the pleasure it derives from sight, hearing, smell, taste, touch. When the soul rejects and denies that which it can derive through the senses, we can quite well say that it is dark and empty. What is there left? So, St. John speaks of this state as night; this is the night of the senses, or of the sensual part of the soul. Remember, purification consists in voiding and stripping the soul of every desire.

Without this mortification the soul no more achieves progress on the road to perfection and to the knowledge of God and of itself, however many efforts it may make, than the seed grows when it is cast upon untilled ground.... Any desire, although it be but for the smallest imperfection, stains and defiles the soul.... Voluntary desires must be driven away, every one howsoever small it may be.... And the reason is that the state of this Divine union is the soul's total transformation in the will of God.

The soul wills only what God wills. "For if this soul desired any imperfection that God wills not, there would not be made one will of God, since the soul would have a will which God had not." In all these matters, for a good understanding of them, we ought to go back constantly to the human soul of Our Lord, and so judge what the soul of the just man ought to be like.

All desires of the good things of life, food, money, honors, family, health, all must be eradicated. Nor in his lengthy exposition does the Saint soften these harsh prescriptions. It is only God Who counts it all. We can say, by way of anticipation, that God arranges things from the best, and anyone who leaves father, mother, family for His sins receives a hundredfold even in this life. St. John himself "loved thy countryside... he had an exquisite sensibility, he was one of the greatest poets of Spain; he had a profound tenderness for his brother Francis the poor mason, and a deep delight in his spiritual children." But the soul must not think of things like that. She must take the plunge. Again, what is left? As far as things that can be perceived by the senses are concerned, there is nothing. As far as the senses are concerned there is nothing. As far as the senses are concerned, the soul is empty and it is night for it.

Next there is the higher part of the soul, where reason presides and acts. Jesus had no thoughts, imaginations, memories other than those of the Divine person in Him. So must it be with every man in union with God. The man who strives for full union with God must have no thoughts, no imaginations, no memories, no desires whatever but those which God operates in him. He must discipline himself so that he does not think of anything, remember anything. This is to but all taken very literally and exactly. All particular knowledge must go.

His soul becomes empty. Only one thing remains, one thought one activity. He knows that God is there; he knows this is what God wants; he trusts Him and hopes in Him; he loves Him without knowing how, or why, or even that he does love Him. He cannot see God he knows that He is there. But it is all darkness.

* * *

Beginners will make use of meditation. This exercise is possible and easy, even for busy lay people. It means practicing oneself in thinking about God and Divine things. The time comes when the soul must leave off meditation. So far, we are speaking of what the soul does through and by its own efforts, always aided, as said above, by God's grace. We must bear in mind that all the time God is in the soul, secretly working Himself. The time will come when He will take over and do everything Himself. To prepare itself and make ready for that, at the proper time, the soul must quit meditation. St. John gives very explicit instructions how to know when that time comes. This is one of the most critical moments in the whole journey of the soul to union with God. It is so shocking to the soul to be told that it must not even think about God, it must not think about anything. The reason for this is because it is now time for God to begin to take over and operate in the soul. If the soul is thinking about anything, even about God and Divine things, these thoughts fill the soul, and it is not empty, ready to be filled with God, so that God can operate through the man's reason and thought in a manner resembling the way He reasoned and thought in Christ's soul.

So the soul must abandon meditation. St. John is most clear and explicit about this. He comes back to it again and again, he hammers it in. Tt is an utter impossibility to make any further progress, unless the soul gives up meditation. There will be all sorts of differences among souls. Some will arrive at this point sooner than others. The majority of those who start out do reach this stage, and usually in a short time. The reason why a great many of them advance no further is because they keep on at meditation when they should drop it, and remain quiet, attentive to the touches of God, and the breathing of the Holy Spirit. Some souls, after they have left meditation, will have to return to it at times until they are firmly entrenched in the stage.

* * *

This is, in outline, what the soul has to do by its own efforts on the way to union with God. The prospect is not one of pleasant enjoyment. Only experience can tell us what will happen to a soul which follows faithfully the directions here laid down, experience and a divinely inspired understanding of what God tells us in the Holy Scriptures. St. John of the Cross had both, and he tells us what the life of that soul is like. It is a life of anguish and bitter suffering; at times death would be a joy. It is true that at times sweet joy pervades the soul, and gentle touches of God, spiritual consolations and comforts, but only at times; but even these, the soul must not desire them, must even turn from them and take no pleasure in them. She must strip herself to the skin, yea, she should strip off her very skin. No, it is not a pleasure journey.

* * *

And this is not all. In fact, it is only the beginning, and the easiest part of the way. The work of the soul's own efforts is finished. When it has annihilated all the desires of the life of the senses, empties itself of all these, and purified its rational life of understanding, memory and will, its work is done. We have here the explanation of the whole doctrine of mortification in the discipline of the Church.

* * *

Now God Himself takes charge. The word, the Son, the Second Person begins to operate in a new way in the soul. He had been there all the time, and working too. He is hidden now too, but this time He is not seen because the light of His presence is so intense it blinds the soul, and the soul is in utter darkness, can see nothing because of the excess of light. This state of the soul is what is called contemplation, infused contemplation, because God, as it were, pours His presence into the soul. He does not yet bestow upon the soul that love in which it so longs. Far from it; that union cannot come until every slightest imperfection is burned out of the soul. And she is still very imperfect, poor, weak, defiled, wretched. She walks in twofold darkness of night. She can see nothing of God because of the great light of His presence; that is one darkness. She sees her own wretched condition and unworthiness, and how unfit she is that He should have anything to do with her; she is sure she deserves nothing but to be cast out of His presence into the bottom of hell. This is her greatest suffering. Human words fail utterly to express what the soul endured in this condition. The sufferings up to now, though indescribable, are as nothing to what she enters upon now. She is filled with black darkness, and this is the kind of darkness.

The soul did all she could do by her own efforts to purge away the grave defilements of her nature. She is still far removed from that purity required for God to unite Himself to her after the manner in which He was united to the human body and soul in Our Lord. And the soul must resemble the soul of Christ. She herself can do no more. It is God Who does the rest. In the first stage of purification, God purifies the soul of every imperfection. She does nothing wherever; there is nothing she can do except not interfere with God's word in her.

She went to work at the lower part of her nature, the sensual part, and cleaned and scoured it, cut and burned, to make it pure and clean; then she did the same for her understanding, her memory and her will. It was all so bitter and terrible, it seemed beyond human endurance. Now God starts to work. It is as if what she did was nothing at all. God now purifies her sense nature and her higher nature of reason. She is like impure gold and He puts her in a furnace and burns her until all the impurities are burned out. No tongue can tell, or pen begin to describe, what sufferings this entails. And all the while, she so realizes her less-than-nothingness that she is sure God must hate her. This is the worst suffering of all. As if it were not enough, the Devil never ceases to torment and use all his wiles and artifices to mislead her. This state of the soul, the first stage of contemplation, is called the Dark Night of the Soul.

That blackness and suffering, the pain and anguish are not continuous. The Divine Word loves the soul. He would not be doing this if He did not. Sometimes He imparts to her touches of unutterable sweetness, and she experiences bliss beyond words; she knows not whence it comes or how. But these moments are like flashes of lightning in the darkness of the night.

When He finishes with the purification of her soul, she will be fit to go straight to God. It is really the sufferings of purgatory which she is going through. Souls which suffer this purification to the end, if they die then, go straight to heaven without passing through purgatory at all. Very few souls experience it to the end.

* * *

St. John of the Cross composed a poem describing the progress of a soul from the first beginning until the final consummation in full and perfect union with God. Competent authorities rank it as one of the greatest love poems in all literature. The four works we are studying were written to explain the poem. It is a love poem. This must never be lost to mind. It is the love story of two who fall hopelessly in love with each other, become betrothed, and finally become one in the consummation of marriage. It is hard to go to extremes to the stark realism of the lover and his beloved, the bride and her spouse, and their union in marriage. The bride is the soul which has passed through the two dreadful nights of purgation, and is now all ready for her lover and bridegroom. We can learn something of that Divine betrothal and marriage of God the Son with the purified soul, not because this latter resembles the former, but because earthly marriage, the pure love and union of man and woman, is an image of that heavenly marriage of God with the soul. And it is only in this way that the true nature of human marriage can be understood. People marvel at how the mystics speak of love better than anyone else, when they have no experiences from human love themselves. It is because they in love with God.

Picture to yourself the most perfect communion and union of the most perfect lovers possible, the joy and happiness with each other you are infinitely below the peace, the pleasure, the joy, the happiness of this union of the soul with God. Eye has not seen, nor ear heard nor has it entered into the mind of man to conceive it. All those who are blessed despair of talking about it.

At the beginning of the betrothal of the soul to the Word, the Son of God, God reveals to the soul great things of Himself, makes it beautiful in majesty and grandeur. The soul has a vision and a found taste of abundant and inestimable riches, and finds there all the repose and refreshment desired; and attains to the secrets of God, which is the food of those who know Him most; it is conscious of the awful power of God, tastes of the wonderful sweetness of the Spirit, finds its true rest and divine light, drinks deeply of the wisdom of God, which shine forth in the harmony of the creatures, and the works of God. The most subtle and delicate knowledge enters with marvelous sweetness and delight into the innermost substance of the soul, which is the highest of all delights. Still, we are not to think that what the soul perceives, though pure truth, can be the perfect and clear fruition of heaven. In the betrothal, the peace is not yet perfect. And the Devil can still attack it.

Spiritual marriage, beyond all comparison, is a far higher status than that of betrothal. It is complete transformation in the Beloved whereby they surrender each to the other, the entire possession of themselves in perfect union of love. In this union of love, so far as it is possible in this life, the soul becomes God, by participation. St. John believes that no soul ever attains to the state without being confirmed in grace. The nature of God and the nature of the soul are so united, that without undergoing any essential change, each seem to be God. The Bridegroom reveals His secrets to the bride. The chief of these are the sweet mysteries of the Incarnation, the ways and means of redemption, which is one of the greatest works of God. He infuses love and increases it, without infusing and increasing distinct knowledge. The soul now, in a certain sense, is like Adam in paradise who knew no evil. It is so innocent that it sees no evil. Such a soul will scarcely intermeddle in the affairs of others, because it forgets even its own. Love has set the soul on fire, and transmuted it into love. God is pleased only with love. All our works, all our labors, how grand soever they may be, are nothing in the sight of God, for we can give Him nothing. It is the property of love to place him who loves on an equality with the object of his love. Hence the soul is equal to God in love, she loves Him with the same love with which He loved her. She would not be satisfied with anything less.

The understanding of such a soul is the understanding of God, its will is the will of God, its memory the eternal memory of God, and its delights the delights of God. And the substance of such a soul, while all the time being other than the substance of God, for it cannot be substantially changed into Him, nevertheless is united with Him, absorbed into Him, is God by participation. He will do for His beloved bride anything she asks. Until this state is reached it is necessary to make acts of love. Now it is not necessary that the soul should occupy itself in other and exterior duties (unless they be matters of obligation) which might hinder, were it but for a moment, the life of love in God. This is true even though they may minister greatly to His service; an instant of pure love is more precious in the eyes of God and the soul, and more profitable to the Church, than all other good works together, though it may seem as if nothing were done.

* * *

"O that men would understand how impossible it is to enter the thicket, the manifold riches of God, without entering into the thicket of manifold suffering, making it the desire and consolation of the soul; and how that the soul which really longs for divine wisdom longs first of all for the sufferings of the Cross."

This is the spiritual doctrine of St. John of the Cross. There it is, complete, standing above the vicissitudes of time in its universality, as true and valid today as it was in the sixteenth century, and it will always be the same. It may cause surprise that there is no mention in it of things one would expect, saying prayers, attendance at Mass, or saying Mass, visits to the Blessed Sacrament, novenas, Stations of the Cross, indulgences, not even Confession and Holy Communion. What of them? In answer to this question this much can be said: St. John of the Cross said Mass like an angel; his life was a life of prayer; like One other he passed whole nights in prayer; the great work of his life was hearing confessions and guiding souls in holiness; the Blessed Virgin was his very mother, on two occasions she saved his life by a striking miracle, his devotion to her was intense and lifelong; his whole order was dedicated to her. His spiritual doctrine stands by itself, it can be used with supreme confidence by those who know nothing of his life; but any interpretation of it which conflicts with his life would obviously have to be an incorrect one. Prayer and the Sacraments have their place in his teaching.

When this is said, it must be insisted on that the central principle in his doctrine is this, for a man to lead the Christian life perfectly (normally speaking, God can work miracles in special cases), there are certain things that he must do by his own efforts, and there is no way out of it. He must ruthlessly annihilate in himself everything that is not God, all desires, and everything else. He must do this himself. There are things that God does, and others He leaves to man. Man has to do these. For example, suppose one has worldly ambitious to shine among men. He must give that up by efforts. He cannot expect God to take that desire away from him. It would be like a farmer being so pious that he would kneel beside his bed and ask God to put in his crop and harvest it for him. God could do that, but He does not do things like that.

* * *

How far is this teaching of St. John of the Cross applicable today in America? He would say it is in every respect applicable to every one, and everywhere. It is not an expedient technique; it is solid doctrine, founded on Divine Truth. It is true, only a rare few have reached the final stage. It does not follow that those who do not attain that union are not friends of God. St. John thinks a great many could go much further than they do if they knew better what they should do. Insofar as they do advance in the love of God this is the way they must go, whether they know it or not. This is capital. Then is no progress in spirituality except by way of mortifying and purifying the soul. This doctrine is valid in its entirety for all ages, and all classes, and conditions, rich or poor, strong or weak, married or single, old or young.

Naturally, some states of life are more suited to the cultivation of the spiritual life than others. This is the seed, cause and explanation of religious life in the Church, and why St. Thomas holds it the perfect state of life. It was for this very purpose it was planned. It is not that all religious are holy, or that others are not holy. It means that religious life most lends itself to the attainment of perfection. The intense physical pleasure, and the cares and worries of married life, make it harder to give oneself wholly to God. Only mortal sin turns man away from God. Otherwise, he is a friend of God. If he is to go up higher, normally he must want to do so of his own free will and with that same freedom make those efforts here laid down. In him cling fast to that principle, and follow it, and he will not wander around but always head straight to the goal of perfect union with God if not as perfect as possible in this life, then, at least finally, in the eternal kingdom of God.

HENRY CARR, C.S.B

The Unwise
A STORY

IN THE VESTIBULE OF HIS ESTABLISHMENT, Tobias Bunnell teetered slowly on his heels and stared moodily through the glass door at the weather outside "Bunnell's Funeral Parlor" bathed the lawn in pink neon; by its light he could see the hazard drizzle drilling on the walk. Thoughtfully, he diddled his upper plate with his tongue, jingled the coins in his pockets and reflected that it was one hell of a night for a wake.

For thirty years the only furniture dealer and undertaker in five north-western Connecticut villages, Tobias often took a personal interest in his soirees; he had, in his time, buried whole families. In the present case, he felt no such interest. As Judge of Probate in Judea, the deceased, Charlie Benson, had ruled against Tobias years ago in a property suit. Tobias had put down Charlie as a cozy article; he was scarcely saddened now by Charlie's fatal heart attack in his feedstore two days before.

Tobias looked at his watch and again at the rain. Eight-thirty, and only seven people in the parlor. Judea was a dozen miles away; half of the relatives would stay home; the other half show up late. They'd hang around waiting for something to happen — the thing would drag along till eleven.

He was surprised in his thoughts by a young man bounding up the porch steps, stomping his feet, vigorously slinging the rain off his hat and presenting himself gravely at the door. Tobias straightened, gently opened the door and, in as funeral a tone as possible for a fat little man in a wrinkled brown suit, asked:

"Relative of the deceased?"

The young man smiled faintly. "A nephew."

"Ah!" breathed Tobias, taking his things. The trench coat and pin-stripe suit looked out-of-town. "So sad about your uncle," he was saying. "Came so sudden . . ."

The young man was surprised. "You knew my uncle?"

"Charlie? Known him for years. Fine man." Mentally Tobias seated him with Mrs. Thurber, the sister from Litchfield, and the niece from Cornwall Bridge. "Care to sign the book?" he asked casually, indicating with a wave a register on a bible stand. He waited while the young man advanced to the book and wrote scratchily: "Roger Sprague, New Haven, Conn." Then he said, "This way, please," and led the young man through what had once been a living room, where the other guests sat in fidgety little groups, to the alcove where the casket was.

The young man followed reluctantly; he had never seen death. His eyes blinked in the unreal amber glow of the torch-bulbs; the visitors watched him indifferently. As he approached the alcove, the odor of embalming touched his stomach.

Tobias stood at the head of the coffin. "There he is," he said. The young man hesitated, stepped forward to kneel, checked himself. There was no kneeling bench. He looked around; no cross, no candles. A budget funeral? Then he remembered. The congregational ways of his father came back to him. He felt rebuked; a Yankee turned Roman.

"Natural, ain't he?" remarked Tobias in a stage whisper.

"What?"

"Looks natural, don't he?" repeated Tobias conversationally.

"Oh yes, yes...."

Roger Sprague had not seen his uncle for years; he stared at the shrunk skull, the knotted hands unnaturally folded on the still chest, the sparse, gray hair inappropriately cushioned in satin.

He thought: this is my uncle Charlie, my mother's brother. How he is. He is quite dead. How different, when we tromped down the hay in his barn. It was hot in the mow. We kids got tired and he called up to us to git movin'. His voice was hard and strong. In his feedstore, the grain row was dark — we scooped out handfuls from the bins and ate it, while he talked over a legal point out front with a neighbor. His voice was deliberate, then he leaned against the counter, exploring little sideroads of the law. Till we stumbled and made a noise and he caught us and told us to scat. Then his voice was loud, he took big steps. How dead he is now.

Tobias shifted his teeth. "Your aunt, Mrs. Thurber, is here," he observed "Mebbe you'd like to say hello."

The young man did not answer: "and at the hour of our death." Our death. This, then, he thought bitterly: hands, lids folded, wrenched out of the corner of our lives — pray for us now, when we are delivered up to the undertaker with the loose upper plate.

The mood of prayer evaporated. He reflected that Uncle Charlie, could he hear, would wince at the popish sentiment. He turned to the undertaker.

"I don't think she'd recognize me," he said. "It's been years . . . "

"Time to get acquainted," suggested Tobias, and led the young man in the parlor.

Mrs. Thurber filled the center of the couch. Large, washed and muscular she sat back in wide-legged complacency, incongruously knitting and airing her views to two high school girls flanking her on either side.

"In Science, of course," she was saying, "we don't hold with the gloom view of death. Mrs. Eddy says . . . "

"Mrs. Thurber," interrupted Tobias, "here's your nephew, Roger Sprague.

The three looked up at him.

"Hello, Aunt Ruth," said Roger gravely. Tobias sidled away.

"Roger!" She recognized him, beamed brightly. "It's nice to see you I never dreamed — isn't it awful? Seems like the only time the family — is down, Roger. You remember your cousin Natalie, don't you?"

"Hello, Roger," muttered the thin girl on the right, indifferently. The heavy lipstick accentuated her round, child's face; memory stirred in him of a fist fight over a bicycle, years ago. Was she eighteen yet? Obviously, she was being "mature."

"Hello, Natalie, how are you?"

He pulled over a camp chair and sat before them. Somewhere in the back of the house, a doorbell buzzed softly.

"And this," said Mrs. Thurber, nodding graciously, "is Natalie's friend Mary Curran. Mary, Roger Sprague."

"How do you do?" murmured Mary Curran, in a precise, chaste voice. Her eyes met his an instant; they were steady, quite blue. They fluttered withdrew from his stare.

He was alerted; the name . . . where . . . ? He shuffled through his thoughts but could place her nowhere. He gave up, confused by her presence.

"How do you do?" he repeated mechanically.

She looked again, smiled hesitantly. She was slight, feminine; her heart shaped face, framed in soft, light hair, breathed an astringent, clean scent. Her mouth was coral, moist, parted slightly. She sat forward in her precise way; her thin, long fingers clasped loosely on the dirndl skirt pulled modestly over her knees.

He sensed a warmth carefully withheld. He felt himself fill slowly with a vague desire. He thought: *thou art fair . . . thou hast dove's eyes . . .* Reluctantly he noticed a scar on her forehead, snaking crazily along the hairline. Where . . . ?

"Poor Uncle Charlie," he said abruptly. "It was a shock . . . " He shook his head sadly. A group of middle-aged men passed through the alcove; they whispered among themselves. The others in the room stirred briefly like leaves ruffled by a breeze. One or two nodded to the newcomers:

"Lo, Bill."

"Hi, Fred."

"Poor Uncle Charles," repeated Natalie.

"You, were very fond of your uncle?" Mary Curran asked the young man.

"Yes," he answered. "Though, frankly," he corrected himself, "I . . . "

"Roger hasn't seen his uncle since he was twelve," explained

Mrs. Thurber, searching for a dropped stitch. "His people moved to New Haven."

"Are you from Judea?" asked Roger.

"No, Cornwall," said Mary Curran. Then added, as though answering the real question, "I came to keep Natalie company. She was a little . . . afraid, I think." She smiled at Natalie to show she was explaining, not criticizing. Natalie smirked lamely.

"I suppose I feel *respect* for Uncle Charlie," resumed Roger. "To me, he was always sort of a monument, a pillar of respectability and . . . well, decency."

Mrs. Thurber giggled. "Roger, that's about the nicest thing you could've said. Coming from a nephew, I call that a real compliment."

Nobody could think of anything to add to that. The conversation withered. They smiled blandly at each other, looked out at the late arrivals. Mrs. Thurber waved hello to a friend across the room, fished up slack on her yarn and began a new row. Natalie appraised a young man standing in a group. Disturbed by Roger's interest, Mary Curran examined her hands.

"I'm afraid," Roger ventured, "I broke up your conversation by coming over."

"Oh, it was nothing," answered his aunt. "We were just discussing death."

"Oh," he responded gravely. "It gives you something to think about, doesn't it?" No one agreed. "I mean," he went on, "here we are, talking so calmly . . . and in the next room . . . "

"Yes?" challenged his aunt.

"Oh, nothing. It's just that . . . it doesn't seem appropriate, somehow. I mean, some prayers . . . or some sort of service . . . "

"Fiddlesticks!" interrupted Mrs. Thurber, knitting rapidly. "Everyone's here to pay his respects. Charles lived a good life — an honest official and townsman. Now he's gone to his reward. We ought to rejoice for him. Why, if he could come back now, he'd want people . . . that's why I can't get used . . . I expect him to get right up outa that coffin any minute and scold us all for bein' gloomy, and then go lookin' for his pipe." She bent over and inspected her work.

"I didn't mean it that way, Aunt Ruth," said the young man contritely. He felt absurd. "You're not Yankee, are you?" he asked the girl suddenly.

"No," she answered, surprised. "Why?"

"You'll be pleased to hear, Mary," said Mrs. Thurber with emphasis, patting her work in her lap, "that you have a fellow-Catholic in Roger. Came home from college a convert."

"Really?" said Mary Curran. "That *is* interesting." She looked at him warmly, questioningly.

"Oh yes," continued Mrs. Thurber, "it was the gossip of the family."

"It's hard to keep secret," said Mary Curran, smiling at the young man. Feeling talked about, he retired from her gaze.

"Why did you ask . . . about being Yankee?" she encouraged him.

"I should think you'd find a Yankee wake rather . . . different," he remarked.

"Not especially," she answered coolly. It evidently displeased her to take sides.

"You don't feel that something is — lacking?" He was blundering, he knew it. "I mean," he stumbled, "a wake should be something more than sort of get-together, don't you think? Because death is important, so absolute, something final . . . "

Pain crossed her face. She tried to smile, failed, looked away. "I agree with Mrs. Thurber," she said, studying the rug. "We should rejoice with your uncle. Death is final — but it is not a tragedy."

Had he hurt her, said something wrong? He did not know, could not fathom the tension he felt. He had only been making conversation, he just wanted to say that death had supernatural implications — he had thought she would agree.

"You know, Mary," said Mrs. Thurber, yanking up yarn, "you

sound just like Mary Baker Eddy. Have you ever read *Science and Health*?"

"I don't think so," answered the girl.

"You ought to, I'm sure you'd like it. I was reading just this morning."

"Evenin', Ruth," said the first of the three men. "Rotten weather, ain't it?" They stood uncertainly beside the sofa. They wore the left-overs in solemn expressions — they had just come from the alcove.

"Why, Bill Ormsbee, hello!" Mrs. Thurber stood up quickly. Natalie jumped up to join her. An outsider, Mary Curran remained seated. Roger looked at her as though to say: Now we can really talk. Her glance did not answer him. They sat in silence a moment.

"I'm afraid I was unkind," he said uncertainly.

"I'm afraid so," she agreed. She had lost her repose; her thin hands topped absently with a handkerchief.

Desire flooded him again. He wanted to sit beside her, ask her forgiveness....

"I'm sorry," he said soberly.

"Don't see Candace anywheres," Bill Ormsbee was saying, looking after.

"Bill, you wouldn't know her," condoned Mrs. Thurber rapidly "She's in a state. She depended so on Charles . . . "

"Natalie Benson, Jim Appleyard." The second man was introducing to the third.

"It's so hard," resumed the young man earnestly, "to know what to say sometimes. These people, my relatives, I mean — they regard me as sort of a renegade, a traitor."

"That's a pity," answered Mary Curran. She seemed preoccupied, unwillingly to pursue the thought. She watched Natalie and Appleyard as though hoping to join them.

"Yes, it is," he went on quickly. "You see, Catholicism has given me so much. So much that I want to share with them" She asked, looking at him oddly. She was listening to him again.

"So many things," he replied. He leaned forward, eager to explain. "About the sacramental view of life, I mean, and the Mass, and the magnificent liturgy of death."

"Do you know it?" she asked gravely.

"Oh yes, I've read it many times. I think there's no poetry like it — especially the preface: *Unto Thy faithful, O Lord, life is changed, not taken away...* "

Yes, yes — very beautiful," she interrupted, in a small, tight whisper. She frowned, looked away again as though in pain.

"That's their great loss, you see — the sense of sacrament," he hurried on anxiously. "They denied the Sacraments, of course — my people, I mean, Yankees — in the very beginning. But still they had a strong sense of sin and hell and the hereafter. When they became 'liberal,' they lost even that. So now their religion has no content, and at their own funerals, they can only discuss how 'natural' the corpse looks. You do know what I mean, don't you?"

Mary Curran was silent a moment. Then she answered: "Unfortunately, it's not confirmed to Yankees."

"Perhaps not," he faltered, feeling that he had overshot the mark. "But I was trying to bring out... "

A wheezing, croupy, interminable cough startled the whole parlor. Ormsbee was doubled up; he spluttered and turned red. Appleyard thumped him on the back while Mrs. Thurber looked sympathetic and the rest of the room watched in alarm.

"Are ya all right, Bill? Asked Appleyard.

Ormsbee subsided with a gasp, pulled out a handkerchief and blew his nose. "God," he joked, "ya never know. Sounds like I'll be next."

"Bill! What a thing to say," chided Mrs. Thurber.

"'Strue, ain't it? Here today, gone tomorra. Weren't we kiddin' Charlie just last week about him runnin against me fer first selectman?"

"Ya know," said the second man, "I just can't believe he's gone.

The others returned to their conversations.

"That's it," continued the young man talkatively, groping for the thread of his argument, "the sacramentality of life. It was a revelation to me — an immense, sublime fact. It's the only thing that can sanctify our lives — our deaths — whatever we are. And that's why we of the Faith have such a responsibility . . . " He trailed of idiotically — her distress was plain. "But this is not new to you, of course," he ended.

"Oh, you're right," she said wearily. "We of the Faith need to be reminded of these things, too. We grow up so slowly to the greatness of our ideas."

"Excuse me Mary." Aunt Ruth stood beside them. "I hate to interrupt this nice chat, but there's a cousin here from York State who's never met Roger." She gave the young man a meaningful look. He stood up unwillingly. "He'll be back in a few minutes, Mary," she shot over her schedule, and piloted the young man across the room.

"I simply had to interfere," whispered Mrs. Thurber hurriedly on the way over. "I could see you were upsetting the girl. Really, Roger — although it's my fault, I suppose I should have warned you — you've got to be more careful what you say to the girl. That's the Mary Curran who saw her sister killed in that awful smash-up last year. Here he is, Arnold. Roger, this is your second cousin, Arnold Ohmen from Rheinbeck. Arnold, can you imagine Clarissa Benson having a son this size?"

Pleasantries were served all around. They stood in a group surrounding Ohmen, a gaunt farmer apparently the feature because he was seldom seen He said little, confined himself to nodding his head and muttering "ayeh ayeh," so as to hide the cud in his cheek. His Adam's apple, sliding on the long neck, periodically betrayed him.

"Studyin' law eh?" "Nothin' like education. Ayeh . . . ayeh . . . Anything in the world for fella . . . "

Roger Sprague was not listening. He stood there,

uncomprehendingly stunned by the knowledge his aunt had supplied.

Mary Curran — that was the name. even the New Haven papers has carried the account: " . . . an eyewitness stated. The driver, Ralph Lucas has started down Warren Hill about fifty miles an hour. Passing out four cars Lucas, blinded by the fog, continued on the left side of the road and smashed head-on into the car coming up the hill. The deceased, Agnes Curran, was thrown from the vehicle and crushed against the railing. Her sister, Mary Curran, also in the vehicle, suffered shock, three broken ribs, and laceration of the head. She was rushed to Hungerford Hospital where her condition reported critical. Deceased was to have married Lucas this Saturday. Lucas who escaped with minor abrasions, is missing and is sought by police for questioning. Interment of the deceased, Agnes Curran, will take place at nine o'clock Saturday morning at . . . "

That was the name, all right. Had they caught Lucas? Useless to speak late — probably not. A G. I. gone nuts — never showed up at school again anyway. It had shocked the campus for a week.

Mary Curran . . . his conversation with her no longer puzzled him. His agitation; he realized now what it hid. He understood her pain when she said "Death is final, but it is not a tragedy." Did she believe it? So firm a faith seemed impossible. He marveled at her strength, her patience.

"Candace, of course, is a Woodruff," his aunt was saying. Methodical she spun her web. Ohmen added "ayeh" and swallowed furtively at appropriate intervals. "The Woodruffs were always like that," she went on. "Got it from their grandfather, old Enoch. Come to think of it, *he* was a Benson on the mother's side. . . . "

How she must despise him, thought Roger Sprague. Everything he has said had been hideously inept. He loathed his own blind, opinionated zeal. He sank into a pool of shame, humiliated by his egotism. His faith was unreal, idiotic. What did he know of sanctification?

He looked across the room for Mary Curran. She sat as they had left her, eyes cast down, her head bent a little, like a bruised bird. Tobias Bunner moved along the wall, loudly banging camp chairs shut — time to go home.

"Ayeh," nodded Ohmen, "we're all gonna miss old Charlie."

"Excuse me," said the young man, and left the group. He crossed the parlor, sat down beside Mary Curran.

"I owe you an apology," he said gently.

"Do you?" She looked up absently.

"I'm afraid I was very tactless, before. You see, I didn't remember that terrible accident . . . "

"Oh," she said, looking away again. She gave no sign, merely acknowledge that now he knew.

"Please forgive me," he begged.

She tried to collect herself, to turn her attention to the young man. Her kind, blue eyes searched his face for something — expression? Sentiment? — he couldn't imagine — then turned inward again in spite of herself. She had hold of some reflection she was loathe to leave.

"It's all right," she murmured softly. She fingered her handkerchief, studied its design a moment, added, "It wasn't an accident, you see."

"Wasn't . . . ?"

"I don't think so. I've wondered . . . They'd been quarrelling, Ralph and Sis." She stared straight ahead, reliving the scene. "Sis was angry — I think she was beginning to realize — poor Ralph . . . He drove faster and faster. I asked him to slow down. Just before the crash, Sis cried out, 'My God! Here it is!' And Ralph yelled back, 'See what your God can do for you now.'" She paused, closed her eyes.

"What a blasphemous thing . . . "

"Was it? She turned, regarded him curiously. "Perhaps God did do for her," she whispered. She turned away again, musing. "Perhaps . . . foreseeing her marriage . . . God was kind and took her away . . . " Her breath caught on a sob. She composed herself, asked, "Don't you think so?"

"Yes, I do," answered Roger. "In the sight of the unwise," he quoted slowly, "she seemed to die; but she is at peace."

He smiled tenderly at Mary Curran. Her grief and her acceptance seemed to him a figure of the hundred hurts of all those whom, like her, he had never really known: Aunt Ruth, Uncle Charlie, the people in this room, this town, the whole, unhappy world. A vast pity engulfed him.

He felt now he somehow understood.

NEIL MACCARTHY

"God helps those who help themselves,"
Mr. Bleep was heard to say.
He helped himself to another drink,
And quietly passed away.

INTEGRITY

On this the day
that saw thy birth
Sing the new song
of ransomed~
Earth:

DECEMBER 1947

25 CENTS A COPY, VOL.2., NO.3

NE OF THE DANGERS that confronts an apostolate dealing with social problems is that the preoccupation with the social order can become as complete in the apostle as it is in those who seek their beatitude in it. So complex a thing is the modern social scene that it exercises an enchantment over those who work against it as well as those who move with its side. Hate can be as binding as love. The fanatical prohibitionist is as much a slave to drink as the chronic drunkard. The complete revolutionary is one with the reactionary in this: that they both are hypnotized by the performance taking place in our daily three-ring circus.

The feast of Christmas should shake us loose from the fascination of the passing parade. Our idealism no longer should focus through the eyes of Adam, the man pre-eminent, the dominator of the world, but rather, since this great thing has happened, we must look upward and outward through the eyes of a Divine Infant. From manger Christ saw a world alive God.

The Christ-Child is the center and periphery of a new order. Never again can the world of man be the same, and things are no longer what they seem. What was once but a stable for animals, is now a Temple of God. What was once merely an ass is now a sacramental, reminding men from henceforth of the Natal Vigil. What was once a shepherd is now a Prince, brother to Christ the King. What was once a minor town of a minor tribe is now the seat of Christendom, the root site of God's new order for His children. What was once steel, or wood, or clay, now is gold to be beaten into chalices and mirrors to cup and reflect the glory of the Word Incarnate.

Why try to regain the heights of Eden now that Christ has lifted us up above the realm of man and set our feet in the foothills of Divinity? We have been adopted into the Divine Family by the magnificent blessing of Christ's becoming our blood Brother. It would be the most false kind of humility now to try to be a nice sort of homo sapiens, to regain a merely human dignity, to reorder the world under the dominion of human reason. To do this would be to besiege a fortress already taken. It would be a false piety to call Adam "Father," and to stand in awe of the mystery of man or the works of men, now that the Creator has condescended to make Himself one with us.

Yes, we have men and the works of men, their laws, their order and their sciences, and these things are jewels. Now that Christ is with us these jewels at the disposition of a Prince. They are jewels in the crown of a King Who brings a new order to a new Principality.

From now on, whenever men place one brick upon another it will be in affirmation or in denial of the God-man. The denials will not more detract from His Glory or His Authority than does a shadow lessen the power of the sun. From now on, the light is there in the four corners of the sky, and there is no darkness that can ever put it out.

THE EDITORS

* * *

The editors and staff are more than happy to comply with the traditional custom of well-wishing at this season of the year. During the past year we have met many of our readers and have exchanged sizable correspondence with many more of them. These pleasure experiences have left us with the certainty that we enjoy a relation with our readers more friendly and intimate than is the usual lot of publishers.

So, when we do express our fondest wish that the graces and blessings of the Nativity be great among you, our only regret is that we cannot exchange these greetings face to face.

ALL OF US

Sitting In Darkness

JIM CHATFIELD BUTTONED UP HIS SHEEPSKIN, pulled on mittens, and opened the kitchen door. Reluctantly he stepped out into the night. The cold hit his nose like the jab of a stick. A polar wind cut across his knees. He slammed the door.

Hunching his collar around his ears and turning his back to the wind, he tacked clumsily across the dooryard to the barn, a tall farmer humpy with clothes, stumbling sleepily to chores on a winter morning.

Overhead, a motor droned frostily. Furtively, he glanced up. The scars, crystal and aloof, winked vacantly in their icy vastness. Mindless, myriad, they spilled across the upper darkness like strewn glass. The red and green outboard lights of the dawn and mail to Boston crawled tinnily through Cassiopeia.

Well, no snow on Christmas — Jacky couldn't use the sled today.

The door to the milkroom yielded stubbornly on rusty rollers. He stepped quickly inside, letting it slide shut behind him while he groped for the light. The whitewashed walls of the little room stared stonily at him in the harsh glare. His breath steamed like dragon smoke. Mechanically, he turned on the milking machine motor; the soft *slug, slug* of its exhaust warmed the silence. The stacked milk cans, the pails, the galvanized sink, the cooler filmed with frost, looked cold. He shivered, turned on the hot water tap. While waiting for the water to warm, he snapped on the radio.

God rest you merry, gentlemen...

Wearily he twisted the knob.

... and may all your Christmases...

Irritably, he twirled it again. The theme song of the Corn Husken filled the room, floated out into the barn. The cows were waking; they arose slowly, breathing heavily and rattling their stanchions. He touched his fingers to the water experimentally, luxuriated a moment in a warmth. Then he lifted the teat-cups off the sterilizer rack, rinsed them briefly and slipped the rubbers on the pulsator.

Where the heck was Jacky?

Scowling, he assembled the milking machines and carried them out into the barn, at the end of the alley between the two rows of rumps. The animals stirred, swished their tails lazily in placid expectation of grain. As he started back to the milkroom, a low moo followed by quavery, nasal blat made him hesitate.

Jim Chatfield grinned.

He sauntered over to the maternity pen in the corner and leaned happily over the high-boarded side. There she was. His new foundation dam: Ardleigh Highbrook Mariette — Big Brown, to him — sprawled in the hay in swollen contentment, chewing her cud. And snoozed curled at her side, the thriftiest Guernsey calf you ever saw; heifer calf too. His mouth smirked a little — here was a Christmas present he had earned — then tightened as he recalled the night before.

Big Brown had started bellowing about ten; the calf was stud. He'd had to tie a rope to its front feet and pull it out. It was blue — he almost lost it. His wife had come down about eleven, had found him chaffing the heifer with a towel.

"Are you going to take care of cows all night?"

"I got to clean up—she ain't dropped her afterbirth. Why—something wrong?"

"Oh, no. only, the tree isn't all decorated yet. And the children's presents..."

Not a word about the calf. Could he help it if it had to be born on Christmas Eve? Raise it right, milk nine thousand pounds some dry.

"Merry Christmas, Pa!" The barn door slammed, letting in a cool blast.

He left the pen, strode down the alley to the boy.

"Merry Christmas, Jacky."

"I said it first, I beat ya!" Grinning, he came up to his father, thin child of ten, in an old coat too short for his growth. Shining with delight and the cold, his face was almost as red as earmuffs.

"How come you're late?" Hands on hips, feigning disapproved he towered over the boy.

"I didn't peek! Honest, Pa!" The grin faded. "I didn't go near...

"Atta boy." He smiled broadly to show he was kidding. The child beamed—he got it. "Now look, son. That big old milk truck's gonna be standin' out there in about an hour. So let's hop to it and git squared away. Then we can go up the house and look at the tree and see what Sanny Claus got ya. Okay?"

"Okay, Pa."

"Shoot the grain to 'em, boy." He dismissed the child with an affectionate pat.

"Pa?"

"Yes, Jacky?"

"It's Christmas, Pa."

"So?"

"Can I give the girls an extra measure of grain?"

His father chuckled. "You do that, boy," he said. "You do that little thing." He turned and strode toward the milkroom. "Merry

Christmas, girls," the boy sang out merrily, rounding the mangers toward the feed-chute.

Jim Chatfield smiled as drew off some water in a bucket, spilled a squirt of CN in it, and yanked a couple of towels from a rack. The kid was all right, thought of the animals. He considered with pleasure his advantage over his neighbors. Poor old Lundberg — four girls. And Mercalf's only boy working in a factory. But Jacky was a farmer. It was in him — you could see it.

And now, in keepin' with the spirit of the season, Hank and his musical saw are gonna give us that grand old hymn, "Away in a Manger"...

Stupid radio. Why did he have it on? He seldom listened to it. Habit, he supposed. Made noise. Thawed out the barn.

He dropped a towel in the bucket, slung one over his shoulder and went out in the dairy. He straddled the manure gutter, began washing Dynamo. Through the stanchions, he could see Jacky bent over his grain tub, dumping scoopfuls of the brown meal in the mangers, chatting playfully with the cows.

"There you are, Dynamo, that's for you. Moneybag, you stop stealin', I'm gonna give you yours in a second." The tub scraped on the concrete walk as the boy dragged it from one animal to the next.

Jim Charfield finished rubbing Dynamo's bag, set a milking machine between her legs.

"Pa." The boy had stopped for a breather.

"What is it?" He plugged in on the airline, slipped on the teatcups. The pulsator bobbed rhythmically: *fft, fft, fft*...

"Was Jesus really born in a manger, like they say?"

"Sure, why?"

"What did Saint Joseph do with the cows in the stanchions?"

"Just let 'em walk around, I guess. Hold still, Susie." He slipped the other machine on the cow across the alley.

"They'd plop all over the barn, if he did that."

"Mebbe it was a different kind of a manger." He bent over to wash moneybag. She jumped at his touch.

"Like what?"

"Like a hay-rack fer young stock." He examined the cow's udder "Hello — Jacky, run in the milkhouse and git me the Bag Balm."

"What's the matter?"

"Moneybag's got a cut teat."

"Oh." The boy ambled off. "All the same, it don't seem like a very good place to put a baby."

"The Bag Balm!"

"Okay, okay." The boy quickened pace.

Frowning, Jim Chatfield changed the machine from Dynamo to Moneybag. She shifted her weight uneasily. He squatted beside her, blocked her legs with his arm so that she couldn't kick off the machine.

"Easy, baby, easy," he murmured, stroking her side soothingly. Darned old sway-back; second time in six months she'd stepped on herself. The leg came up swiftly, whacked him like the blow of a plank "Damn you, take it easy!" he bellowed.

Humming with the radio, the boy came up to him, set the can of ointment on the floor. "Shouldn't cuss on Christmas, Pa." he joked.

"You get that machine off Susie before her whole udder get sucked in, and never mind about me!" bellowed hid father.

The boy crossed the aisle, quickly changed the machine. The radio blared on.

Well, Hank, what dis Santy leave in yer stockin' this mornin'?

Why, a sack of that big Red-G layin' mash naturally. Ha, ha, ha . . .

The two worked in silence a moment. The boy returned to his grain tub. His father pulled the machine off Moneybag, began massaging her with ointment.

A small voice asked, "Pa?"

"What is it?"

"Do you think a Paris Comet is as good a sled as a Flexible Flyer?"

"I dunno."

"Bobby Hickox says it is."

"Yeah?"

"He says it's made by the same company."

"Mebbe it is."

"Pa."

"Yes?"

"Ya know what I wrote to Santa Claus?"

"No, what?"

"I said: 'If ya don't have a Flexible Flyer, a Paris Comet is all right.' That was in case."

"In case what?"

"In case he doesn't have enough Flexible Flyers to go around."

"Oh." Jim Chatfield stepped across the alley, unhooked the milker. Susie lowed complainingly, strained against her stanchion. "Better git some grain over here," he muttered, stumbling off to the milkroom with a machine in either hand.

"Git your nose outa there, Bucky, I got work to do," the boy was saying. The tub bumped along the walk. He sang softly to himself: "Jingle bells, jingle bells . . . "

Wearily, Jim Chatfield took the covers off the machines and set them on the drainboard of the sink. He wrenched the lid off an empty can, dropped the strainer in place, and poured through the hot frothy milk.

You couldn't win. No matter what you did, you couldn't win.

Big Brown had been a buy—no doubt about it. Even old Lundberg, who never had a good word for anything, had nodded his head as he looked her over, growling, "Yaw, yaw," in his Swedish way. But money spent was money spent, even for a bargain. It had meant no new truck that fall. He hadn't minded, had even congratulated himself, what with the price of trucks, and all.

365

But he hadn't figured things would be so skimpy at Christmas.

He slammed the covers on the machines, returned to the barn, began the monotonous cycle again: wash, dry, milk, wash, dry, milk . . . *fft, fft, fft* . . .

He thought about the tree in the parlor — even that looked pindling. He'd been sawing wood . . . he and Jacky had gone up to the woodlot in the afternoon . . . it was getting dark, they hadn't had much time . . . When he'd got around to trimming it, he guessed he hadn't fussed with it like he should — getting the calf born had taken the starch right out of him. And at the foot of the tree, the presents: a couple of gee-gaws for the baby, a sweater and a new cook pot for the wife . . . and Jacky's old sled, fixed up and painted over.

. . . and now, for our regular five-minute newscast, we take you direct to . . .

"I'm finished, Pa." The thin figure stood beside him, shivering slightly, fists jammed in the torn pockets of the too-small coat.

"Take a rest, son."

"Pa." The boy's face was solemn.

"Yes."

"You know that Bobby Hickox says?"

"No, what?"

"Bobby Hickox says" — the boy spoke gravely, watching his father's reaction — "that Santa Claus is your old man."

"That so?" Jim Chatfield stopped to take off a machine. What'd you tell him?"

"I told him he was full of baloney," the boy answered fiercely. His father was silent. "Pa.", he asked anxiously, "You're not Santa Claus, are you?"

Jim Chatfield stepped out on the walk. He stood facing the boy. For a moment he said nothing. Then he shook his head slowly, "No son," he said sadly, "I ain't no Sanny Claus."

He placed his hand on the boy's head and gave it a little shake. The boy smiled back uncertainly. Jim Chatfield bent over, picked up the machine and lugged it off to the milkroom.

It is almost noon here in Europe. Worshippers are crowding the churches of the city, but as they hurry through the streets, there is little joy on their faces. Fuel rations have again been cut. Emergency shipments are being rushed from the Ruhr, but heavy snows hamper all rail movement. The communists threaten . . .

Jim Chatfield banged the lid off an empty, transferred the strainer and heaved the full can into the cooler with a splash. The agitator was broken; he churned the icy water with a sawed-off canoe paddle.

He remembered the last time he and Jacky had been down store, he'd been buying a box of filters. The counters were littered with Christmas stuff.

"Can I look around, Pa?" the boy had asked.

"Sure, sure. Go ahead, Jacky." He had resumed his discussion with Burt about the coming auction over on Chestnut Hill.

"Pa! Pa! They got it — the sled I was talkin' about! Can I show ya, Pa?" Grinning from ear to ear, the boy had dragged him over to a stack of sleds. "No, not that one, the big one! See how the runners bend around? Streamlined, Pa. do ya think Santa Claus might bring me that one, huh?" He had glanced at the tag: $7.95.

Eight dollars would have made the boy's Christmas. Had he been a stinker, for eight lousy bucks?

He tried to persuade himself that he had not. He told himself that Christmas was supposed to be something more than a lot of junky toys that cost too much. Christmas was the birthday of a Baby Who was born poor on purpose to show people how to live right. Wasn't that what he was trying to do? He wasn't looking for a million dollars; he was only trying to build up the farm, make a living. Why, with this new calf, and the other stock he'd raise out of Big Brown, he'd make enough milk to buy a dozen sleds for Christmas. Why, in a few years . . .

But he did not believe himself. The time for new sleds was now not in a few years. He sensed that the "something more" that Christmas meant was not in him. He saw himself as an unfeeling man, who pushed his wife and children and begrudged them Christmas as a nuisance that interfered with the work.

Well, there was nothing he could do about it now. He'd have to take his medicine; stand by the boy at the tree and watch his joy die, watch him try to smile, make the best of it, be a little man. Next year, maybe . . . but there was nothing he could do now. Except let the kid down easy. He assembled the machine, went out into the barn.

Oh come, all ye faithful . . .

The boy's back was to him. He stood as he had left him, looking off down the alley, hands still dug into the old coat, his shoulders hunched against the cold.

Jim Chatfield plugged in the machine, slipped the cups on Sally, then straightened up and draped his arms over the cow's spine. He did not look at his son.

He asked: "Hear that feller on the radio?"

The child, lost in thought, recollected himself. "What? Oh . . . yeah . . . some."

"Tough, over there in Europe."

"I guess so."

The two were silent. Jacky looked at the floor, traced an arc on the concrete with his shoe.

The father began again. "Looks to me like a lot of them little boys and girls over there ain't gonna have much of a Christmas, this year."

The boy frowned. Troubled, he looked at his father. "Won't Santa Claus take care of them?"

"Don't hardly seem so."

"Why not? Doesn't he want to make them happy? Isn't Santa a good man? Mom says he's a *saint.* A saint wouldn't let the little children be unhappy, would he?"

"Well, son, I'll tell ya." He dropped his voice to a confidential tone. "There's so many poor folks over there, so many kids without any toys, or warm clothes, or shoes . . . I wouldn't be surprised if Sanny Claus just didn't have enough things to go around."

The boy thought it over, said stubbornly: "It don't seem very fair."

"No, it don't, son." Jim Chatfield stepped out in the aisle, fished the rag out of the pail of disinfectant and slowly began washing another cow. "That's the way it is sometimes, Jacky," he said grimly over his shoulder. "All them people over there, hungry and cold and just askin' for a good, hot meal or a blanket fer the baby . . . and all us folks here, warm and plenty to eat, prayin' to God for new automobiles and dolls and sleds and things." "He dropped the rag in the bucket, massaged the cow dry. "Yessir, like you say, Jacky, it ain't fair. Sometimes it seems like folks here ferget all about Jesus bein' born in an old barn. "He crossed the alley, changed the machine.

The boy watched him absently. Then he said: "You know what, Pa?"

"What, son?"

"Maybe some little boy in Europe needs a Flexible Flyer more than me, huh?"

"Wouldn't be surprised, Jacky."

"You know what, Pa?"

"What, son?"

"If I was Santa Claus, I wouldn't give me a Flexible Flyer. Or a Paris Comet, even. I'd give it to some little boy in Europe, that's what I'd do!"

The man looked down at his son. He studied the thin, earnest face.

"Would you really, Jacky?"

"I sure would, Pa. And Christmas morning I'd hide in a corner, or in the chimney, quiet like a little mouse, and I'd wait for that little boy to find that sled, and I'd be laughin' inside and I'd . . . "

"Jacky," said his father, giving the boy's shoulder a squeeze, "you're all right. Now I tell ya' what — let's you climb up in the mow and throw down some hay, and I'll finish up milkin' and then we'll feed the girls and have all those chores done, and then, when we go up the house, we'll have lots of time to look at the Christmas tree before we go to church. What d'ya say?"

"Okay, Pa." The boy smiled quickly, plodded off toward a ladder in the corner of the barn.

His father watched him go. He quickly uncoupled one of the machines and strode out to the milkroom with it. He set it on the floor, peered sharply out in the barn to make sure Jacky had disappeared up the ladder. Then he went over to a calendar hanging on the wall, tore off the month of December and turned it over. A stub of a pencil hung on a string beside the calendar, he snapped the string off its nail, twisted the pencil out of its loop. In large, backhand letters on the back of the torn sheet he printed: TO JACKY FROM SANTA. With the point of the pencil, he jabbed a hole in the paper, ran the string through the hole. Then, holding both ends of the string, he went out in the barn tumbled down through the square hole.

"That enough, Pa?" called a muffled voice.

"No, no, a lot more, Jacky." Quickly Jim Chatfield went over to the maternity pen, opened the gate and stepped in. Big Brown lifted her head, lowered at him suspiciously.

"Ssh!" he whispered. He knelt beside the calf. She regarded him with sleepy indifference. Nervously, he ran the string under her muzzle around her neck, knotted it. He stood up, surveyed the effect. The note hung crookedly under her chin like a ridiculous bib.

Jim Chatfield smiled. "Ya little peanut," he murmured. He left the pen, walked rapidly back to the milkroom. He poured the milk slowly through the strainer and listened. He could hear the boy scrambling down the ladder.

He lifted the strainer out of the can, slammed on the lid, called out: "Jacky!"

"Yes, Pa?"

"Throw a coupla forkfuls to Big Brown, will ya?"

"Okay," the boy answered.

Jim Chatfield stood by the cooler. He listened again. He heard the boy mutter to himself, heard the hay swishing along the floor he dragged it past the mangers towards the pen.

Jim Chatfield reached for his sheepskin.

"Pa! Pa!"

"Be right back, Jacky. Gotta bring the truck around."

Jim Chatfield stepped out into the dawn. The milkroom door slid shut behind him. He stood there a moment, blinking in the gloom. A gust of wind caught him in the face, making his eyes water.

The stars were all gone. He looked toward the East. It was getting lighter now.

NEIL MACCARTHRY

The Darkness of the Renaissance

A sanctified hath shone upon us; come ye
Gentiles and adore the Lord; for this day a
great light hath descended upon the earth.

WHAT IS THE GREAT LIGHT WHICH
descended upon the earth the first Christmas? It is He "Who
is the image of the invisible God, the first born of every creature." This light is the very Word of God, consubstantial with
the Father, filled with the brightness of the Divinity. Great indeed
is this light which descended from heaven and illuminated the
minds of men. For "no man hath seen God at any time: the only
begotten Son who is in the bosom of the Father, he hath declared
him." By this Word Who alone has known the Father, is the glory
of the Father revealed to the minds of men. In an inspired voice
of the Church proclaims: "A light shall shine upon this day, for
the Lord is born to us: and He shall be called wonderful, God,
the Prince of Peace, the Father of the world to come: of whose
reign there shall be no end."

With Christ the Father has given us all things; "Who hath
delivered us from the power of darkness, and hath translated
us into the kingdom of the Son of his love." For it is by Christ
that "He hath given us most great and precious promises: that
by these you may be made partakers of the divine nature." For
to "as many as received Him, He gave them power to be made
the sons of God, to them that believe in His name."

Having been made partakers of the divine nature, men were
empowered to live the very life of God. Thus, we have a new
principle of knowledge, not merely the light of human reason,
but the very Word of God, that Divine Word in which God

knows all things. For in Faith this Word is communicated to the soul. By it the human intellect knows God, not merely as He can be known from His creation, but as God knows Himself, a perfection which human nature of itself could never attain.

But the light shineth in darkness. And the darkness did not comprehend it." What is this "darkness?" Does not the Church pray that "we who have known the mystery of His light may attain the enjoyment of His happiness in heaven"? Why is this light a mystery? A mystery is dark, but here we have a light which is called a mystery. Is not the noon-day sun dark to the eyes of an owl? This divine light is dark to us because its very brilliance blinds our feeble minds. For the human intellect is the weakest of all intellects and is able to bear but a little light. Relative to the light of God it is indeed darkness and that is why the very brightness of this light unless he recognizes this weakness and assents to that which his intellect cannot see, just as a child accepts many things his father teaches him, even though he cannot comprehend the reasons. We accept the Faith in just that way; for it tells us many things about God in His most intimate life and as yet we cannot see how these things are so. Accordingly, we assent to them solely on the word of our Heavenly Father Who by the impulse of His grace moves our wills to command the intellects' assent. Hence to live a life of Faith, a divine life, a man must die to his natural light. Do not the Saints tell us that we must seek Christ in the darkness of Faith, leaving behind our understanding, memory, imagination — all our natural activity? Is this not to die, for a man to give up his own understanding and live by pure Faith? And did not Our Lord say, "... he that will save his life, shall lose it: and he that shall lose his life for My sake, shall find it"? This was what those Pharisees and Sadducees refused to do who came to Our Lord and "asked Him to show them a sign from heaven." Did they not want a sign that they could understand? They would accept Christ if they did not have to renounce their understanding.

II

Once this marvelous light had illuminated the earth and shown us a perfection in comparison to which all natural perfection is as nothing; once man had been told of the incomprehensible prodigality of God Who offered to make him His son, to elevate him to a divine life, to give him a participation in God's own knowledge; is it to be thought that men should merely ignore Christ and His promises, should continue to seek a natural perfection as though Christ had not become incarnate? Yet this is the problem with which we are faced in considering modern civilization. We are told that the Renaissance, the beginning of the modern era, was a "return to nature," an attempt to shake off the "bondage" of Faith. In the light of the Faith, is not this account incredible? It is evident that in comparison with the gifts which God has made, ours by the Incarnation, the Devil with his shoddy wares is in an unenviable position. (And surely Satan is the only one who could have been the instigator of so terrible a thing as the Renaissance.) What has he to offer that could entice men from God? Is it to be thought that he would use the promise of a merely natural perfection? Perfect as that is, it is but a remote participation in the perfection of the divine life. Natural knowledge is but a shadow of supernatural truth. And even if Satan were such a poor salesman (and how can we think he is when we see the effective methods he has taught modern advertising?), he could not offer men that, for nature correctly understood leads to God, its Author. The Devil is a fool, but he is not stupid. He knew that once men had been raised to a participation in the Divine Word, the first of all lights, they could never be satisfied with merely the light of human reason.

To understand Satan's tactics let us consider the prototype of all temptations: "And the serpent said to the woman: No, you shall not die the death. For God doth know that in what day soever you shall eat thereof, your eyes shall be opened: *and you shall be as gods,* knowing good and evil."

Was not the same promise made at the time of the Renaissance? Were not men persuaded that only by turning from God and His Holy Faith would they attain the perfection of knowledge; that freed from the darkness of Faith, all things would become clear to them? At this time, the modern myth of an *infinite* progress in knowledge was born. They thought they were returning to nature, but Aristotle would have blinked at what they called "nature." In the natural order metaphysical is the highest science. Did the Renaissance, then, turn from theology to metaphysics? Everyone knows such was not the case. Rather, the natural sciences, mathematics, history and poetry, became the principal intellectual disciplines and were regarded as the highest knowledge. Why was this? Was it not because these disciplines are most proportioned to our intellects? United to a body, our intellects can best understand the natures of corporeal things. Even metaphysics, a natural discipline, is dark to us because of all natural knowledge, it is farthest removed from sense. For that reason, Aristotle said that it is more divine than human. (We must remember that God is the principal object of metaphysics.) If a man lives long in a cave his eyes become attuned to the murk around him. Objects in the cave become clear to him while he can barely see the world bathed in sunlight. But is he not mistaken if he then claims that the gloom of the cave is really bright and the sun is dark? In the same way, as long as we are tied to sense, material objects are clearest to us. And the things of God are very hard for us to penetrate. But we are surely foolish if we claim that the things that are clearest to us are really the brightest. For God, on the other hand, Who knows Himself in His Divine Word, it is just the opposite. That which is more intelligible to Him is also the most intelligible in itself. And it will be so for us in beatitude when strengthened by the Light of Glory we shall see God face to face. He Who is the most intelligible being, the source of all light, will be most intelligible to us. God will no longer be dark to us by an excess of brilliance. (It is as though an owl were fitted with a marvelous pair of spectacles through which he could look directly into the sun.) Through Christ we are promised this greatest of all gifts; but we must remember that now we already possess the seed of this life for St. Thomas tells us that Baptism is a "certain beginning of eternal life." Indeed, the Life of Faith and the Lift of Glory are essentially one and the same, for in both we know, in and by the Divine Word, in the one face to face, in the other "as in a mirror, darkly."

Hence to understand the Renaissance, we must understand this that which is most intelligible to a divine light is most intelligible in itself. This is true for God, first of all. But it is potentially so for those who follow Christ. In beatitude, it will be actually so for them. Now do we not see what the men of the Renaissance were really saying (they did not understand it, but Satan who put it into their heads did) when they turned from Faith, and even from metaphysics, the highest wisdom in the natural order, and made those disciplines which are most intelligible to reason the highest knowledge? They actually thought that those things which are most intelligible to reason are the most intelligible in themselves. This doctrine *means* that reason is the divine light. (Rationalism is truly a most unreasonable doctrine.) "And the serpent said to the woman . . . your eyes shall be open: and you shall be as gods."

Do we not begin to see what this celebrated "return to nature" really was? By a master stroke, so he thought (for this greatest of fools never learns that God uses these master strokes for His own purposes), Satan offered men the fruits of Christ without the conditions Christ exacts. Our Lord promised infinite light, but only if we are willing to die to ourselves, to forfeit our natural life. "Unless the seed falling into the ground dieth, it cannot bring forth fruit." Satan is the great flatterer. He does not tell us, as Christ does, that our natural reason is darkness renounce our natural understanding. No, he persuades men that they indeed should "be as gods," knowing as God knows, not by denying their natural light but by making it he ultimate light. Similarly, Satan held out to men the infinite freedom which is ours through Christ. But he said that we would gain the "freedom of the sons of God," not by obeying God's laws and dying to our own will, but by negating all law, all discipline. And just as Christ promised that those who would receive Him, by dying to their own will and light, should be made the sons of God: " . . . as many as received Him. He gave them power to be made the sons of God, to them that believe in His name, who are born, not of blood, nor of the will of the flesh, nor of the will of man, but of God"; so the Devil promised that the true rebirth to a life of infinite perfection would take place only when men renounced the yoke of Christ and were born "of the will of the flesh and the will of man."

III

St. John tells us that "All things were made by Him (the Word) and without Him was made nothing that was made." But men were so deceived as to think that only by turning from this Word could they attain the knowledge of that nature which is His work. Once such a monstrously perverted doctrine had been accepted, we should hardly expect that men would gain the understanding of nature they desired. We have seen how distorted the knowledge of nature was in the Renaissance; and this initial error is working itself out to its full consequences in our time, characterized as it is by the utter loss of natural truth.

As we know, the Faith is a participation in God's knowledge; St. Thomas says it is a "certain impression of the Divine knowledge in us" Now God is the uncreated light, the source and fount of all secondary lights, such as the light of reason. All the while the Renaissance thought it was turning to light, from the source of all light. Having done this, it was inevitable that all derived lights would in time be denied. When the tree is cut, down the branches wither.

What was begun then is nearing completion for us. On looking at modern doctrine, what strikes us most is the absolute and universal denial of reason, the cultivation of the irrational — even that remnant of reason which the Renaissance preserved is gone. If reason is respected by anyone, we would expect that it would be the philosophers. But John Dewey, the dean of American philosophers, tells us that philosophy has its origin in the imagination. The French philosopher, Bergson, teaches that instinct and intuition give us our only valid knowledge. And this is brought home to us by the American, William James, who remarked that Bergson had freed him from logic, i.e., reason. To choose one other example from many, we have the contemporary cult of Existentialism which derides reason and cherishes the irrational.

Perhaps modern art is more familiar to most of us. One thing is certain, a painting by Picasso is not recognizable as a likeness of anything in nature. It is not clear what it is. Surrealism provides another example. Or again we might consider modern music, which is characterized by excessive dissonance and a lack of any intelligible harmonic resolution. Compare the obscurity and harshness of Stravinsky, Hindemeth or Schonberg with the clarity of Mozart. For Mozart, consonance was a first principle of music; for the moderns, dissonance holds that place. The same manifestations occur in the poetry of today which is proverbially difficult and obscure. What we notice in it is a tendency to formlessness, the lack of an ordered form which is inevitable when the imagination is divorced from reason.

But experimental science is most familiar of all, and indeed is the motivating force behind the manifestations of irrationality in these other fields. Now modern science has one great characteristic: it does not claim to have any absolute and final knowledge (and further says that no other discipline gives us such knowledge). Its conclusions are always subject to change; indeed, scientists expect them to be displaced. A scientist would shudder with horror if it were said that any of his knowledge is necessary and unchangeable. Knowledge to him is infinitely perfectible.

The rejection of reason is not the only thing to be noticed in those examples. Do we not observe that the various human faculties are denied the very objects to which they tend by nature? All men desire to know and to know with certitude. But modern science says that we have no certain knowledge. The ear naturally seeks consonance, but in this modern music it hears only dissonance which is dark to it. For every faculty darkness is substituted for light. This is nothing less than a destruction of nature. See what sacrifices Satan asks of those he deludes; he does not ask that they merely mortify their nature but that they annihilate it. And the Renaissance thought that Christ asked for too much.

To understand modern doctrine more precisely we must make use of a somewhat technical point of philosophy, technical but not difficult. St. Thomas tells us that there are two kinds of infinite, one on the part of matter, the other on the part of form. Matter is infinite in the sense that it is able to be determined, informed by many different forms. Of itself, it has no form but it can receive the form of animality, humanity and even non-living forms such as a rock, etc. When it is determined by any one form, it becomes finite, i.e., it combines with the form to become *one* determinate kind of thing. But matter considered is itself, not united to a form, and it is in virtue of its form that we know it. Form, too, is in-batch of concrete is capable of being made into many things, of receiving many different forms. It can become a house, a burial vault, a church, a statue, etc. Now since we can only know by forms, matter as destitute of form is absolutely unintelligible. We can only know it as it is, united to a form, and it is in virtue of its form that we know it. Form, too, is infinite, for of itself it is common to many things. But it is made finite by being received in matter, i.e., it becomes the form of this particular thing.

Matter is an infinite which is lacking in all perfection; accordingly, when it is determined to become some one thing it receives a perfection. Form, on the other hand, is not perfected when joined to matter, but rather it is limited. Therefore, form which is infinite because not limited by matter is an infinite of perfection. St. Thomas goes on to say that God is a self-subsisting form, that the form of the Divinity is not received into any matter (or any potency of any kind) and so is not limited, made finite. Hence, God as infinite and unlimited cannot be grasped by a finite intellect. This is why God is unintelligible and dark to us. Matter too, as infinite, is unintelligible to us, not as in God's case because it is too intelligible, but because it simple lacks all intelligibility. To sum up: there are two infinites, God and matter; one is infinite because of its perfection, the other because of its imperfection. Both are unintelligible to us; God, Who is most intelligible in Himself, because of an excess of intelligibility; matter because it is intrinsically and essentially unintelligible.

Now anyone familiar with modern thought knows that the one thing universally agreed on is that there are no forms (essences) such as we have described. The moderns use the term "form" but by it they mean *material structure.* For example, all would deny that there is such a thing as human nature, in the sense of an essence which is present in all men, as is presupposed when we say that Christ redeemed man. Nor we can understand why men of science tell us that they have no absolute and unchanging knowledge. When science is reduced to the investigation of matter (material structure) divorced from form, it can give us no certain knowledge, for the object known is indeterminate and changing. Consequently, knowledge of it cannot be eternally true, but is as undetermined as its object. But it is this denial of form which makes the object of knowledge a quasi-infinite object, which makes it unintelligible and inexhaustible as an object of contemplation. And because the object known is formless and dark, it is impossible to have any literal, determinate knowledge. But in every instance, the fact that our knowledge is unclear and inadequate to express the fullness of this infinite object is used to insinuate that this is necessarily so because of the inexhaustible profundity of the object. For example, contemporary literary criticism insists that what a poem says can never be fully expressed in a literal paraphrase. And they are right in this, but not, as they intimate, because the poem's meaning is too profound to be expressed, nor because it gives us a truth above logic, as they frequently say. Rather it is because a poem is a material (sensible) image and this as material is intrinsically lacking in intelligibility. Historical scholarship gives us another illustration of this pursuit of the infinite of matter. In our time scholarship has become a search for an endless number of facts; material facts as such, not as illuminated and made intelligible by rational principles. Indeed, any attempt to interpret or explain the fact in the light of abstract principles is frowned upon as departing from scholarly objectivity. Once again, we have this quasi-mystical contemplation of a material and therefore inexhaustible object.

What are we to make of all this? Can we conclude that modern man has ceased to be a rational animal? We would deny our own principles if we said that. Man is rational by nature and that means he has to have reasons for what he does. Even lunatics are most ingenious in finding reasons for their aberrations (bad reasons it is true, but still reasons). The human mind cannot seek darkness as an end in itself, in virtue of our rational nature we must necessarily seek light. Is this not true for those who embrace the darkness of Faith? They know that through this darkness they will attain the eternal and uncreated light. Does this not tell us why the moderns embrace the darkness of matter, why they seek the irrational and unintelligible? In truth it is only by seeking darkness that we shall ever see the Infinite Being. But are not the moderns also seeking the infinite? Is not that why they devote themselves to the investigation of matter?

Let us not be so blind as to accuse them of seeing darkness and unintelligibility for its own sake. We should remember that it was with the promise of infinite knowledge that the Devil lured men from Christ, infinite knowledge without paying the price of darkness. He told them that their intellects could comprehend all things. This he could only do because Christ had promised men that through Him they would know as God knows. But as Satan knew, men must inevitably fail in this blasphemous undertaking and we today are the witness of the frustration of the lie that was the Renaissance. But men are still seeking infinite light, for after Christ, after the great light which this day hath descended upon the earth, they could be satisfied with nothing less. But being unwilling to seek it in darkness, they sought it without Christ. See to what a depth of degradation it has led them! They have inevitably lost, not only supernatural truth, but even every natural good, the very nature to which they so triumphantly "returned"; see how terribly the Devil tricks those whom he deludes, for now they are seeking this infinite light in darkness, and infinitely greater darkness than Christ asks, for this darkness destroys nature. Is it not clear to the eyes of Faith that in seeking the infinite of matter, in running after the unintelligible and irrational, by a horrible diabolical delusion, men are seeking Satan, not Satan for his own sake, but Satan masked as Christ? This should not surprise us. St. Paul told us that our struggle "is not against flesh and blood, but against principalities and powers, against the powers of darkness in high places."

Do we not see how abundantly Our Lord's words have been fulfilled: "And I, if I be lifted up from the earth, will draw all things to Myself." For since His coming men have been unable not to seek Him. How wonderfully it manifests His Divine power when we realize that even Satan must imitate Christ if he is to attract men. But even more, seeing the diabolical origin of the errors around us, we must realize that "this kind is not cast out but by prayer and fasting."

Our Lord said: "I am the light of the world: he that followeth Me, walketh not in darkness, but shall have the light of life." Does not history verify this abundantly? Let us learn well that since the coming of Christ, the "light of the world," we can no longer live merely a natural life. Either we will embrace the Divine Word in the darkness of Faith, desiring *only* that Word and all else for His sake, or we will embrace the darkness of the light with which Lucifer will destroys us. For he that does not follow Christ, the eternal light, Who has come into the world to be our light that we might know the Father, "walketh in darkness and knoweth not whither he goeth."

WILLIAM DAVEY, T.O.P.

The Light in the Darkness

*Oh God, Who hast made this most holy night to
shine forth with the brightness of the true light, grant
that we may enjoy His happiness in heaven, the
mystery of Whose light we have known on earth.*
—COLLECT FROM FIRST MASS OF NATIVITY

IT WAS IN THE MIDST OF DARKNESS, SYMBOL-
ical of that which darkens the soul, that Jesus was born. It is
at the moment when the sun has reached the lowest point of
its course, and is re-born again that the "Sun of Suns" is born
each year at Christmas. The sun of nature and the Sun of Souls
appear together.

It is this important message that the Church wishes to impress
on us during the Christmas season. Yet most of us fail to understand the real significance of the Christmas story. It is essentially
a festival of lights, symbolic of the Light of the World. We have
retained some semblance of the symbolism in the Christmas tree
lights and the lights in windows; but we do it only because it has
always been done, and we are ignorant of the real meaning of it all.

Christmas is, therefore, a season of light. Christmas ceremonies the world over evolve around lights and fires — burning candles, blazing logs, illuminated tress. The lights on our Christmas

trees and in our windows have a significance. It is well for us to remember that.

The use of the symbolism of light did not originate with the Church. Like most of the other Christian customs it has been part of the folklore of mankind since the days of the cave-dwellers. The feast of Christmas at mid-winter coincides with a feast the pagans celebrated at the mid-winter solstice in honor of the birth of the sun, which they worshipped. The association of light with the darkness of mid-winter has been a religious tradition all through the ages and in all great religious. The Jewish calendar marks at mid-winter the feast of Channukah in honor of the capture of Jerusalem by the Maccabees. Prayers are said in the synagogues at sunrise and sunset, and in the homes a taper is lit every night, until by the eighth night eight candles are burning in token of ever-increasing strength.

The Holy Family was a pious one, and like all good Jews lived liturgically. So today, all good orthodox Jews live liturgically. To live so means to live the life of the Church in every phase of life. Our work, our play, our study, our meditation should always be directed to the honor and glory of God, to the Blessed Trinity, the Blessed Virgin and the saints and the martyrs. The Christian way of life is the liturgical way of life.

Because we no longer live liturgically is, without doubt, the reason why the celebration of Christmas has in our time no apparent connection with the birth of Christ. Advent slips by unnoticed by most of us; we live through the season in a welter of confusion, of crowded streets and shops, in worry over Bill's size in socks, or whether Gladys would prefer the pink silk negligee, or the perfume that the salesgirl assured us would surround her with the lure of a movie queen; we spend anxious moments wondering whether Aunt Sue will like the embroidered piano scarf that was left over from last year, and if it is possible to get anything decent at all for Aunt Minnie for less than a dollar and a half; and on the Holy Eve itself as we hear the old traditional carols being chanted and while the priest reads to us once more the age-old story of the birth of the Christ Child in the manger our thoughts are on the carefully wrapped packages under the tree, and whether Junior will really care for the electric train that cost the better part of a week's salary. We have heard the Christmas story year after a year and it means nothing to us; we listen and we do not heed. We go on about our business, feverishly attending to a hundred inconsequential details and heaving a sigh of relief when it is all over.

It is often said, repeated over and over each year: "Why can't the Christmas spirit last throughout the year?" It cannot last and never will last longer than three days, simply because it is not the true Christmas spirit. The glow of comradeship, of tolerance, of benevolence, is produced by the suggestions of the festivity surrounding us at every turn: the crowded streets, the holly and mistletoe that transform the drabness of business quarters, the gaudily decorated shop windows, the carol singers that greet us in department stores and public buildings, and the constant repetition of that grossly misquoted chorus of the angelic choir, "Peace on earth, good will to men."

That misquotation is the key to the whole sorry affair of a modern Christmas. We have lost the true meaning of the day. The Christmas spirit is more likely to come out of a bottle than from the heart. The angels promised, on that first Christmas, "Peace to men of good will." But there is little good will abroad these days. Rather we are confronted with a sentimental longing for a brotherhood of man. But brothers must have a father and a family must have a head. There can be no family of nations until there is a father of all nations, yet we will not accept this. Each year the Church observes the birthday of the Father of Nations and we do not accept Him. We talk about Him, we know His story, we give Him lip service, but we refuse to bow down and accept His laws; we refuse to give Him even the ordinary respect that we give our earthly father.

It was not haphazardly that the early Fathers of the Church arranged the yearly liturgy. It was with a sense of timing, a dramatic instinct which caused them to draw on the accumulated mystical experience of man and incorporate it into the Church's devotional chronology. Jewish symbolism and pagan imagery suited the purpose of the early disciples exactly; to dramatize the sources of life, the phenomena of nature, and through these visible signs the better to illustrate to their flocks the hidden meanings of the life of the Church and of Christ and the mysteries of the Redemption. The early Fathers were poets and artists, musicians and mystics, and their combined genius guided by the inspiration of the Holy Spirit, created the magnificent fabric of Catholic culture into which are embedded the precious jewels of the Mass and the Sacraments. Woven around these priceless treasures are the canonical hours which sanctify each hour of the day and night, chants and prayers, the prismatic thread of seasonal colors and the intricate designs symbolic of the cycle of nature: the equinox, mid-summer and mid-winter, the harvest and the sowing.

The brightest symbol of all is the Christmas one. The story of the birth of the Light of the World is told to the world by the flickering light of the candle, the emblem of the frail Child who brought with Him into the dark world the promise of a brighter future and Whose light spread over the earth in a blaze of glory. It is on this lesson that we should meditate at Christmas; not on gifts, parties, trees. Christmas is a home festival, unlike other Catholic feasts which are community affairs. The family attend Mass together, sing carols and pray around the crib, but we have forgotten that now. Even when there is a crib in the house it is very often dwarfed by the Christmas tree and the pile of gifts. It might be better from the spiritual point of view to dispense with Christmas presents altogether (although if this were carried to its logical conclusion a "recession" might result). There are days set aside especially for the exchange of gifts: Epiphany, for example, when friends exchange money, fruits or sweets in imitation of the Three Wise Men from the East; or the feast of the original

Santa Claus, St. Nicholas, December 6, which is the day set apart for the children when they are honored with gifts and special entertainment; or New Year's Day which always has been the time for gifts to employees and public servants.

The mediaeval Christian, and the Catholic peasant today, continued into their homes the symbolic observances of Christmas. There was no need for anyone to go out on Christmas Day. Carols were sung around the crib, the story of the search of Mary and Joseph for room at the inn was told in little plays or charades accompanied by traditional chants and dialogue. The candles were lit with great care and the Yule log was set ablaze with much ceremony and blessings. Life at home amidst a Catholic family could be one of constant joy and interest. It should be shocking to a Catholic to see the long lines of children before a movie house on Christmas Day, of all days.

The feast of the Epiphany, which the Irish call "Little Christmas," is also a day of interesting customs. The exchange of gifts to represent gold, frankincense and myrrh; the Twelfth Night cake which is divided among the family and guests to signify that to each goes the portion of the Lord, and into which is baked a coin. He who receives the coin is Twelfth Night King and reigns over the household and is given special privileges on that day, symbolic of the royalty of the Magi. It is in homely festivities of this sort that the life of the Church enters our homes.

In our times, when the world is under the pall of misery, destruction and hunger, the symbol of the Child Jesus, the Light of the World, has tremendous significance. We have woefully neglected the symbols of the Church, sign posts along the Christian Way. Christmas will reveal its meaning to us when we concentrate on the on the Church's customs and do not dissipate our energy in frantic last-minute shopping, expensive gifts, huge Christmas trees. There is more hope for the world in the symbol of a flickering candle than in all the deliberations of the United Nations.

LEONARD AUSTIN

The Family Feast

"ARE YOU GOING AWAY FOR CHRISTMAS?"
asked the massive blonde, as she covered her typewriter.

"What, all of us? You'd want Noah's Ark!" replied the junior
as she applied the first lipstick she had ever owned with a fine,
slashing technique. "My married sister and her kids are coming,
and my friend and her baby and the woman next door and Peter's
girl because they live in digs and can't get home and . . . "

"A real old-fashioned Christmas," remarked the massive blonde.

"Well, you can have one where there's kids, can't you? I always
say Christmas is nothing without . . . "

"What are you doing, Grace?" asked the willowy brunette.

The massive blonde turned around, "Oh, just as usual. Stew
in our own juice. Mum likes to be just ourselves on Christmas
day. You always go away, don't you?" There was a suggestion of
envy in her voice.

"We're going to Bournemouth to my uncle's hotel. We had a
lovely time last year — there was an R. A. F. Station near, but it
won't be there now. Still, it's better than just sticking at home
nowadays. You can't get anything now."

"We've got a turkey my sister won in a raffle at her office." said
the massive blonde, "but we couldn't get any drinks."

"We got a parcel from America, from the G. I. that was fond
of my sister," said the junior, "so we got a simply swell cake and
nylons. Just like pre-war. Are you going home, Ursula?"

"Home's my flat," replied the girl in glasses.

"Your people, then?"

"I haven't any, only aunts and uncles, and they haven't got
room. I suppose. They all live in the country."

"I thought you went to friends," said the massive blonde.

"Sometimes. I think they think I go to relations and my relations think I go to friends."

'Why don't you ask some lonely person to spend it with you?" suggested the massive blonde helpfully.

"I tried to, but they all had somewhere to go."

"Still, it doesn't seem right to be by yourself — Christmas is the family feast, though to be sure no one can have a decent Christmas now."

"And I haven't got a family!"

"Well, after all," said the willowy brunette brightly but tactlessly "you wouldn't want to go where you felt you were an outsider, would you?"

"God forbid!" exclaimed the girl in glasses with energy. "I prefer my own company."

"Scrooge!" said the junior, who had not long left school.

"I've a good deal of sympathy with Scrooge," continued the girl in glasses, as she packed up her belongings quickly and ran off, hoping no one had seen that her eyes were wet.

She heard that they did not start talking again immediately after she had left the room. They would probably say she was getting on, after all, and it was sad, but they always thought people brought it on themselves, and she was thirty-eight. She made her way through the crowds to Trafalgar Square, and while she waited in the queue, tried to pull herself together and failed.

Christmas was more unbearable every year. Before the war, her mother had been alive and her sister in England. Now her sister had married an Australian and gone to join him. During the war she had worked in a government office directly concerned with the war effort, and as someone had had to work over the holiday, she had volunteered to do so after mother's death, and taken someone else's fire-watching duty in the evening. Last year the war was over and she had hoped someone would remember she lived alone, but none did, or if they did it was only to add that they would simply *love* to have had her but…(mother is ill, or my sister's having a baby, or my brother's been de-mobbed that week, or nothing decent to eat, as you know and so on). She had finally rung up everyone she could think of, wishing them a happy Christmas and hoping . . . it was always the same, with a post-script that after all no one could have a decent Christmas now. It was not the dinner she wanted. She would have brought her own meat ration and eaten it there rather than feel left out. She had rooted out all the lonely people she knew, but they all had friends they went to. She seemed to be the lonely person in London. At the last time, a girl-friend, shocked at the thought of her spending a lonely Christmas, had put off her own friends, to whom she always went, in order to spend it with her, a kindness which Ursula never forgot. But this year the girlfriend was in Germany with the Control Commission.

If only she could bring herself not to mind being left out. She had no objection to her own company all the rest of the year, but at Christmas it was different.

The next day was Christmas Eve, and she went shopping. So did everyone else, and she spent most of the morning in queues of various kinds at the butcher, the greengrocer, the tobacconist, and the baker. Somehow the shops and stalls had managed to decorate themselves seasonably with home-made paper chains. Children were spending the money they had exacted for singing two verses of "While shepherds watched . . . " through the letter boxes and were getting in everyone's way. She caught scraps of talk in the shops and queues: "Just ourselves, you know . . . " "So we shall have drinks anyway . . . " "But it doesn't matter about the food really — if you've got kids, they enjoy anything . . . " To think — they've never known a real Christmas — I mean, pre-war, Poor little things." The poor little things did not seem unduly depressed but still got under everyone's feet. She felt she would never enjoy another Christmas as long as she lived. She would never be able to forget that someone, somewhere, was being left out, because it was the family feast and he or she did not belong to anyone's family. For that was what it had come to mean — the feast when outsiders were shut out, not the feast when strangers were brought in, as they once had been. She tried to remind herself that the Holy Family had been shut out too, but did not find much comfort in the thought. If only they would let her forget that it was Christmas, she would not feel so bad.

The queue at the confectioner's was so long she could not face it, and stood for some time in one for oranges, but the supply ran out before her turn came. Still, she had a pretty good load, one way and another. One year, she had lost her ration book and could not get an emergency one because the Food Office shut on Christmas Eve. She had been faced with a Christmas dinner of vegetables and last year's bottled plums, but fortunately the grocer produced a tin of Spam quietly and with an air of great secrecy when no one was looking.

In the afternoon she went to a cinema to kill time, and take her mind off herself, and when she came home, she got herself a meal, not too late because of Midnight Mass. Next door they were throwing a party, a wildly hilarious one, with the help of a cracked piano and a great deal of song. Few things are more depressing than listening to someone else's party. Children were singing carols in the street.

At eleven she set out, in good time to be sure of a seat, with a small New Testament in her pocket to read till Mass began. She arrived at the Cathedral and it was nearly empty. The people drifted in in twos and threes, shapeless and impersonal in the vast gloom. Few of the lights were yet lit, and she found it impossible to read the small prior in her New Testament, so she let her mind wander instead. Dim figures came in, genuflected and took their places, filling up the vast, unfinished building. The high arches of uncovered brick seemed to lose themselves in a faint haze.

The Cathedral filled slowly. The people passed up and down the aisles looking for places. They pressed into the aisles, now that there were no seats left, and filled the chapels and leaned against the great square piers. The sanctuary lights were turned on and the organ began to play, filling the building with great billows of sound. It did not matter that one was alone.

At twelve o'clock, the Mass began. The ancient ritual, the solemn Latin, led light back into the past. She was with the Christians who had been present at the same mystery in the low chambers, crudely but lovingly painted with Christian symbols (the fish and the loaves, the orante, Saint Peter and Saint Paul) hollowed out of the ground under Rome among the tombs of their fathers. She was with Agnes and Cecily, Cosmas and Damien, John and Paul — friendly names from a vanished world, a world in which Virgil was a modern poet and his tongue the common speech, a yet unfallen Rome before Monica and Augustine were born or thought of. But they had been present too, and Francis and the English martyrs of Elizabeth's reign who said Mass secretly in garrets and cellars and were put to death for it. What a little thing time was. A thousand years in thy sight are but as yesterday . . .

The Mass was over now. In the Cathedral, great clouds of sound from the organ rolled up into the dark arches while a priest said the second mass and a few people stayed on. The rest of the congregation hurried home through the bitter, empty streets.

Once home, Ursula heated some cocoa and drank it while she undressed quickly. Then she got into bed and turned off the light. Everything was quiet now, quiet and dark.

The next day she got up late and ate a leisurely breakfast by the fire. She had opened her few presents as they had arrived during the past week. Out in the street, some children were running up and down and shouting, and, indoors, mothers and elder sisters began to be very busy.

She went to High Mass at the little parish church across the way. It was filled with families with young children mostly, who had not been able to go to Midnight Mass. Many of them were wearing gaudy new head scarves, bright gloves and gay buttonholes pinned to shabby coats, which were obviously Christmas presents; and the child in front had a new doll to keep her quiet.

The row of children in front of her, inadequately controlled by their father, fidgeted and whispered. The priest gave a short address in which he admonished them to remember the significance of the feast while they enjoyed themselves with their families, and hoped they would have a very happy Christmas.

After Mass all the children fell over each other to get out first, and pranced up and down in the street outside, bragging about their presents, and mothers and elder sisters hurried home, those of them that were not home already, to get dinner.

Ursula went back to her flat and cooked her steak and sprouts and warmed up the mince pie, and after the plates were cleared away, she settled down with a book by the fire. It was very cosy and peaceful, once you could shut the world out and forget what you had not got, and no one could remind you of it.

In the afternoon, she went for a long walk along by the river as far as Battersea Park. Fathers were taking their offspring for a walk, and she remembered a game they had used to play on Christmas afternoons of counting up the number of obviously new ties to see who could get the highest score. In the evening she went to the ballet. It had been a tolerably pleasant holiday.

* * *

"Did you have a nice Christmas?" asked the massive blonde next morning.

"Very nice, thank you. Did you?"

"Middling. Go anywhere?"

"No. Just pottered about at home."

"So did we. You can't have a proper Christmas now, with no drinks and rationing, can you? Did you have a nice Christmas, Peggy?"

The willowy brunette drifted in looking the worse for wear, lugging a heavy suitcase. She sat down with a groan.

"Swell, thanks," she said faintly, and began to make up her face.

"Hullo, Ursula," cried the junior, bursting in with her coat hanging open and her hair all over the place. "Did you go any-where after all?"

"No. I stayed at home."

"Oh, what a shame. You ought to have to come to us. I told Mum you lived alone and she scolded me for not asking you. I wish I'd known."

"Thank you very much, dear. You're a lamb, but you know, I was quite happy."

"Still," said the junior, "it doesn't seem right being alone at Christmas."

"Oh, it isn't so bad, when you don't fret over what you haven't got."

"Yes, but Ursula, *Christmas!* It isn't right — you ought to enjoy yourself. It's the whole *point* of it."

"But I did enjoy myself. I was quite happy."

"But I don't mean that. You ought to have *fun.*"

"She likes being alone," said the willowy brunette. "Don't you, Ursula?"

"Well, all I can say is you *ought* to of," said the junior with emphasis. "It's all wrong."

"After all," said the massive blonde comfortably, "It wouldn't do if we were all alike, would it?"

"No, I suppose not," said the junior doubtfully, "but after all — still I'm glad it wasn't so bad after all."

What a nice little thing she is, thought Ursula, as she waited for a bus at the end of the day. So natural and so thoughtless and so kind. She could not explain that she also had been with her family — with Agnes and Cecily, John and Paul.

And yet in spite of this it had not been like Christmas at all. The junior was quite right. Ursula had been happy because, except when she was at Mass, she had been able to forget it was Christmas. But Christmas was not intended to be kept as a purely religious feast anymore than it was meant to be a secular one. Either way of keeping it was a perversion. It was, as everyone said without thinking, the family feast, and celebrated the coming of God into the human family. It should rightly be celebrated by family merrymakers, as well as by prayer and praise, though perhaps not in the somewhat exclusive manner of some good families. And those who had no families must find them. Not only at Christmas but all the rest of the year. Such a self-contained life was not right or natural, and it was well to be reminded of it. But she had become thus detached because, at one time or another, she had been hurt by human contacts, and had severed herself from them. Now she was hurt by having none, and it hurt even when she could school herself to believe that she did not need them. Just once in the year she had all the concentrated pain which for most people is spread over the four seasons. The world had strayed far from the old Catholic Christmas, and had broken it up into little bits, as it had broken up the Faith into little bits. But the remedy would hardly be applied in either case by pretending not to see what was there.

C.M. LARKINS
LONDON, ENGLAND

KRIS GIMBEL'S

Christian customs, business men
    Are seldom loathe to forfeit,
But cling they will to Santa Claus
    Who brings a handsome profit.

'Twas the Day Before Christmas

THE CHURCH OF ST. EFFICIENTIAS ROSE MAG-
nificently in the midst of an entire city block. Its beauty was
enhanced in the summer by the vastness of the cool, green
grass that surrounded it; in the winter by the whiteness of the
untouched snow. Even brash Protestants and unbelievers dared
not take liberties with the Monsignor's lawn—not that he was a
fearsome person, but because he had so skillfully blocked the natural shortcuts with a small hedges and short fences so that they
never really got started. Even the small boys, making "angels" in
the snow in the neighborhood, seemed to shy away from destroying the pristine beauty of the huge expanse of whiteness that
surrounded the church this 24th day of December, 1947.

The Monsignor was justly proud of his church. When he came
to St. Efficientias, the parish plant had been in deplorable condition. With characteristic thoroughness and forethought, he had
planned the remaking of the parish buildings, the church, the
rectory, and the school.

And now, twenty years later, he could look with pride, and
justly so, upon a magnificent church, a convenient rectory, and
a well-equipped school. It had not been easy, and had required
the utmost cooperation of the entire parish. The Monsignor had
been fortunate in securing a devoted corps of laymen, all experienced, successful businessmen, who worked with him and helped
organize his campaigns. As a result of their cooperation and the
Monsignor's hard work, he now had a parish entirely free of debt.

At precisely 7:13 A.M. this day before Christmas, the Monsignor stepped out of the side of the door of the Church. He had
just finished the 6:30 Mass, and he pulled his overcoat tighter
around his spare, thin body. But even swathed in the overcoat,

and huddled against the force of the cold wind, he still had an air about him as he walked down the steps. He strode quickly along the clean-swept walk, wide enough so parishioners hurrying to late Sunday Mass had ample room to pass one another without encroaching on the lawn, but also protected with a fence, small enough to be inconspicuous, but large enough to present an obstacle to hedge hopping. He paused at the street, carefully looking each way, before crossing to the rectory. His routine was the same, day in and day out, winter, summer, spring or fall. His housekeeper knew the moment his footsteps ouldd sound on the porch, the moment his breakfast should be on the dining room table, almost the second he would bow his gray head to say grace, for the Monsignor valued his minutes. He knew that time was valuable, and he did not propose to waste it.

At precisely 8:00 A.M., he was seated in his office, laying his plans for the day. He knew that soon the first assistant would come hurrying through the hall, having finished the 7:30 Mass; and moments later the second assistant would hurry through the same hall, not late but hurrying so that he would be ready to leave the sacristy when the electric clock there stood at ten seconds before 8:15. The Monsignor rejoiced in the evenness of life in the parish, the smoothness with which it ran, the effortless routine by which the different activities, the different parts of it fitted together.

He permitted himself the luxury of reminiscence this morning. He knew his plans for the day, and the assistants knew what their tasks would be. He had learned the value of scheduling, preparing, planning the day's work when his laymen's committee conducted their first campaign. They had made, from the census cards, a list of every wage earner in the parish. Then they had gone down the list, and set an amount for each. He had been amazed at how much they knew of the finances of each parishioner, and still more amazed at how right their estimates had been. It had made a tremendous impression on the Monsignor.

This was the day before Christmas. There would be Confessions in the morning and in the afternoon. The words he had used in last Sunday's sermon ran through his mind:

"There will be Confessions in the evening of the 23rd of December from seven-thirty until nine. On the day before Christmas there will be Confessions in the morning from ten until eleven-thirty, and in the afternoon from two-thirty until finished. We hope that Confessions may be finished by five o'clock. This should be possible if everyone will cooperate, and I know that the loyal parishioners of St. Efficientias will. Your priest, just as yourselves do, would like to have Christmas Eve free."

He remembered the first time he stopped Confessions on Christmas Eve. You would have thought it was a heresy. It almost seemed as though some of his parishioners wanted to be in the state of grace for the shortest possible time before receiving Communion at the Midnight Mass. But it was ridiculous for himself and his assistants to be in the confessional Christmas Eve, with little or no chance to rest before the Midnight Mass. Now the change was accepted, just as was the fact that Confessions were not heard before Mass on Sundays. That was as old-world custom; there was no reason why it should be continued. He had resorted to strategy in removing that obstacle to the smooth running of his parish. He had merely announced that anyone wishing to go to Confession before Mass could notify one of the ushers, who would tell the priest in the sacristy.

The Monsignor felt rather satisfied with his work for the past year. The total number of Communions distributed would be more than in any other year. The financial repost would also be better. He finally felt that he had the parish organized properly so that it would almost run itself, even if he were not at the controls. It had not been easy, of course, and there had been much opposition at first, and even some assistance had to be transferred.

The one who had caused the most trouble was Father Stanislaus, who for five years now had been pastor of the little Polish church on the other side of the city, in the coal dock and gas plant district. Father Stanislaus could never realize that as order was the law of the universe, it should also be the law of the parish. He had objected to almost everything the Monsignor planned, sometimes vehemently, sometimes mildly, humorously, as though objecting with the realization that no change would be made in the plans.

Father Stanislaus had not liked the new accounting system, the Monsignor recalled, even though the Monsignor's public accountant friend had installed it without charge. The accountant had spent much time preparing the proper forms and books to cover what he considered the accounting needs of the parish, and when he had finished, declared that anyone could keep the records without difficulty.

He had made a mistake there, though, because Father Stanislaus couldn't. Or maybe he hadn't wanted to. Yet he was always willing, always anxious to work hard, and the Monsignor had thought that he could learn. But Father Stanislaus had not been anxious to learn the keeping of such records, even simple records. The Monsignor's accountant friend had spent considerable time trying to explain the records and forms to Father Stanislaus. Finally, he had complained to the Monsignor "It's no use, Monsignor," he said. "Father Stanislaus doesn't care, for instance, how much you spend for meals in the rectory. He sees no need for comparative cost figures to show the relative cost of a certain commodity this year as against last year."

And Father Stanislaus thought that most amusing, and laughed heartily. "What does it matter," he asked, "how much we spend for fish on Friday? If it was less last year, perhaps someone gave us a catch of fish; perhaps the cost was less; perhaps we ate eggs instead, or maybe it was St. Patrick's Day. But anyway, what does it matter? These are the trivial things that fill our lives and detract from our main purpose in life." And then Father Stanislaus went off to play golf with a Baptist boy who was in love with a Catholic girl, but who thought priests were bogeymen.

It had been easier with Father Stanislaus gone. He seemed to stir up the other assistants a bit — not deliberately, but by his complete disregard of what he considered irrelevant. He wasn't disobedient; he just didn't consider such things very important, and refused to take them seriously.

And partly because of Father Stanislaus, the Monsignor had waited until his transfer before putting into effect his schedule of office hours. It was accepted now, without question. Every Sunday the Monsignor's bulletin carried at the foot of the page the hours for Baptism, Confession, and office hours at the rectory. The Monsignor had very carefully explained at all the Masses when he first listed the office hours that of course the priests of St. Efficientias were always available for sick calls, at any hour of the day or night. He wanted to be sure there was no misunderstanding about that, as he told the parishioners, "... every business-man must have office hours; otherwise, he is not using his time to the utmost. That is our only purpose in setting such hours as these. Of course, we will always be available in the evenings by appointment." He was sure the parishioners had understood the reasons behind it; at any rate, he knew that they had now accepted the change.

* * *

On the other side of the city, the Church of St. Pastorus poked its gilded cross into the sky from a small hill among the houses of the coal dock workers, and within range of the gas plant. It was not an elaborate structure — it had originally been a Methodist church, but Father Stanislaus had made it as attractive as he could. Some purists objected to it as garish; they complained about the decorations in the church, the multitude of electric lights, the gaudy statues, about the huge statue of Christ alongside the church, with a spotlight playing on it. They didn't know, of course, that the men on the coal docks along the river could see it while they worked the long winter nights, and that it gave them strength and courage, and occasionally routed temptation when their glance happened that way.

Father Stanislaus' lawn was as green in summer as the Monsignor's; there was just not much of it. The church, the rectory and the school were crowded into a quarter of a city block, and there wasn't much space left for lawn. In winter he had more snow than the Monsignor, and the wind piled it high around the church and school and rectory. It was not as clean; Father had the bad habit of encouraging the children to play around the rectory and school, and some of them inevitably strayed into the churchyard.

His day, on this 24th day of December, 1947, began too early. About four o'clock in the morning, there was a banging on his door. Hurrying down the stairs, Father Stanislaus stumbled through the accumulation of baseballs, bats, and footballs that still cluttered his hallway and switched on the porch light as he opened the door.

"Father," said the taxi driver on the porch, "Joe Hulobowicz is our in the cab, dead drunk. I took him home and his wife won't let him in the house. What'll I do with him?"

Father Stanislaus shook his head. "Poor Joe — and poor Mary and the children. Is he very drunk?"

"Dead drunk, Father," said the taxi driver. "They got their bonus tonight, and it was too much for Joe."

"Wait here," said Father. "I'll go with you back to his house."

He raced back upstairs to dress, and returned in a few minutes.

At the Hulobowicz house, there was a light in the kitchen window and Father Stanislaus went around to the back. Through the window, he could see Mary Hulobowicz, her head on the table, either asleep or sobbing quietly, so as not to wake the children.

When he knocked, she jumped. "It's Father, Mary," he called.

She opened the door and he stepped inside. "Joe's outside in a car," he said.

"He can't come in," she said, almost hysterically. "This is the last time, Father. If he can't keep away from whiskey on Christmas Eve . . . "

"Mary," said Father Stanislaus slowly, "Joe has his weakness — and I have my weakness, and you have your weakness. That's our human nature, but Joe doesn't fight his. Tell Joe I want to see him before Confession this afternoon. I'll get him straightened out, Mary."

She wavered, then nodded her head in agreement.

"I'll bring him in," said Father Stanislaus; "you get a bed ready for him."

He went out the back door again, and with the help of the taxi driver lifted Joe Hulobowicz out of the cab. While the driver was slamming shut the door, he dropped two folded bills into Joe's pocket. He knew Joe's drinking habits — until he ran out of money — and he did not want to see the Hulobowicz family penniless on Christmas Eve — and the coal company could wait. They were accustomed to that by now.

Back in his rectory, he wearily climbed the stairs for a few hours rest before his day began in earnest. His daily Mass was at eight o'clock, and as usual he was late for it — and the lateness ran into everything he did during the day. His afternoon Confessions were scheduled to begin at three o'clock; but it was three-fifteen before he appeared. Joe had come around, and Father Stanislaus had straightened him out; and after that Father had telephoned some of the tavern keepers to make sure that Joe stayed straightened, at least for a while. His afternoon Confessions were supposed to end at five, but there were still twenty to be heard at five, and with others coming in it was six-fifteen before he finished and had a chance for a bite to eat.

At six-thirty, the Baptist boy of five years before, who was in love with a Catholic girl, but who had thought priests were bogeymen, called with his first-born and his wife, to pay his

Christmas respects to the priest who had converted him. Father Stanislaus played with the little girl for most of the time the couple were there, for he loved all people and most of all he loved children. They started to hurry off, knowing he had many waiting for Confessions, but he stopped them for a minute and left the room. He came back with a hand behind his back and gave the little girl a stick of peppermint candy, and then another and another and another, until her hands were so full, she could hold no more, and still he gave her more and more. And he laughed with children's delight at her happiness and joyful bewilderment in trying to hold all the candy and yet take the new sticks that were being offered her.

After they had gone, he went back to the confessional again. He knew from experience there would be many coming to Confession that night. Some parishioners rather bitterly referred to it as the overflow from St. Efficientias, but Father Stanislaus would have resented that. A priest is a pastor of souls, and every lost soul, every soul in a state of sin, is a lost sheep, to be brought back to the fold.

He had a little respite between the late comers for Confession and the early comers for the Midnight Mass, and in the quiet solitude of the church, in the company of God, he read his breviary, switching off the light above him in the confessional whenever the outside door opened, patiently awaiting the God-given privilege of restoring another human soul to God's grace.

* * *

At the Midnight Mass, both the Church of St. Efficientias and the Church of St. Pastorus were crowded. In the former, as the electric clock in the sacristy showed ten seconds before the time of the Mass, the two altar boys left the sacristy, followed by the second assistant who was Master of Ceremonies of the Mass, followed by the Monsignor who was Celebrant of the Mass. And the bell tinkled on the second of midnight. The well-trained altar boys, their faces shiny bright, every hair in place, performed with the usual precision of the Monsignor's altar boys, lit the front of the church, where they could more closely follow the Mass, fur-coated women and a few well-dressed men opened their St. Andrew's Missals to the Mass of the Catechumens and knelt as the Monsignor began the prayers at the foot of the altar. With liturgical exactitude they followed the Monsignor's even pace, cued by *Dominus vobiscum* and the electric chimes, run on split second timing by the altar boys.

Father Stanislaus was still hearing Confessions at midnight, and it was five minutes past the hour before he was able to leave the confessional. He hurried up the aisle to the sacristy, where six altar boys were waiting for him. He glowed as he smiled at them, from unruly hair more or less firmly watered and brushed into place, down past spotlessly clean but mended surplices to a surprising variety of shoes, brown, black, tennis and heavy boot. At twelve-seventeen the first two altar boys stepped out of the sacristy, then two more, and two more, and then Father Stanislaus. As he began the prayers at the foot of the altar, some of those in the church took out worn prayer books to follow the Mass. Three old women, in the first pew, with shabby black coats, and heavy shawls for their heads, continued saying the Rosary; effortlessly the beads slipped through their fingers, as though they said the Rosary all day long, and perhaps they did.

The bells did not ring on time, and sometimes the server forgot his job and had to be nudged by another; but when Father Stanislaus whispered *HOC EST ENIM CORPUS MEUM,* the church was hushed and they could almost hear angels' wings beating about the altar.

It was Christmas, 1947, in the Church of St. Efficientias and in the Church of St. Pastorus. God had come, once again, as a little Child to *all* His people.

FLOYD ANDERSON

Plea to All Men

Stranger who drinks with me at the Inn of the World
A lonely glass against the evening's gloom,
Do not the stars draw closer in their heavens
Than we are close within this little room?
Shall we never speak to one another?
Eternity hastens while we sip our wine.
Shall we sit staring coldly, O my brother,
Seeing I know your pain, as you know mine?
Can we not talk of the one hope that spurs us
Leaping from soul to soul in broken flame?
Will there be tears of joy upon our faces
That, far from home, one calls us still by name?
And when the hour draws on, and fires are dying,
Will you not lean across the dark and say:
Take then this little gift of comfort,
I have not come so far myself today.
We have only tonight, my brother,
Till the long quest for bread and beauty ends!
Can we put by our pride and knock like children
At the one gate that makes us more than friends?
O do not hide from me your journey's anguish.
Tomorrow we may both be lifted up
Because we broke the pilgrim's bread together
And drank of faith within each other's cup.

ELIZABETH M. ODELL

My Marriage Course

BOOKS ON MARRIAGE ARE PERENNIALLY POP-
ular. Young people contemplating Matrimony are always eager
for some pointers on this new life. Marriage courses have come
into demand at many colleges and universities and even in our
high schools. They are usually well attended. The seriousness
with which the subject is studied shows that in this day of light-
ly-entered marriages and too-frequent divorce and infidelity,
youth still seeks to realize an ideal relationship between man
and woman. The young look to older and wiser minds to help
them avoid the pitfalls which beset modern couples entering life
together. The trouble in many of these books and courses is that
the heads which conceived them are older but not nearly wise
enough. They lack the Christian ideal which alone can make
marriage the great and beautiful union to which Christ raised it.

If I were to give such a marriage course, I would base it in
part on material from several books which I have recently read.
So! You Want To Get Married! by Dorothy Fremont Grant and
The Art Of Happy Marriage by Rev. James Magner would help
me marshal up the pertinent facts, proper attitudes and practical
details which should be considered. Both books treat the same
material, but in a different manner. They are both good as far as
they go but they do not go far enough.

Mrs. Grant's book is written in an informal manner and
intended for young women. Her style is attractive. Her language
is simple, yet modern in phrasing so as to appeal to the sweet
young things to whom it is directed. Father Magner addresses his
work to a more general audience. His treatment is much more
comprehensive, so that we might take it as one of our texts in this
theoretical course. Among the subjects discussed are the court-
ship, details of the wedding, the purpose of marriage, the proper
place of sex, the very practical matters of money and children.

All of these matters are important and should be carefully considered by young men and women before marriage. In fact, they should be considered before one has become so blindly infatuated that such things do not seem important when compared to this "great love."

An entirely different treatise on matrimony is contained in a little booklet, *Companions for Eternity*, a translation of a work by A. M. Carré, O. P., published by Blackfriars Publications, Oxford. This booklet I would label as a "must" in my marriage course. It is, as the author tells us, based on three conferences given to students in the Latin Quarter in Paris. It is the "statement of the Catholic case for marriage in terms suitable to their psychology." He shows us married love in all its beauty and with all the difficulties which beset it, since it is a union of two sin-prone creatures. The full implications of marriage as a vocation, as a state of life, are made clear. St. Paul has compared marriage with the union between Christ and His Church. Father Carré shows us how the grace of the sacrament is always with us in the humble everyday life to help realize in the Christian home the same beautiful love, devotion and sacrifice as that which exists between Christ and His Church.

The last part of the booklet treats of the mission of the man and that of the woman, and of how they complement and fulfill each other.

I have already said that I would recommend the first two books to young people considering marriage, but still sufficiently whole of heart to realize that reason as well as emotion must prevail when choosing a partner for life. *Companions for Eternity* could also be read by them with profit, but I would especially recommend it to engage or married couples and urge them to read it together. It will help them to gain deeper insight into this love which God has given them. They will learn how best to cooperate with the grace of Matrimony so that their love may grow and take on the characteristics of divine love. When two people are intensely interested in saving each others' souls and each is willing to make the sacrifices necessary to help the other grow in grace, the practical problems previously mentioned will be more readily solved. Questions of planned parenthood and of keeping up with the Joneses will not even arise if the first purpose in their minds is to serve God and each other.

These last remarks may indicate that I consider the spiritual approach of Father Carrémore important than that used by Mrs. Grant and Father Magner. In a sense, I do. The latter two presuppose, for the most part, that young people who are entering marriage today will face pretty much the same problems as their parents faced. They ignore the fact that our whole social order is in a state of revolution. The United States has been slower than European countries to feel the change, but events are moving faster and faster. God alone knows in what sort of world our children will grow up. The old standards of security are vanishing. Couples today must choose whether they will sacrifice independence of thought and action to a system of mass production for the sake of a weekly pay check, or develop and use their talents and abilities so as to best serve God and their fellow man and trust in God's Providence to help them provide their daily wants. Whichever choice is made will have a profound effect on their attitudes and manner of living and a corresponding effect on the children.

On the matter of security, one point in Father Magner's book stuck me particularly. He recommends that married couples keep a bank balance of not less than five hundred dollars. Mrs. Grant suggests that they save ten per cent of their income. Both ideas are very good. However, the people they know must have different earning capacity from those with whom I am acquainted. I am not referring to the very poor or slothful people. I know five couples whose marriages are better than most. Both man and wife are well educated in each case. They have fairly remunerative work. They have good will and strong faith. All are trying to carry out the Pope's suggestions for a truly Christian marriage.

On the other hand, I know many couples who are following more worldly ideas. They are aiming to get ahead by small compromises with the best way of doing things. They are not bad but more "liberal."

No couple of either sort has ever, to my knowledge, had as much as five hundred dollars at one time. Those of the first group have found themselves burdened with the expense of having a baby every year or year and a half. (They average five children to a family.) Those of the second group average two and a half children. They have trouble in saving because they are trying to keep the children well dressed and to keep up a certain social position from which they hope to go a little higher. It is all very well to save ten per cent of a week's wages, but it is difficult to do so if the weekly wage does not supply quite enough to go around. This is the usual case today for a working man with a good-sized family. It is in many cases the reason why wives work outside the home. It is the exceptional woman who really wants to punch a time clock. All this leads to the social problem of giving a working man a living family wage, which I shall not discuss here.

Those strongly tempted to choose security and worldly advancement at the expense of ideals and principles should realize that as our world is going, they will probably not have their reward either here or hereafter. Our country is the last stronghold of capitalism and the tide of battle here is going against it. The threatening spread of communism, the prospect of atomic warfare, the terrible unrest of whole nations. All these make our faith in the continuance of life as we have known it seem rather silly. Families without strong spiritual foundations and dependence on God are going to go under in the coming storm, as indeed many have already gone under before the advance wave of materialism and paganism.

Husband and wife can do much to gain God's favor and blessing on their union by their individual and family prayers. Saying night prayers together is one of the best I know for marital harmony. It is impossible to hold a grievance when you habitually kneel together and say the *Our Father*. These prayers can gain in efficacy when we have a heavenly advocate praying along with us. Holy Mother Church has recognized many married saints who might be taken as family patrons. The Holy Family is, of course, the ideal.

I have recently read of another in a biography of Blessed Margaret Clitherow by Margaret T. Monro. She was an English convert to the Faith during the perilous days of Queen Elizabeth. She was a young housewife noted for her charm and vivacity. However, she did not hesitate to choose death of being crushed, rather than the comparatively easy one of hanging, in order to spare her children the ordeal of being forced to testify against her. Her children illustrate her great influence for good in the remarkable fact that, although only fourteen, twelve and ten respectively at the time of her death, and although brought up by Protestants (their father was a Protestant), the two sons became priests and the daughter became a nun. Blessed Margaret has been chosen as a patroness by two Catholic women's groups in England because her difficulties, particularly in securing Catholic education for her children, in many ways were like those which Catholics in England are facing today. Modern Americans who may also live to see days of persecution, but will, in any case, face the difficulties of living in an unbelieving world, will do well to add to their family prayers, "Blessed Margaret Clitherow, pray for us."

As a conclusion to my marriage course, we would read aloud the instruction which is read before the marriage service, although we will already be familiar with it. I would urge these young people to make a ceremony of rereading it along with their marriage vows on each wedding anniversary. The beautiful words of Holy Mother Church will help them recall, in the midst of everyday routine or even drabness, the idealism with which they began their life together and help them start another year with renewed zeal.

DOROTHY WILLOCK

Christ with Us

THE DRY WOOD

By Caryll Houselander

Sheed & Ward

Men are weary of seeking truth in the fulness of factual information (they have reached the perfection of statistics and research, but their heads are still void of wisdom). Men are also weary of living on past glories or in the future of the "progress" myth. They are nauseated by the unrealities and fictions and sentimentalities with which they hide from the enigmatic reality of the here and now. They will give their allegiance only to those who can explain life in the intensity of the present moment. They are moved, therefore, by the pseudo-realists who say, "Here is *real* life — it is one vast sewer of despair," because that's what their own lives look like to their own superficial view. Or they will give their allegiance to a Christianity which can take the garbage can of contemporary life and show Christ present now, redeeming now, transforming now, the rich and the poor, old and young, Protestant and Catholic and Jews and pagan refuse of our own apartment houses and offices and parishes. This is Caryll Houselander's gift. She can see Christ behind the smoke screen of our human sins and limitations. She can cut through the camouflage of secularism to show men as they really are, desperately in need of God, and to show Christ dispensing Himself to humanity through His Church.

The Dry Wood is Caryll Houselander's first novel, set in a slum parish of London. It is a story of sanctity and sin and God's grace moving men's hearts, in a setting of intense ordinariness. Hundreds of little touches of ordinariness shield the novel from any slight falsification of facts, so that Christ may show through more clearly. When the pastor hears Confessions, he is yet bothered by his rheumatism. The pious of the parish are often tedious and self-righteous. The rectory housekeeper is fittingly called "The Test of Faith." The parish church is a monument of cluttered ugliness and bad taste, and the author seeing that, yet sees that to some it looks beautiful even when it isn't, and that it is often in reality beautiful. She sees the candles like stars at a High Mass and the altar boys like little cherubim. There isn't a grain of sentimentality in the book, but it is filled with awe and compassion and love, and great deal of wonderful humor.

The story revolves around a central character and a thesis. The focal character is a seven-year-old who is crippled and mute from birth. The thesis is that twentieth century sanctity is child-like sanctity and that the sufferings of pure and innocent children are needed to redeem a world sunk in vice and pride.

The author's compassion and humor take the bitterness out of her sometimes very penetrating criticisms of such things as over-emphasis on liturgical reform, and youth movements which pour all their budding apostles into the same mold.

To my mind the best thing of all, in a book which is excellent throughout, is the charity and clarity with which Caryll Houselander views Solly Lee, the book's most despicable character. I doubt if there can be found anywhere as good an analysis of the destitution of the modern Jew.

CAROL ROBINSON

THE GREATEST CATHERINE

By Michael de la Bédoyère
Bruce

St. Catherine of Siena might well be chosen the patron saint of our times. She was *the* lay apostle of her day. She loved God passionately and gave wholly of herself in bringing Christ's message to her fellow men. She too lived in troubled times but had the courage to speak up to her contemporaries, whether kings, Cardinals or Pope, in urging them to reform their lives in order to combat the evils of their day. We are all called to be saints, not "men of distinction" or protagonists of the "new look," so let us stop "playing safe" and be strong and uncompromising in restoring all things in Christ.

Catherine Benincasa was born just six hundred years ago into a humble working man's family in Siena, Italy. Her early devotion to prayer and penance incurred the wrath of her family but she soon won them over. She joined the Third Order of Saint Dominic, cared for the sick and the poor, and converted many sinners. Although outspoken, she was intelligent and charming and soon had many followers. Her country was being torn by wars; the people were restless and rebellious. It was the beginning of the breakdown of a balanced and united Christendom. Catherine urged the use of spiritual weapons to restore peace and order. The problem of her day was to bring about reform in the Church whereas the problem in our day is to reform the temporal order, to reintegrate religion and life. What we can learn from Catherine is the tremendous power of spiritual weapons.

Michael de la Bédoyère is the ideal person to give us a clear insight into Catherine's character and personality, her significance to this generation, because he himself is an active lay apostle, editor of the *The Catholic Herald*, and author of *Christianity in the Market Place, No Dreamers Weak,* and other books calculated to stimulate vigorous Catholic Action.

DOREEN O'SULLIVAN

Christian Commandos

FISHERS OF MEN
By Maxence van der Meersch
Sheed and Ward

Today nations are fast becoming buried under the mire of materialism which threatens to extinguish the one light that can bring order out of chaos — the light of Christ in the hearts of men.

Materialistic paganism which knows no class distinction is sweeping through the working world and leaving behind despair in the souls of men who should be following the footsteps of the Worker Who years ago left them the means of finding peace on earth.

Since the priest cannot enter the factory gates or office doors as a direct means of influence, it is the young worker himself who will have to become an apostle of his fellow men and with God's help lead them out of their darkness. This is the purpose of the worldwide Young Christian Worker (Jocist) movement. For anyone not acquainted with this movement, no treatise can so clearly set forth its principles or realism, idealism, and action as does *Fishers of Men*.

Van der Meersch, one of the leading French contemporary novelists, depicts with compassion and understanding the struggles of a young French worker, Pierre Mardyck, who arose out of the sordidness of his life to lead a campaign for Christ. The setting of the story is in France but in its essence the story is international for whether it be France or the United States, the young apostle will encounter similar hatred and ingratitude for the part he has chosen to play in this conquest of souls. The success of the J.O.C. does not manifest itself in sweeping members on to glory, but out of apparent worldly failures, it raises its members to undreamed of spiritual heights.

The movement permeated all aspects of Mardyck's life, rescuing him from vice and giving him a purpose for living hitherto unknown. The discovery of man's intimate relationship with God gave him the strength to face the opposition encountered at home, the antagonism of the communists at work, and made a beautiful thing of his love, and success of a marriage which, if measured at a materialistic scale, would have been tagged impossible.

With complete candor, Meersch paints a realistic picture of the spiritual growth of this working boy; a picture that perhaps would shock a few super-sensitive minds, but so would the corrupt conditions of the American working man — hope founded

415

in Pierre Mardyck and thousands like him who cry: "Christ's apostles, that is what we are! Fishers of men, that is what we are! We, far more than anyone else, come to save that which was lost! And our suffering and our labors shall once again redeem the sinfulness of the world."

MARY STAPLES

What Did Chesterton Have?

PARADOX IN CHESTERTON
By Hugh Kenner
Sheed and Ward

It seems now that many, if not most, of Chesterton's numerous readers looked at him much in the manner of a group of South Sea Islanders watching an aviator servicing his plane. The group of natives smile as the pilot checks the air in his tires. They laugh boisterously as he swings the propeller. They howl with glee as he lubricates the engine. They roll on the ground, holding their sides as he fills the tank. It is amazing how ludicrous the activities of a competent man can be, if you haven't the least idea what he is about. Well, Chesterton was like that. The task that he set himself to, and somehow accomplished, was as foreign to the modern mind as aeronautics is to a South Sea Islander. Chesterton saw that reality was all of a Oneness. The modern man looks upon reality as a chain of reactions as unrelated as the sections of a news reel; Chesterton saw reality in the full round. The modern mind comprehends nothing until it is reduced to the dull dimensions of length and breadth. It is the nature of the Chestertonian vision that concerns the author of this book.

That Chesterton should utilize paradox to a sometimes unbearable degree, is no more surprising than a fisherman should smell of fish. Chesterton was trying to get to the roots of things, and the roots of things are buried in paradox. The most profound statements that a man can make are of necessity paradoxical. This is true whether you say "In one God, there are three Divine Persons," or, "the strength of a martyr lies in his weakness," or, "one cannot see the problem if he is too close to it."

Chesterton saw this analogical aspect of reality before he saw anything else. As the author points out, Chesterton intuitively grasped the universality of paradox. For the human mind, paradox is a two-bladed instrument as indispensable to the philosopher, as a scissors is to a tailor.

Mr. Kenner inquiries into this analogical nature of being. He goes back to Aquinas and points out the agreement in principle and similarity in method between these two defenders of the Faith. Then he analyzes the various uses to which G. K. put his spiritual weapon. The paradoxes that Chesterton saw made him prone to use paradox rhetorically. It furnished plots for his short stories. It was the journalistic *peg* upon which he hung his essays.

The author admits, as well he must, that the Prince of Paradox at times made too much of a good thing, But, he hastens to insist that it *is* a good thing. If you drown in Chesterton's paradox, at least admit fairly that you are drowning in an oasis. His contemporaries sit themselves down at either end of a see-saw, and, at that, a see-saw without a fulcrum. One mind sits upon authority; the other upon individual freedom. One cries out for justice: the other cries out for Mercy. One Chesterton lies in this: that he saw in the acts of His Creator apparent contradictions. He saw that this Creator was a God Who could neither deceive nor be deceived. He concluded that these apparent contradictions were the blessed revelations of a merciful Father to children who can only see as through a glass darkly. He sensed behind the curtain of paradox a Beatific Vision which hid itself lest it blind us.

ED WILLOCK

A Not Unlikely Saint

MATT TALBOT, ALCOHOLIC
By *Albert H. Dolan, O. Carm.*
The Carmelite Press
Englewood, N. J.

One hurried and over-simplified explanation of why people drink so much today is that when you rob men of absolutes, they will become absolutely plastered. If a man cannot expend himself in a major cause, he will deplete himself in a minor tavern. This tiny booklet advances neither of these arguments. It merely tells how a man gave up drinking by doing the thing which, when suggested, is usually called, "impractical." This man turned to God in a spiritual, social, and physical way. To escape the tavern, he went to church. For conversation, he talked to God. For stimulation, he drank deep of the Holy Ghost. For his trouble, he has undoubtedly merited heaven, and will, if millions of prayers are answered, be canonized by the Church.

The Church is the most reluctant institution in the world to canonize a saint. Of the many called to canonization by the daily press, the Church chooses but a few. Matt Talbot was not the kind of man that the press would glorify, but he is the kind of man that many a journalist could profitably imitate, not in their work but in their leisure. The Church knows a good thing when she sees it. The teetotaler thinks that giving up drink is the least that a man could do. The Church, having had more experience with men, knows that giving up drink often calls for heroics. In the case of Matt Talbot, it called for, and got, heroic sanctity.

Talbot can teach by his example and intercede by his merits for all those who know they are incapable of avoiding drink. He is the logical patron for Alcoholics Anonymous. He resisted the appeal of the tavern and of the advertisement. He switched to Calvary because Calvary is lighter.

This booklet is a brief sketch of his simple and beautiful life. This is not so much an example of what a man can do if he tries, as it is an example of what God can do if we let Him.

ED WILLOCK

Workers Hungry For God

DEAR BISHOP
By Catherine de Hueck
Sheed and Ward

This is short (96 pages), very readable, and packed with meaty, thought-provoking material for everyone, priest or layman. The priest because it deals with the lost sheep of his flock; the layman because he is often the only one who can reach them and bring them back to the fold — they are usually beyond the reach of the shepherd.

The book grew out of two experiences of the Baroness de Hueck — her early life in this country when she had to work like the Katzie in her book; and an assignment during the war from a member of the American Hierarchy — to find out what American youth thought of God, His Church, churches in general and their reaction to communism and democracy.

The answer was discouraging, among the saloons, the restaurants, the hotels, the factories; "desert," as she calls it. There aren't the ninety-nine saved and one lost; but the ninety-nine lost, and "no one caring about the workers, right where the workers are . . . My backwash, blowsy streets. A wilderness waiting for a new sort of missionary. Shades of Father Marquette, Father Jogues, and all the martyred Jesuits! Who is to follow in your footsteps?"

A beginning has been made in France, where priests are down in the blowsy, backwash streets with the workmen, working with them in factories, shops, stores; celebrating Mass with fellow-workmen at night, whenever it is possible. But isn't this primarily a job for the layman, working with the clergy? Who else can reach these people? Most of them would shy away from a priest as from pestilence. They can only be reached by someone working with them, in their own environment, whom they will recognize as one of their own, in whom they will have confidence, whom they will trust, whom they will believe. A beginning has been made through the Jocists, the Catholic Worker, Friendship House, and such activities. But the surface of what can be done has only been scratched.

Get *Dear Bishop* and read it. It is guaranteed to dispel complacency, goad to action, and renew our charity toward our brother sheep who are lost in a cement desert.

FLOYD ANDERSON